KOSMOS

Kosmos

CONNECTING WITH NATURE

Don Pierce

Heartwood Path

Contact:
Heartwood Path
info@heartwoodpath.com
805-689-7042
www.heartwoodpath.com

ISBN/SKU: 979-8-9857352-0-8
EISBN: 979-8-9857352-1-5

To my daughters, Jennifer O'Neal and Courtney Logue.

Contents

Read This First

Although anyone may find the practices, challenges, and understandings in this book to be useful it is made available with the understanding that neither the author nor the publisher are engaged in presenting specific medical, psychological, emotional, sexual, or spiritual advice. Nor is anything in this book intended to be a diagnosis, prescription, recommendation, or cure for any specific kind of medical, psychological, emotional, sexual, or spiritual problem. Each person has unique needs and this book cannot take these individual differences into account. Each reader is encouraged to engage in a program of treatment, prevention, and cure only in consultation with a licensed, qualified physician, therapist, or other competent professional.

Introduction

REMEMBER THE PRIMARY POSTULATE

There is a postulate at the heart of the Heartwood Path that is so powerful it enables participants to, at once, become happier and to add beauty and sustainability to the natural environment. Serving as our foundation of reasoning, discussion, and belief, this primary postulate is stated as follows:

"The greatest trustable truths of one's life arise during one's sensing of the Now in nature."

This revered statement guided us as we chose each of the topics and activities in this series of books. It also was a determining factor for how we created its main methodology, which you will be doing by the end of the first learning station.

As you will learn, your sensing of the Now is trustable because, coming from your own experience, it gives you undeniably accurate information. Doing this sensing in nature allows you to tap into an incredible source of intelligence.

Without producing any pollution, being mindful of the Now in nature reduces stress, anxiety, and disorders. It produces deep joy. It supports sustainability. It creates a reverence for life. And it binds all things together into balanced, peaceful, and trustworthy relationships.

Without a purposeful program that encourages regular moments of awareness of the present moment in nature, one is prone to looking for unhealthy replacements. One becomes prone to all sorts of heinous substitutions, including substance abuse, excessive consumption, and other defilements that damage oneself, other people, and the planet.

Our propensity to replace frequent moments in the peace of natural areas with indoor distractions and stories that are detached from the wisdom of nature collectively causes what Dr. Michael Cohen calls "Earth Misery." This malady is marked by remarkably consistent and corresponding increases in mental illness, obesity, resource deficits, pollution, stress, species extinction, and more (2018).

Given its demonstrable ability to reduce Earth Misery, keep the primary postulate of this series of courses in mind as you move to your first taste of the Heartwood Path. Do so, just for the fun of it. Do so, just for your own happiness. Do so, just for the good of the environment.

A Taste

LEARN ABOUT YOUR SELF BY APPRECIATING NATURE

This sample experience will give you a good introduction to the Heartwood Path. Along this pathway of learning, you will encounter numerous topics such as the structure of integrity, how living in accordance with universal principles can keep you from always fighting against pre-established long-term natural and cultural patterns, anchoring the unique gifts of your individuality, working well with others during social or environmental advocacy, and persevering.

Each book leads the reader along a course dotted with numerous learning stations we call "waypoints." Thanks to online and print technologies, these waypoints do not have to occur in stuffy classrooms. They occur whenever you are ready and wherever in nature you like. Each waypoint has thought-provoking text followed by a related and engaging activity. By both reading the subject matter—indoors or outdoors—and by doing the activities outdoors, in a natural area of your choosing, you will be able to become happier while also contributing more effectively to the beauty and sustainability of the world.

As you use the Heartwood Path to flourish you will naturally become an eco-centric elder. You may even choose to become an eco-centric life coach. Such elders and life coaches seek to overcome the biggest problem humanity has not adequately addressed:

Too many of us are not maturing psychologically or spiritually.

Along with merely growing into physical maturity—the kind of old age we can visibly see in the outer world—we need to also grow and develop within the invisible inner world; that is, we need to become comprehensively mature (both inside and out) to the point that will be necessary if we are to become what the world truly needs and the Heart-wood Path develops: eco-centric volunteers or eco-centric life coaches capable of helping others with their comprehensive development.

Often in life, it's easier done than said. So let's dive right in. Great happiness comes to those who find that place where their own happiness meets the world's hunger for natural beauty and environmental sustainability, and that place begins with this Introductory Experience at the beginning of the Heartwood Path.

To A Revelatory Activity That Is Worth Repeating Over And Over Again...

HumaNatureConnect Activity

Throughout the Heartwood Path you will learn why it is so important—to both yourself and to nature—to do the following steps of the Start-up Protocol during each of the activities that follow.

Start-up Protocol For Heartwood Path Activities

(With Introductory Remarks)

- Read The Text — Use your literary sense, your mind sense, and your reason sense to move towards happiness and sustainability by reading the Heartwood Path text but also go outdoors to the backyard or to the backwoods, where the higher levels of negative ions in the air will improve your mood and sense of well-being. Determine how the topic of the waypoint affects you and your world.

- Attention Restoration — With a pen and journal in hand, go to a natural area that is attractive, has a variety of plants and animals, and is tranquil enough to leave room for reflection.

- Source — Spend time wandering without an agenda in nature or, if you don't have time to receive nature's magic in this way, follow the instructions in the text at each waypoint—the learning stations along the Heartwood Path. Not doing the activity will let unencumbered nature work its spell on you. Doing the activity will most likely be a faster route to greater happiness and environmental sustainability—the inseparable purposes of the Heartwood Path.

- Attractive Natural Being — Once you are in a natural area (the wilder, the better), look to find a natural being that is attractive to you and remain near that being until the end of the activity. Along the Heartwood Path, to halt the further objectivization of nature, natural objects, big or small, are called "natural beings—" as a way to acknowledge their ability to feel and to perceive things.

- Appreciation And Gratitude — While communing with the natural being, appreciate its beauty and how it's attractiveness makes you feel as you inhale; and, as you exhale, be grateful for its presence and its sharing of a great trustable truth. The more appreciative and grateful you are, the more you will be open to receiving information, guidance, and healing from the natural being.

- Consent — Once you find an aspect of nature that is attractive to you continuously for at least ten seconds, think of your continued attraction as your chosen being's consent to have a connection experience that will help you function optimally; receive information, guidance, and healing; and establish in your mind a more helpful egalitarian relationship with the natural being.

- The Natural Senses — Beyond seeing, hearing, and the three other commonly recognized senses, use as many of the fifty-four Natural Senses as you see fit and prepare to document the ones that you use in your journal. In your mind, form a bridge of awareness that spans from the reality of the natural scene you are visiting for this activity to the inner world of your own mind space. Use any or all of your natural senses—those that you share with beings in nature, such as the sense of thirst, the sense of gravity, the sense of color, or the sense of spiritual oneness (for a complete list go to the Appendix). This commonality in the ways of feeling and perceiving is why the natural senses are useful for building rapport with nature, for expanding upon your ability to perceive holistically, for communing with your chosen natural being, and for getting the most out of the prescribed activities. During my guidance sessions for those doing the following activity, for example, I may suggest that my client work on using any or all of the following: the natural sense of play, the natural sense of creativity, or the natural sense of moods.

- Great Trustable Truth — Experience what is happening at the present moment in nature, paying particular attention to the role of both beauty and balance; remember that impressions you form about attractive natural beings and natural areas, coming from your experiencing of them in the Now, are trustable; and recognize that the natural processes and features witnessed are a source of special, substantial, and irreplaceable truthfulness about both nature and yourself. To find a great trustable truth, look around the natural area to see what clues are available to your senses—from natural beings and not from yourself—regarding overcoming obstacles, what it means to be successful, and what traits help the natural being be successful. Let a great trustable truth come to you by being aware of your present moment with an attractive natural being. Having recognized certain positive traits in your chosen natural being, write down how you would like to possess these same or similar qualities yourself. Verify the revealed great trustable truth by writing in your journal: "I know (write-in this moment's great trustable truth) is true because I am experiencing it."

- <u>Recall</u> — Place the great trustable truth and any other insights that you discover in a mental lock-box so you can later record them in your journal.

If you do the Heartwood Path's activities—and not just read it's text—you will likely feel much better than you do when you are isolated from nature. So let's get the good feelings flowing! It is now time to do the premier prescribed HumaNatureConnect Activity, presented here because of its popularity as a real eye-opener for each participant.

Comparing Nature To Self

Find a pleasing spot in Nature. Look around and determine which of all of the natural beings you find to be most attractive. Study this being for a few minutes. Appreciate it's attractive qualities. Make a mental or written list of reasons why you picked this particular natural being. Pinpoint not only the being's favorable qualities but also why, for you, such qualities add to this being's attractiveness.

Create a sentence that reads:

"I love this (insert the words that identify your chosen attractive natural being) because it is (insert words that refer to the qualities you like about the natural being)."

Then, create a parallel sentence that reads:

"I love (insert the word "myself") because I am—(insert the same qualities as before)."

Typically, the preferred natural being has the same attributes that Heartwood Path participants would like to help bring forth in themselves. For this reason, this activity is a remarkably good way to reveal often subconscious positive attributes you would like to see develop in yourself. The attractive attributes of the natural being that are appreciated by the participants are usually qualities that the participants do not know they would like to see emerge in themselves. In this way, this activity is a very good way to learn about hither-to unrecognized and unappreciated aspects of your emerging sense of self that, now that these attractions are brought to light, you can develop further. Let us say, for example, that you are attracted to kelp (a prevalent seaweed), especially the way it is both anchored to the seabed and the way it is free to move in the ocean currents. This attraction may tell you that, until this moment, you did not recognize that you seek to be married to a spouse that, at once, gives you the anchor of a safe and secure household but also does not substantially limit your freedom of movement, your attitudes, or your activities. Knowing this, you now have a better chance of finding a suitable mate by looking for someone who can allow you to have both your required security and ample freedom.

In this activity, always state "I am ____" rather than "I would like to be ___". "I am___" makes the sentence an affirmation, which is best stated in the present tense. Stating what you want to be in the present tense is a powerful motivator. Example: "Just as the coconut is hard, I am willing to face hard facts."

Follow-up Protocol

For best results, write down your impressions of this activity in your journal, using as many of the following components as you see fit. Afterwards, share your interpretations with others. For this Introductory Experience, do not be too concerned if questions arise about the following Journal Components or the Heartwood Path Exchange. It is best to take the Heartwood Path one step at a time. Our Follow-up Protocol (our post-activity suggested actions) will be explained next.

Journal Components

- General Description — writing a general description of how you did the activity and what happened.
- Freeform — writing, in freeform, what you found attractive about your natural being.
- Three Qualities — writing down three qualities you found most attractive about your natural being.
- Three Learnings — writing down three things you learned from this activity.
- Self-esteem & Trust — writing down how, if at all, this activity changed your self-esteem or trustfulness of Nature.
- Changes To Self — writing down what aspects of your self, if any, were changed by this activity.
- Honor Yourself — praising yourself and your commitment to making another stop along the Heartwood Path good for yourself and the world.
- I'm A Person Who . . . — writing down three different so-called "G/G Statements" using the following format: "This connection experience tells me that I am a person who_____."
- Feelings If Activity Taken — writing down a sentence about how you would feel if you lost your ability to experience this connection.
- Nature Compared To Self — creating a sentence that reads: "I love this (insert words that identify the attractive natural being) because it is (insert words that refer to the qualities you like about the natural being)." Then, creating a parallel sentence that reads: "I love (insert the word "myself") because I am (insert the same qualities as before)." *If only one follow-up component can be done at any one waypoint, do this one. It reveals a lot about the participant quickly. In group settings it is a very good way to get pertinent conversation underway.*

- <u>Two-Word Summary</u> — writing down two words that summarize your response to this activity.

The Heartwood Path Exchange

Swap Your Ideas, Impressions, Photos, And News With Others

- Post your impressions and photos in the Comments at the bottom of the page (if you are using the website edition).
- Read the Heartwood Path book series as an individual or engage with others in a Heartwood Path course. The first book or course—**Kosmos**—offers an overview of the Heartwood Path and gives you an important introduction to communing with nature for information, guidance, and healing.
- We call groupings of people who are doing Heartwood Path activities together "salons (in the same way the groups of women who organized the French Revolution were called "salons"). Create your own salon that meets regularly online, by phone, or in person.
- Discuss your impressions with trusted family members and friends.
- Post your impressions on this specific waypoint on our Facebook Page.
- Join the broader conversations on our Facebook Page.
- To see what conversations you can inspire, share your photos and impressions about anything pertaining to your journey down the Heartwood Path on your Facebook page, on Instagram, and on other social media accounts. If you like, include "#heartwoodpath" wherever pertinent.

Heartwood Path Axioms

Key Assertions From Waypoint

i.

Read the thought-provoking Heartwood Path text, but don't stop there.

ii.

Improve your optimal functioning by communing with nature as you are instructed to do at each learning station of the Heartwood Path.

iii.

Find guidance, information, and healing by always completing the Follow-up Protocol after each of the activities found along the Heartwood Path.

iv.

Great happiness comes to those who find that place where their own happiness meets the world's hunger for sustainability and that place begins with this Introductory Experience at the beginning of the Heartwood Path.

v.

Along the Heartwood Path, to halt the further objectivization of nature, natural objects, big or small, are called "natural beings" as a way to acknowledge their ability to feel and perceive things.

Nocturnal Pilgrimage

For best results, write down your impressions of each night's dreams in your journal using the Heartwood Path Dreaming Time Protocols found in the Appendix. Afterwards, consider sharing your Dream Tending with others.

As often as you possibly can, sleep well before moving from one waypoint to the next. Sleep long (preferably eight hours) so that you are amply refreshed before pondering the text and doing the activity at each waypoint along the Heartwood Path.

Pay attention to your dreams. They are full of fruitful discoveries. For this reason, begin now to record your dreams in a journal. Help with your journal entries and additional techniques for reaping benefits from your dreams will unfold in the Nocturnal Pilgrimage sections of each waypoint.

There you have it: your first of hundreds of experiences—all aimed at making you happier in a sustainable world. From the start, get in the habit of doing the activities while you are outside, even if you read the waypoint text while you are inside.

If you have any questions along the way, do not hesitate to contact us. The easiest way to get started is to give us a call. We will guide you through the next steps or answer any questions that may arise. Besides our free help to beginners, we also provide a complimentary session of what we call "Guidance." Without any obligation, first-time participants and those contemplating signing up for ongoing Guidance can receive free help from an experienced staff person, including, for matters regarding technique or content, Heartwood Path creator Don Pierce; and, for administrative and technical matters, Heartwood Path CEO Courtney Logue. By asking for help, you will be taking an important first step towards greater happiness, greater effectiveness, and improved environmental sustainability.

Guidance

It is best to go down the Heartwood Path with a guide who can answer questions, show you how to discover more, help you solve problems, offer inspiration, and encourage you to dig deeper and keep going. Perhaps you may wonder how a piece of information discovered along the Heartwood Path applies to you. If so, a Guide can help. Perhaps you would like to share your own experiences and perspectives with someone who listens well and does not judge. If so, sign-up for Guidance. It happens in person, on the phone, and online. The fees are very reasonable. Go to our Guidance section or Store, both online, for more information, for prices, and for easy ordering. So confident that our Guidance will be inspiring and helpful, we offer a money-back, no questions asked guarantee if you are not, in any way, satisfied. The most economical way to receive Guidance is to purchase the printed books and receive unlimited Guidance. It may not be a requirement, but we are sure that you will gain greatly from your Guidance sessions.

Start off right. Use the following contact information for ways you can receive orientation help (about getting started on the Path initially), Heartwood Path Guidance (about your own on-going spiritual growth), or other assistance:

Text or call.

Courtney Logue

(805) 689-7042

email: courtney@heartwoodpath.com.

or

Don Pierce

(618) 632-5600

email: don@heartwoodpath.com.

If you are not inclined to reach out to us at this point, go now to the next waypoint: "Preparations At The Trailhead." It too will help you get started.

1

Preparations At The Trailhead

DRAW NEAR TO ATTRACTIONS IN NATURE

Here at the beginning of the Heartwood Path, imagine that you are approaching a large, attractive wood-hewn sign that welcomes you to your time of discovery and offers all the necessary information you need before heading forward. Don't pass by the important messages on this two-sided sign. Begin reading on the front side:

Welcome To The Heartwood Path

This course of study will make you and your environment better. You will become happier as the Heartwood Path gives you a route for your personal development. Along the way, your growth as a more compassionate person will result in a healthy environment that endures.

These benefits will emerge as you learn what it takes to form certain types of impressions about nature near your home. Remember, this book is not a course in natural history alone. Such a course would have you dwell upon natural aspects in the outer world only. It is also not a course in psychology alone. Such a course of study would only have you dwell upon cognitive aspects in the inner world only. The Heartwood Path is a course of study that has you dwell upon the bridge between the inner and outer world, and that bridge is the collection of impressions you form in your mind because you are communing in specific ways with attractive natural beings. As such, we will be practicing a type of eco-psychology and, eventually, conservation psychology.

It is becoming increasingly clear in scientific circles that reality is not just the stuff that is viewed passively in the outer world. Reality is also, and perhaps more so, determined by our inner world predictions which affect our interpretations which, in turn, help to inform our collective consciousness of reality.

It is, therefore, fitting that we focus on the impression, the bridge between the two worlds, which is made from both outer world be-haviors and physical systems and inner world individual intentions and more-than-individual ethics, mores, social codes, and religious or spiritual beliefs. Why not be informed by wholeness? The impression, molded by both the inner world and the outer worlds, offers a glimpse of a more complete and accurate reality.

The physical world that we have come to know does not exist with-out our consciousness of it. Conversely, the inner world—the realm of one's intentions and our agreed upon ethics and religious beliefs—depends on the existence of the outer world.

When doing Heartwood Path activities do not dwell only on the attractive natural beings you encounter and do not dwell only on thoughts unaffected by an attractive natural being. Instead, form a sort of draw bridge that spans and includes your inner world and the outer world. Comprised of both your own intentions and ethics plus the per-ceived qualities of attractive natural beings, this draw bridge lets you in on good, beautiful, and true aspects of wholeness. And that's how you find remarkable guidance, amazing health, and valuable information. But only if you also learn to understand and be receptive to certain typically overlooked aspects of the natural universe.

Everything you gain from the Heartwood Path—the inseparable arising of increased happiness, increased effectiveness, and a healthy and sustainable environment—depends on your understanding of six aspects of the natural universe. We will use an acronym developed by Dr. Michael Cohen of Project Nature Connect when we refer to these vitally important but typically overlooked natural components: "NNIAAL." Your first introduction to these elements, which together allow nature to intelligently impart health, information, and guidance to those who have learned how to be receptive, will occur along the Heartwood Path in the activity that follows.

Beyond learning more about NNIALL, here, at this waypoint, you will discover the reason the Heartwood Path came into existence. We provide this information because the purpose of the Heartwood Path is exposed when it's origin is unveiled.

As in the Introductory Experience, later in this waypoint you will continue to be guided by the Start-up and Follow-up Protocols. Use these to continue to heighten the benefits of the Heartwood Path for both yourself and the environment.

The benefits of the Heartwood Path—listed at the beginning of the next section of this book—will begin to be yours as you make your way through the following sections of this orientation: Reasons, Book/Course Benefits, and Impetus.

Reasons:

Why Do People Read Heartwood Path Books Or Take Heartwood Path Courses?

Some people read Heartwood Path books just for fun. Some people read Heartwood Path books to enhance their happiness. Some people read Heartwood Path books just to improve the environment. Some people read Heartwood Path books for all of these reasons.

People who engage in pilgrimages down the Heartwood Path receive a broader perspective. They also receive increased happiness, increased effectiveness, progress towards a sustainable environment, and an increased ability to persevere in their acts of altruism. No untrue claims of simplicity here. It takes a long, carefully conceived course of study to deliver on these promises.

To help participants maintain their enthusiasm for their transformative learning, we will not use stuffy classrooms. Much of the time spent on the Heartwood Path occurs in the beauty of the great outdoors.

People are naturally drawn to attractions in nature. They are attracted to learn more about what they encounter in the natural environment, which is beautiful and diverse because the beings in the natural landscapes are attracted to be and behave in ways that both draw attention to themselves and enhance their chances of survival.

Those who participate in the Heartwood Path enhance their awareness of attractions outdoors. In time, their attractions often turn to strong feelings of love. While spending time in nature is soothing, the unavoidable witnessing of environmental problems make people fearful, concerned, and attracted to protect what they have come to love. When they see more clearly how their beloved beings and natural landscapes are endangered, their compassion, which may have previously been limited to their own family or to their own kind, grows to include all sentient beings.

With practice, those who go down the Heartwood Path are able to enhance their skills of compassion. This doing for others makes them feel a sense of accomplishment, a feeling that they cannot match through conspicuous consumption or routine entertainments. As they do more to protect natural attractions, they become saint-like in their helping of others. To this end, the Heartwood Path puts one's attractions on a positive course that leads to environmental sustainability and a powerful type of happiness described below.

Book/Course Benefits:

Here's What You'll Receive

The Heartwood Path does not lead to the "common" temporary satisfactions that come from everyday entertainments and conspicuous consumption. Instead of these momentary indulgences, the Heartwood Path will lead you to find "uncommon happiness;" that is, happiness that is abundant, abiding, and authentic.

The "Triple A" happiness that is found along the Heartwood Path arises from a very specific three-part circularity: a circle of outcomes where any one part leads to the other two parts. In this way along the Heartwood Path:

1. environmental sustainability leads to individual maturity and easy and enduring assistance to others;
2. personal maturity leads to both environmental sustainability and easy and enduring assistance to others; and
3. easy and enduring assistance to others—leads to individual maturity and environmental sustainability.

These benefits sound a bit serious and heavy; but, as you will discover in this introduction, getting to them is actually very pleasurable and fun.

One thing is certain: from here on you will grow and your self-concept will change. You can allow nature to carry you where it may. Or you can engage in the specific text and series of Heartwood Path Activities. Those who follow the Heartwood Path will be moved beyond the ordinary and become uncommonly happy. And the world will become better off because you are making the necessary effort.

Impetus:

Why The Heartwood Path Came To Be

After working for over a decade fighting ill-considered water projects, preserving wilderness, and helping to build the safety net of environment protection laws, only to see our work jeopardized by a political change in Washington D.C in the early Nineties, I came to the realization that it will be necessary to change the hearts and minds of the voting public if lasting protections are to be secured. Despite this political change, I somehow kept my chin up and pressed on despite overwhelming odds. When famed conservationist David Brower asked me to "write a piece" on how to prevent activists from burning out, and when I noticed that the numerous solutions—including meditation, yoga, and spending time in nature—were good for everyone (and not just for activists fighting burnout), the three decade-long effort to chart the Heartwood Path began.

We call those who follow the Heartwood Path "eartHearts." Join them in their effort to increase individual happiness by protecting the planet one person at a time.

That concludes everything presented on the front side of the trail-head sign. Now, imagine going around the sign and beginning to read what is presented on its backside. Keep reading. Being prepared will help you get the most for your time.

Tips For Traversing The Heartwood Path: Ways The Heartwood Path Creates An Integral Self

This book, **Kosmos**, provides the overture. The next book, **Logos**, sets you up to have uncommon integrity and to be successful in the world by giving you an understanding of how to go with the flow of the universe. The third book is **Egos**. It helps you maintain your own inherent and unique gifts as you work on causes, especially environment sustainability and protecting the beauty of nature. The fourth book is **Ecos**. This book awakens you to the relationships that form your Greater Self and teaches you how to best receive guidance, information, and healing from nature. Enjoy your learning and growth while you read these four books; each available now. But, before you jump ahead, your learning and growth will be considerably more pronounced if you take the time to understand the very important topic of the next section.

Consent

Due to our past and present tendency to abuse nature, when you visit an attractive natural area in peaceful friendship it is critical to be attracted to the beings in the natural area while making assurances that you will cause no harm. If you are not skeptical of speaking to natural beings (or images of natural beings) verbally make the assurances that you will be respectful and caring to the natural being. If you cannot at this point set aside your skepticism, make such assurances to yourself as prompts for the emergence of a cooperative and empathetic psychological persuasion that will be helpful to you, the natural being, and the being's setting as you engage in the activity. At a minimum, the seeking of consent puts you in a frame of mind that keeps you from lording over the natural being and, thereby, silencing it or blocking yourself from receiving its information, guidance, and healing. You will know that you have not gained the natural being's consent if you become uncomfortable or if the being becomes in your awareness unattractive. If this happens, simply follow your attraction to another natural being. You will know that you have obtained the natural being's consent (or your own image of its consent) if the being simply remains attractive to you for at least ten seconds. Seeking consent both sets you up psychologically for a beneficial empathetic exchange and honors nature's truth and integrity. Obtaining consent by paying attention to your attraction moves you out of your story-dominated, indoor stagnation and into the sense-dominated outdoor vibrancy that only nature can provide. To see what I mean, compare how you feel when you are un-attracted to how you feel when you are attracted to a natural being. Note if obtaining consent and being attracted enables you to better perceive colors, motions, sounds, new attractions, vibrance, thankfulness, euphoria, peace, and enchantment. Determine if your obtained consent and attractions change for the better how you feel about yourself, the natural being, and the local environment. To feel even better in your state of attraction, promise the attractive natural being and yourself— the two agents presently in your awareness—that you will increasingly love, honor, support, strengthen, respect, help, embrace, and nurture the local and global environment.

Great Trustable Truths Arise During One's Sensing In The Now In Nature

When communing with nature for Heartwood Path Activities, keep your senses open for the experiencing of sensations that are "great;" that is, for perceptions that are out of the ordinary, fabulous, and substantial. Sensations that are special to you are only valid if they are "trustable;" that is, if you can count on their accuracy. Since the sensations we are looking for come from your own experiencing, they are undeniably true; that is, your own experiencing is producing perceptions that are indisputable. What you experience, therefore, is true and can be shared with others as a truth. Truths are statements that are valid, correct, authentic, or sincere. For our purposes here, we shall define the "greatest" portion of the primary postulate— "The greatest trustable truths of one's life arise during one's sensing of the Now in nature—" as meaning not only that the revealed truths are of an extent, amount, or intensity that are above average but also the truths are very pertinent to one's ideal future self. In this way, an admirable factor sensed in nature will be revealed to be really about factors that you want to develop in yourself. Liking the tallness of a tree, as an example for one person, is really about that person wanting to stand tall in her community in the future. Recognizing the diligent work of an ant, as an example for another person, is really about her desire to improve her own work ethic. A different person might admire a tall tree and conclude that she needs to improve her posture or admire an ant and conclude that it is time to improve her relationships in her group. In any of these cases, the next steps after uncovering the nature-inspired insights are, in chronological order, to develop: related qualitative goals (example: "I will be a good team-player"), quantitative objectives (example: "I will be complimented for my team skills four times by December 31st"), and specific plans such as "I will attend four team-building classes by March 15th." The "arise during one's sensing" part of the primary postulate of the Heartwood Path cannot be glossed over, for one's experiencing is not speculative or deniable. One's senses are accurate. Experiential acts are undeniable facts. The "in nature" part of our primary postulate refers to the fact that Heartwood Path participants bring to their awareness great trustable truths *in nature,* which is a source of immense intelligence as evident by its enormous diversity, it's huge web of life-supporting relationships, and its lack of pollution.

Examples of "great trustable truths in nature" include:

"My attraction to anchored, yet flowing, kelp shows me that *I am* a person who wants to be married but not rigidly controlled."

"My appreciation for the solid, upright tree shows me that *I am* a person who is steadfast and respectable."

"My recognition of the nine-second average time between each ocean wave tells me that *I am* a person who pays attention to rhythms and *I am* a good drummer."

Note that in each example it is said "I am___" rather than "I would like to be ___." In Heartwood Path Activities we are working with the power of affirmations, always stated in the present tense. Affirmations are statements said with confidence about a perceived truth. To make your affirmations more powerful, say them over and over, always including the phrase "I am ___." Example: "Just as the leaves produce shade, I am a person who shields my family from harm."

What you learn from direct experience is often better than what you learn from second-hand sources or from reading. What you are told can be misunderstood. What you read can be a lie. Comparatively, what you *experience* with your *own senses* is *undeniably true*. And if what you are experiencing is something *in nature* you are privy to a fabulous source of time-tested *intelligence*. When what you are sensing is unusually positive and recognized as being really about *your ideal future self* the truth is considered to be *great*. For practice, say repeatedly "Just as the natural being is (insert a positive attribute) *I am* (insert something great).

Fulfillment

There is a type of uncommon fulfillment that you can achieve that will be both good for you and good for the environment. What you have to do to achieve this abundant, authentic and abiding form of satisfaction is awaken to the nature of happiness. By this, I mean, that a primary source of your happiness is not within you as a separate being but stems from your unyielding but largely forgotten connection to Nature.

This series of books and courses will take you to a very special place where your own happiness meets the world's great need. You can do this for your own pleasure, for the sake of the environment, or as a new career.

If you are attracted to follow the pacing as suggested, it will take you about fourteen and a half months to receive all the teachings—which are laid out, waypoint by waypoint, along the present course of learning we call the "Heartwood Path." Upon completion, if all goes well, you will awaken to a place that is, at once, full of gladness and marked by ecological sustainability. The daily assignments of this series of books and courses will be rewarding, fun, informative, and transformative.

Do not miss out on receiving these benefits because of the far-too-common lack of understanding addressed in the next section.

The Uncalled-For Yet Not-Uncommon Contention Against One Customary Component Of The Heartwood Path

Allow the natural being to become a personified image in your mind—one that has not only all of its own natural attributes but also the ability to engage in conversation. Here's why doing so ought not be a reason for skepticism.

It will be important for you to remember as you proceed down the Heartwood Path that phenomena are not self-arising distinct entities. They are all formed, molded, and interpreted by a slew of natural senses as they are used by humans. These include seeing, hearing, smelling, tasting, and touching plus forty-nine more so-called natural senses that we will introduce in this book, including, for example, the literary sense that allows one to read and speak. Together, these abilities to perceive—never missing in any interaction—"color" all that exists. In this way, all of the "natural objects" that one perceives are not immutable separate entities but are rather images contrived of the blending of their natural attributes and one's socially-formulated perceptions. If in this book we say "the tree," for example, we really mean one's image of the tree. Since we will always be talking about the image of this or that, we will usually omit the word "image," if only for literary simplicity. Despite this omission, artificial objects and natural beings are always perceived by us as images.

Images of natural beings—whether in your nighttime dreams or in your daytime perceptions—are not mere psychic phantasms. Natural images are living beings that reside in nature, in our dreams, and in our awareness. Throughout the ages, humans have often evoked in these images the human ability to form concepts and to speak. Although it is not uncommon today to hear skepticism about non-humans speaking to us, humans have, over the ages, benefited from such conversations in their dreams, in their celebrations, and in their prayers.

I suggest that you continue and modify this tradition of interacting with personified natural images so that you may flourish—that is, grow and develop in a healthy way and maintain an environment that leads to success and happiness. In your Heartwood Path Activities, respectfully attend to images that come from nature. By doing this attending according to the methodology you will learn along the Heartwood Path, you will be engaged in the helpful and healthful job of reverting so-called un-sensing and illiterate natural objects back into the sensing and communicative fellow subjects they were for all but the most recent earth-destroying period of human history. Don't worry: these conversations will not be held with actual talking animals nor will they occur with isolated mental contrivances in your own inner world alone.

You will instead be asked to form a sort of bridge of awareness between your inner world perceptions and your outer world perceptions and to allow any image of a willing natural being found on this bridge of awareness to have the ability to enter into a variety of forms of give and take, including sometimes the human-like ability to have verbal exchanges. It is on this bridge of awareness, which is a blending of outer world "actualities" and inner world interpretations, that one engages in verbal communication with real world yet interpreted natural beings. It is these verbal interactions that often cause un-learned prospective participants to call the Heartwood Path into question. Remember that it really doesn't matter if statements come from you or from your chosen attractive natural being because there is only a seamless oneness and any separations are delusions. Independent bodies or events are mirages. If real world natural beings come into your awareness as living images, interpreted by you as you see fit, you might as well, if it is helpful to you, let them be sensible and speak. And you will do well to listen and to return the conversation without dominating the interaction. Try asking the personified image of the natural being:

- what it experiences about the topics of discussion at each learning station,
- what it wishes you to know about the topic of the waypoint,
- what does the topic mean in the natural being's world,
- how does the topic affect the environment or the world,
- how might addressing this topic be beneficial, and
- whether the Image of the natural being has any more answers or questions?

Be sure to write out the back and forth conversation with the image of the being about these topics. Do your best, whenever possible, to write in the present tense.

If it helps, feel free to think of our recommended verbal interactions "as-if" they are really occurring. Think of them as imaginary but helpful psychology "tricks" that are done for therapy purposes, rather than as actual real-world verbal exchanges. Sometimes in eco-psychology "faking-it-until-you-make-it" has, in the long run, positive results. If inter-species verbal interactions make you feel like turning away from the Heartwood Path, it will do no harm not to do the conversing. There is plenty of other important work that can be done with positive results.

Much, if not most, of what you gain from the interactions you will have with the natural beings you encounter in this series of books or courses will come to you without the use of the spoken word. The skepticism you may now feel about the plausibility of talking with personified images of natural beings will almost certainly fade as you proceed. And, in any event, as you will soon learn, much of what you will be asked to do along the Heartwood Path will involve only a little heady "verbalizing with" and much more visceral and non-verbal sensing of attractive natural beings. So stay with us.

Online Course Navigation

The Heartwood Path is dotted with hundreds of stops—reflection points or learning stations we call "waypoints." It is recommended that at each waypoint you read its text in a comfortable location, indoors, in your car, or outdoors. You will always be instructed to go outside to an attractive natural being. Follow this instruction faithfully. It is important that nature be able to work its magic on you while you are in its midst. If you are using the online version of the Heartwood Path, notice how you are eased into each Heartwood Path Waypoint by a scrolling digest of 4-6 image boards (photos accompanied by words) we call the "Waypoint Preludes."

Notice how the first Waypoint Prelude after the title image board has a photo of Heartwood Path author Don Pierce and the key prescription for that waypoint (the main task to be performed); notice how there are 2-4 axiomatic Waypoint Preludes (key assertions) at each learning station; and notice how the last prelude at each stop after this one is a one-sentence version of the outdoor activity for that waypoint.

We recommend that you review at least the messages on The Waypoint Preludes immediately before or while you are in nature doing the activities. This review is particularly important if you do not have something else burning on your mind as you move towards your chosen attractive natural beings in their wild places outdoors.

At the end of each set of Waypoint Preludes you will see that you are given two options:

Option 1:

"*Click here to read more."

If you want to spend more time and read more at each waypoint, choose Option 1. Since it provides both the Preludes and the full, un-abridged text, this option provides a more thorough way to go down the Heartwood Path—comprehensive yet engaging, and broken down into manageable portions. The activities at each unpruned Heartwood

Path Waypoint are clear, spelled out with just enough detail, and comprehensive. The comments people leave at the end of each unpruned Heartwood Path Waypoint will add much depth to your experience.

Practice using the links now. You will quickly learn that the best information is in the unpruned edition. Here you will get what it takes to become happier, more effective, steadfast, and capable of helping to protect the beauty of nature and to help enhance the environmental sustainability of the world—all purposes of the Heartwood Path.

Option 2:

"Click here to move to the next waypoint."

If you want to move down the Path rapidly, if you want to read a one-sentence summary of each activity, or if you want to take a quick glimpse of some of the most important topics at each Heartwood Path Waypoint, choose Option 2. If you choose this pruned approach alone, however, you will miss a chance to really apply yourself. Generally in life there is no growth in your Comfort Zone. If you choose the easier pruned route, you can always opt for more information at the end of any series of Waypoint Preludes.

Wander In Nature Aimlessly Or Do The Activities

Each of the activities found at every Heartwood Path activity will suggest that you move outdoors and into a natural setting. Conduct each interaction with nature according to the steps outlined in the Start-up and Follow-up Protocol (each described subsequently) as you see fit.

Ten-In-Ten

Be sure to remove any impediments that might keep you from getting out into nature on a daily basis. One good way to insure that you build into your life time for communing with nature is to immediately create a list of ten places—the wilder the better, from your backyard or from the backwoods—that you can go to within ten miles of your house (and/or ten minutes from your house). Keep this list handy. These "Ten-In-Ten" places will soon become treasured sites that you will visit often as you travel the Heartwood Path for healing, information, and guidance. The Ten-In-Ten list is created just to get you started and to remove the impediment of not knowing where to go, at first. You are always welcome—and encouraged—to also use natural places not included on your Ten-In-Ten list.

Doing And Processing Each Activity

Our Protocols are suggested actions. They are not mandatory, but they are important. Do not skip over them. The more you do, the better.

Follow your attractions. Do not over do it. More involvement will yield better results. By carefully following the Start-up Protocol prior to each activity, you will experience many helpful suggestions for how to improve your functioning by communing in certain ways with nature.

To receive the biggest impact from each waypoint experience, also use the set of recommended actions that follow each activity. The Follow-up Protocol is divided into two parts.

The first part of the Follow-up Protocol is called "Journal Components." This recurring part of the Heartwood Path will help you process your responses to each activity. This processing is the key to making the Heartwood Path work for you. Often guidance from nature comes to you in fleeting, little, odd bits of inner world or dream world events that are hard to remember. Keeping written records of your impressions from the Heartwood Path Activities brings subconscious feelings and impressions in your inner world out into the light of the outer world.

To engage properly in the Follow-up Protocol while traversing the Heartwood Path, purchase a journal (if you do not already have one).

Buy one that can lie flat for easy writing, has lined, or, if you plan to include illustrations, blank pages. Some Heartwood Path participants prefer to decorate the cover of their journal themselves. Obtain a book to be used as a journal that is small enough for you to pack easily in a bag and transport to and from your chosen natural places.

The second part of the Follow-up Protocol, called "The Heartwood Path Exchange," is a set of recommendations for helping you with the important step of sharing your results with others. By reading what others share on the Exchange you will receive important pointers and, more importantly, a fresh way to see the world.

At each learning station along the Heartwood Path, there is a Nocturnal Pilgrimage section. Here, you can receive food for thought, some of it intended to influence the content of your dreams. Be sure to continue your journey down the Heartwood Path at night by planting something of interest in your mind before you fall asleep, by learning how to influence your dreaming even as you dream, by learning how to find pertinent meaning from your dreams, by interpreting your dreams so you can receive more benefits from your Heartwood Path Activities, and by making thoughtful entries into your dream journal. You will learn how to do all of these vitally important tasks as you proceed.

Sharing

The Heartwood Path Exchange reminds eartHearts to post their impressions and photos in the Comments at the bottom of the web-page for each Waypoint; to engage with others in a Heartwood Path course; and to start or participate in a Heartwood Path salon that meets regularly—we suggest weekly—online, by phone, or in person. The Exchange sections, located after each activity, also reminds Heartwood Path participants to discuss their impressions with trusted family members and friends; to post their impressions and photos in our EartHeart Networking Forum; and to post the impressions they form at each waypoint on our Facebook Page, on their Facebook page, and on other social media sites such as Instagram.

Like the other actions recommended at each waypoint, sharing with others in the Heartwood Path Exchange is a vital step towards your own personal happiness and the sustainability of the environment. Receiving comments about your posts is inspiring. Engaging with others online or in person further expands your knowledge. Participating in the Heartwood Path Forum broadens your perspective. Using Facebook or Instagram to share your Heartwood Path impressions helps you to make a difference in the world. Like being in a really good book club, participating in The Heartwood Path Exchange will help you to better understand the subject matter and your own impressions that are generated during the activities. Don't keep what you learn and feel to yourself. Share your impressions with people anytime and anywhere by using The Heartwood Path Exchange regularly.

While it is best to do most, if not all, of these preparatory and post-activity actions, you are always free to follow your own attractions and do only the ones you prefer. By doing the readings, following the Start-up Protocol, doing the activities, following the Follow-up Protocol, participating in the Heartwood Path Exchange, and engaging in the Dreaming Time Activity at each of the waypoints, the Heartwood Path will not only improve your happiness and the quality of your local environment, it will also improve your mental, physical, and spiritual abilities by consistently showing you many inspiring, transformative, and healthful ways to commune with nature. These ways will be revealed to you as you progress.

Critical Learning

In the Start-up Protocol that follows, begin to change your stagnating, self-defeating pattern of remaining far too much in your sedentary, word-dominated, indoor world. Continuing to do so gives you, among other things, the disastrous perspective that nature is full of objects that are separate from yourself. By doing this initial activity, you will begin to see how this viewpoint can be discarded by getting up from your indoor furniture and communing in a revolutionary way with fellow natural beings outside. You will also very likely learn some important things about yourself at this and the other waypoints that follow.

You have now completed reading the trailhead sign for the Heartwood Path. To mark your involvement, drop your name and contact information at our virtual trail registration box at www.heartwood-path.com, download the free certificate of participation or purchase the wearable Heartwood Path badge. Let's jump right in with an activity.

To A More Complete Perception Of Nature...

HumaNatureConnect Activity

Start-up Protocol

If this is not a day when you prefer to spend time in nature without an agenda, do the Heartwood Path Start-up Protocol found in the Appendix. Then return here to do the remaining portion of this activity:

Learning About The Components Of A Helpful Holistic Perspective Of Nature

Obtain a more complete impression of nature by finding a natural attractive being outdoors, remaining with it during the activity, perceiving the surrounding natural environment, and then begin trying to become aware of each of the following often overlooked aspects of the natural universe—**NNIAAL**.

1. **Namelessness.** The lack of words/namelessness/the non-literate aspects of nature. Notice how nature communicates using actual rather than symbolic modes of expression. Ask yourself whether your persistent use of words has caused any separation between

yourself and nature and whether the use of words—mere symbols—limits your expressiveness about real beings and doings. Write your answer in your journal.

2. **Now**. The consciousness of now, the eternal present aspect of the appealing relationships in nature. Ask yourself if your time spent ruminating about the past and planning for the future is taking away from your chances for actually enjoying your life, then write your answer in your journal.

3. **Intelligence.** Nature uses its self-organized intelligence to create attractive, healthful optimums of life. Given the intelligence evident in nature (think of the beauty, diversity, and harmony it creates without causing pollution, for example) how would you respect and appreciate any guidance you receive from nature (if you could learn how to receive such a gift)? Put your answer in your journal

4. **Alive.** The earth is alive. All of it's beings can be regarded as if they were cells of one giant living organism. Living things perceive and, through its various beings, so does the earth. Taken as a whole, this organism—the earth—has a whole range of perceptive abilities: it's rocks have enough perceptive power to "know" when to speed up or slow down their molecules based on the ambient temperature, it's mammals provide for the earth's emotions, it's reptiles reptiles display reactions such as fight or flight, and people—also participants in the functioning of the earth's body—use reason and symbols to deliver self-aware and sophisticated messages. How do your human conceptual abilities make you special? Given what other beings can do, how do your human conceptual abilities provide only a portion of the earth's ability to perceive? By focusing so much on human concepts, what do you think is lost by too often neglecting the emotions of mammals or the reactions of birds, for example? In what ways do you feel the earth is alive or not alive? Record your responses in your journal.

5. **Attraction.** Beings in nature do what they are attracted to do and, in the process, become appealing. Think about the previous sentence carefully and look for examples of its truthfulness in nature. Can you appreciate how beauty plays a vital role in what Dr. Michael Cohen calls Natural Attraction Ecology, and how communing with attractive beings puts you in sync with how nature creates it's best optimum of life? Do not worry if you are unsure of your answer to this question at this point. Save your response so that you can later look at it (perhaps after the end of the third Heartwood Path book/course) to see how much you have learned about the importance of attraction in nature.

6. **Love.** Love is dominant over meanness in nature. Darwin's well-known "survival of the fittest" theory makes nature seem brutish, but careful examination reveals that cooperation is an even more pervasive force in nature than is brutality. There are two types of rhinoceros in Africa, for example. One grazes on grass, the other browses on the leaves of shrubs. This arrangement minimizes conflict between these two powerful beasts. Look for similar examples of conflict-avoidance in nature in your area. Write down these examples in your journal. Also, write down which is more dominant or pervasive in your life: conflict, competition, cooperation, or kindness. Write down how you would feel about obtaining guidance from a loving source rather than from a hateful one.

To make sure you understand NNIAAL, relate this concept to your chosen attractive nature being by recording in your journal your answers to the following pertinent questions:

1. How is your attractive being nameless? What harm would it do (to you, to it, or to both of you) if you gave your natural being a name or called it by some name?

2. How, if at all, does your attractive natural being live in the past or in the future? How does it, if at all, live solely in the Now?

3. How, if at all, is your attractive natural being intelligent or part of an intelligent plan?
4. How, if at all, would you describe your chosen attractive natural being as being alive?
5. Why do you think it is important to find attractive rather than unattractive beings for your Heartwood Path Activities?
6. How is your chosen attractive natural being an exemplar of love? If your chosen being evokes in you a sense of love, how does it feel to be in the absence of hate or fear?

In answering these questions you are beginning to think in a more holistic way, your perspective is broadening, and you are learning about components of nature that will be useful to you throughout your journey down the Heartwood Path.

Follow-up Protocol

For best results, write down your impressions of this activity in your journal using the Heartwood Path Follow-up Protocol found in the Appendix. Afterwards, consider sharing your interpretations with others.

Heartwood Path Axioms

Key Assertions From Waypoint 1.1

1.1.1.

Draw near to attractions in nature.

1.1.2.

Go efficiently down the Heartwood Path to find happiness and environmental sustainability.

1.1.3.

There is a type of uncommon fulfillment that you can achieve that will be both good for you and good for the environment.

1.1.4.

What you have to do to achieve an abundant, authentic, and abiding form of satisfaction is awaken to the nature of happiness.

1.1.5.

As one does more to protect natural attractions, one becomes saint-like in one's helping of others.

Nocturnal Pilgrimage 1.1

For best results, write down your impressions of each night's dreams in your journal using the Heartwood Path Dreaming Time Protocols found in the Appendix. Afterwards, consider sharing your Dream Tending with others.

Your progress down the Heartwood Path occurs both day and night, sometimes while you are awake and sometimes while you dream. Be sure to devote a portion of your day to contemplating the messages you find in the recurring Nocturnal Pilgrimage sections at each waypoint. At these sections, you will often receive food for thought before you retire for the night. Sometimes the concepts from the Heartwood Path text and Heartwood Path activities will show up in some way in your dreams. The impact of your readings and your daytime activities on your dreams is one reason why we give you pointers for how to use your dreaming as a way to receive guidance for your life.

The topic for tonight's nocturnal contemplation is the structure of integrity. Read the next section and find ways to incorporate the structure of integrity into your sense of self and your life.

Integrity

Integrity means both doing what is appropriate and being whole. As such, it is the most important guiding light for those moving down the Heartwood Path.

More important than just doing what you say you are going to do, important as that is, integrity is a repeating theme throughout the Heartwood Path because grappling to achieve it is such a crucial endeavor for anyone trying to get the most from life. Integrity involves reconciling the inner world and the outer world; making sure, for example, that what you are thinking on the inside is reflected by your actions on the outside. It is about one's individual intentions and behaviors and the collective way one is engaged in ethics and all physical systems. There can be no worthy holistic discussion about personal growth without the inclusion of the topic of integrity. We trust that you will soon agree that the Heartwood Path is such a holistic discussion.

Rather than rush down the Heartwood Path, set a slow but steady beat. Give yourself enough time for reflection. It is suggested that you sleep between each waypoint. Be sure to record your nighttime dreams and your daytime impressions dreams in a journal, as suggested at each waypoint. Enjoy what you learn and do at the next waypoint: "Purpose."

2

Purpose

DETERMINE THE SUITABILITY
OF THIS SERIES OF BOOKS

The Heartwood Path series of books has to do with sharing a means of securing human happiness and a sustainable environment. These two laudable goals are achieved through team-building and the conversion of participants into eco-centric elders, or, more specifically, into eartHearts.

Here's an important distinction: Eco-centric elders are leaders who are guided by nature in their service to people and the planet. Eart-Hearts are sort of like environmentalists. Instead of saving the earth one place at a time, as many environmentalists do, eartHearts volunteer to save the earth one person at a time.

Whether they seek to become better eco-centric elders or eartHearts, Heartwood Path participants, most likely being people in their Twenties to Sixties, will, step-by-step, expand their horizons and develop a broader sense of self. The particular form of awakening offered by this series of books means that you will both increase your happiness, improve the effectiveness of your groups, and improve the quality of your environment. The inseparability of these two aims will be sufficiently evident by the end of this series of books/courses.

Prospective participants need only have a yearning to make things better. They need not have achieved—before reading the first Heartwood Path books or before the onset of the first Heartwood Path course—the kind of rare spiritual enlightenment that would make them already a "sage." Many Heartwood Path activities lead participants towards that goal, but only in unsustainable peak experiences, and never as a way to check out from the realities of this world.

Participants prepare themselves for a productive adulthood, productive in ways rarely found in the general population. They are trained to share their newfound knowledge with others.

To be someone well suitable for this series of books, participants need a yearning to attain a psycho-spiritual level of development that is more "saint-like" than "sage-like." Our brand of saints are very good people who still know how to have fun. We will be speaking not of religious canonical saints but of secular saints. We define a "saint" as a person with the following five characteristics: 1) she has a More-Than-Individual, ecological perspective, 2) she has the ability to see what needs to be done to secure a magnificent future, 3) she is willing to stand up against injustice, 4) she is driven without burden to help others, and 5) she wants to obtain some basic life coaching skills and resources that can be used to help others become both glad (uncommonly happy individually and satisfied with their associations in groups) and green (living an ecological lifestyle in a healthy environment and helping others in their efforts to preserve the beauty of nature and secure environmental sustainability).

Beyond such characteristics, the people we seek to develop through this series of books and courses will be those who are willing to become prepared to help others develop an eco-centric perspective—that is, a worldview of concern for all sentient beings and the entire planet. This concern, like all concerns, is mediated by how one understands problems and by what one is willing to do about them. This concern also yields uncommon happiness.

Unless you have some divinely given attributes, people seeking to become saint-like need to work assiduously on their own personal growth. This work often involves partaking in the kind of systematic course of activities presented in this series of books.

For reasons that will be made clear subsequently, almost all the activities in this book series will occur outside in nature. Unless attracted to do otherwise, do the activities in order and build in enough time for reflection by getting a good night's dream-filled sleep between each activity. I call the activities of this series of books "HumaNatureConnect Activities" because, for the most part, they serve to "connect" you—the individual "human"—with the bigger aspect of your own Greater Self— "nature." In doing so, the activities along the Heartwood Path will bring to you and refine for you a component of what I call "Triple A Happiness." This component is "meaning."

Once meaning is extracted from the activities, it is useful to remember the significance of the event. A good way to do this is to bring along with you a pen and writing journal or an electronic mobile device such as an iPhone. If you do not have any of these, now would be a good time to acquire them.

Another way to find the meaning of the activities is to dream and analyze your dreams. We shall call such analysis "Dream Tending," a term coined by Dr. Stephen Aizenstat (2009).

To Start Off Right...

HumaNatureConnect Activity

Start-up Protocol

If this is not a day when you prefer to spend time in nature without an agenda, do the Heartwood Path Start-up Protocol found in the Appendix. Then return here to do the remaining portion of this activity:

Writing A Letter Of Gratitude

Write a letter of gratitude to someone. Make your letter as long or short as you like. Mention specifically what the intended recipient of your letter did for you and how this person's actions affected your life. Determine, once your letter is written, if you are also attracted to deliver your letter of gratitude in person. Note the affect of this letter both on yourself and, if delivered, on the recipient. In writing and delivering your letter you are already en route to "Gladandgreen Junction." This imaginary place, as satisfying as its name implies, is the destination of the Heartwood Path. This journey's end without an end will be described here and there as we continue.

Follow-up Protocol

For best results, write down your impressions of this activity in your journal using the Heartwood Path Follow-up Protocol found in the Appendix. Afterwards, consider sharing your interpretations with others.

The following section will be a regular part of the Heartwood Path. The axioms that you find there will be the most important gleanings from each waypoint. These axioms are encoded. The first digit refers to the Heartwood Path book or course, the second digit refers to the waypoint number, and the third digit refers to the axiom within each waypoint. Heartwood Path axioms help you remember the key points. You may want to look them over before you fall asleep each evening.

Heartwood Path Axioms

Key Assertions From Waypoint 1.2

1.2.1.

By awakening to the nature of happiness that arises not within the individual as a separate being but stems from one's unyield-

ing and largely forgotten connection to nature one can create both uncommon happiness in the individual and beauty and sustainability in environment.

1.2.2.

Saving one's impressions (from one's daily experiences, from connecting with nature, and from dreaming) as daily entries into a chronicle that includes one's personal diary, activity log, and dream journal is an important key to all the gates that lead to happiness and environmental quality.

1.2.3.

One of the vital components of one's chronicle is the expression of gratitude.

Nocturnal Pilgrimage 1.2

For best results, write down your impressions of each night's dreams in your journal using the Heartwood Path Dreaming Time Protocols found in the Appendix. Afterwards, consider sharing your Dream Tending with others.

Be sure to make dream journal entries. The benefits of keeping a dream journal include, dreaming more (by keeping a dream journal you are sending a "strong, silent message to your subconscious mind that dreaming and remembering your dreams is very important to you), remembering your dreams, and discovering repetitive dream cues. Without journaling, you will not be able to continue well in your pilgrimage down the Heartwood Path and you will give up a chance to be transformed positively by your dreams.

Helpful tips for dream journaling include using a pen with a light embedded in the barrel so you can jot down your first dream impressions without jolting your sleep partner or yourself (and losing your dream memory) by turning on a bright light. If you enter and store your notes about your dreams directly into a mobile device or laptop, keep it close to your bed but not close to your head. Be forewarned: keeping a cell phone in your bed may disrupt your direct experience of being in the real world, it may not be healthy, it may be a distraction if it should ring during a dream, and your typing will be loud enough to bother your sleeping partner. Follow your own attractions in this regard and consider turning off mobile devices during dreaming time or using the Airplane Mode. Consider using a tape recorder to record your dreams, if you prefer this option over pen and paper. Make sure your entries remain confidential. Keep them securely stored during the day.

At this early stage, just keep simple notes about your dreams, any way you desire. The main thing here is to get into the habit of maintaining a dream journal. We do have a comprehensive template for keeping a journal of both your awake-time impressions and your night-time dreaming. To begin that comprehensive journaling at this point, however, is probably premature, since you have not yet arrived at the waypoints where such record-keeping is explained. Nevertheless, if you are curious about how we will be recommending how to maintain your journal, go to the Appendix at the end of each book; or, if you are participating online, click on this EartHeart Chronicles Guide link.

Keep these tips and the previous teaching in mind when you head for bed tonight. After you sleep and dream, tend to your dreams by getting into the habit of maintaining a simple dream journal.

When ready, continue to the next waypoint, entitled "Hume-ster."

3

"Hume-ster"

UNDERSTAND ECOLOGICAL GROUNDEDNESS

One's reactions to planetary predicaments ought not be based solely on blind optimism nor on blind pessimism—the two extremes that seem to color much of the public discourse. Some of those involved in the promotion of environmental solutions, for example, are what I call *"boom-sters."* They argue that population growth and technological development are good for several reasons: 1) because people inevitably produce more than they consume; 2) because people are not bound by a carrying capacity of an ecosystem; 3) because people have the intelligence to improve their habitat by inventing technology; 4) because as yet unimaginable ingenuity will result in ecological solutions; and 5) because the free economic market will allow human products and human wellbeing to *boom.* Such a view, right or wrong, has a chance to become popular because it allows people to avoid the psychological discomforts that could accompany the other predominant view, that of the *"doom-sters."* Those who adopt this "doom-ster" viewpoint tend to describe with fire and brimstone a "coming environmental hell in graphic detail" and scare their audience with "dreadful prophecies, then promise salvation through conversion to a new ecological worldview" (Winter and Koger, 2004, p. 19).

The "boom-sters" create hope (which is helpful unless it is blindly unrealistic) and the "doom-sters" create an urgency for action (which is good unless the gloom is so excessive it creates stultifying fear). Given our current environmental predicament, I feel we cannot afford the pessimism that tends to accompany the "doom-ster" perspective nor the naiveté (unfounded optimism) that tends to accompany the "boom-ster" perspective. I propose an alternate perspective—that of the "Hume-ster."

A "Hume-ster" is supportive of the following contentions of Eighteenth Century philosopher David Hume regarding the psychological basis for human nature:

1. desire rather than reason governs human behavior;
2. perceptions are divided into strong and lively impressions, direct sensations, and fainter ideas which are copied from impressions; and
3. ethics are based on feelings rather than on abstract moral principles.

For these and other reasons, many of the theories and practices contained in this book, including the HumaNatureConnect methodologies included at the end of each waypoint, are, intentionally and unintentionally, compatible with the writings of David Hume.

Those who engage in the HumaNatureConnect Activities throughout the Path, for example, are embodying Hume's emphasis on the importance of direct sensation. I believe the element of attraction, so pivotal in all Heartwood Path HumanNatureConnect Activities, can be thought of as one of Hume's "impressions"—a conception that results from outer-world phenomena and are more passionate, lively, and forcible than a more feeble "idea" (Pratt) which arises after an inner world, mental reflection.

Through such inner reflections, ideas, and inner world impressions of outer world phenomena, one may consider that the world's greatest need is the improvement of healthcare worldwide, or a more equitable distribution of food and water, or for improved education globally, or any of a number of actual, significant needs. For our purposes here, let us for the moment determine that all of these needs are secondary to the primary need of environmental sustainability, for without a suitable and sustainable environment there cannot be any significant and enduring resolution of all of the other imaginable or verifiable needs.

Our destination, therefore, is an intersection of "happiness" and "the world's greatest need"—a "place" in your life that is at once metaphorical but also actually reachable. I call this place "Gladandgreen Junction." Let us now break this name down into its three components because, in doing so, we will illustrate the purpose of following the Heartwood Path.

The first component is "Glad." More than a temporary and trivial sense of joviality, the gladness we seek will be called "Triple A Happiness"—happiness that is authentic, abundant, and abiding. For happiness to be authentic, abundant, and abiding for our purposes here it has to have five components:

1. positive emotion (pleasure, rapture, ecstasy, warmth, comfort, etc.);
2. engagement (flow, stopping of time, loss of self-consciousness);
3. meaning (serving something bigger than the self);
4. positive relationships (emotional buoyancy due to other people); and
5. accomplishment (for its own sake).

The second component in "Gladandgreen Junction" is "green." By this I mean a healthy lifestyle, environmental sustainability, a healthy environment, and environmental protection.

The third component is "Junction." We will be looking not for happiness alone, nor for environmental protection alone, but for the meeting and the binding of Triple A happiness and environmental protection.

In leading people to this "place", the Heartwood Path leads to a fantastic sense of fulfillment that arises when a person comes to life more fully. "To find our calling," writes philosopher Frederick Buechner, "is to find the intersection between our own deep gladness and the world's deep hunger" (Second Journey Website). This intersection is a "place" but not necessarily a physical location. It is a "place" that is really a sense of purpose, as in the sentence: "It is not my place to tell you what to do." I borrow the phrasing of the key purpose of the Heartwood Path from a marvelous little book by Buechner called **Wishful Thinking** (1973). Under the heading of "Vocation," Buechner writes;

> "There are all different kinds of voices calling you to all different kinds of work, and the problem is to find out which is the voice of God rather than of Society, say, or the Superego, or Self-interest. By and large a good rule for finding out is this: the kind of work God usually calls you to is the kind of work (a) that you need most to do and (b) that the world most needs to have done" (Buechner, 1973, p. 95).

Except for the joy of tending to family and except for the joy of remaining loyal to one's own principles, I can think of no greater fulfillment than to find that place where you really get a kick out of your work, especially when that work is what really needs to be done for the world. All Heartwood Path Courses lead precisely to this highly charged and rewarding inner world "place" by taking you to your choice of attractive outer world places.

For reasons that will be made clear subsequently, almost all of these activities will occur in a real-world type of place that is not typically considered to be explicitly spiritual or explicitly transformational. Still, the kind of places I will be recommending—places out of doors, ranging from backyards or backwoods—are perfectly well suited for your own *hatching out.* To be a good place for such personal transformation, a location will need to have all or some of the kinds of qualities intimated in the questions included in the following activity (Cope, 1999, 27-32).

To Stand Firm Ecologically…

HumaNatureConnect Activity

Start-up Protocol

If this is not a day when you prefer to spend time in nature without an agenda, do the Heartwood Path Start-up Protocol found in the Appendix. Then return here to do the remaining portion of this activity:

Examining Outdoor Places As Transformational Spaces

For this activity, answer some or all the following questions:

1. What is it about this space that has, if at all, the quality of refuge?
2. What is it about this space that has, if at all, the ability to make you feel safe through constancy in relationship?
3. What is it about this space that, if at all, allows you to be creative and explore?
4. What is it about this space that has, if at all, the capacity to provide a transitional object, much as your baby blanket or teddy bear was a transitional object?
5. What object is there in your chosen outdoor space that is useful in taking you further into your inquiry or towards your goal?
6. How, if at all, is your perspective transitional object—be it a boulder, or a brook, or a beach, or a bird—constant and reliable?
7. How, if at all, are you making sure that you are not deifying (making into a deity) the transitional object.

8. How, if at all, are you making sure that your natural being or setting is being considered as a guide or exemplar and not considered as a spiritual being or as a god.

9. What is it about this space that, if at all, provides you with a way of finding out who you are?

10. What is it about this space that is suitable and not necessarily perfect as a place of transformation? And

11. What is it about this space that, if at all, allows for the acceptance of other paths of development?

Follow-up Protocol

For best results, write down your impressions of this activity in your journal using the Heartwood Path Follow-up Protocol found in the Appendix. Afterwards, consider sharing your interpretations with others.

Heartwood Path Axioms

Key Assertions From Waypoint 1.3

1.3.1.

A needed extra voice for those who speak up for the environment—which have been largely either the "boomsters" who may lead to unrealistic optimism or the "doomsters" who may lead to stupefying fear—can be called the "Humesters"—those who espouse philosopher David Hume's emphasis on desire rather than reason as a preferred way to govern human behavior and his call to use perceptions (which include direct sensations) ideas, and ethics that are based more on feelings than on moral principles.

1.3.2.

More than the other voices, the voice of the Humesters leads to Triple A Happiness—gladness that is authentic, abundant, and abiding.

1.3.3.

Along with helping its participants find Triple A Happiness, the Heartwood Path series of books and courses help participants come to the intersection of one's own deep gladness and the world's deep hunger which can be defined as the need for environmental sustainability.

1.3.4.

One can find the intersection of "gladness" and "greenness," where one finds a natural being in a natural place that feels like a refuge, feels safe, promotes creativity, and provides inspiration.

Nocturnal Pilgrimage 1.3

For best results, write down your impressions of each night's dreams in your journal using the Heartwood Path Dreaming Time Protocols found in the Appendix. Afterwards, consider sharing your Dream Tending with others.

Here's a practice that will help you begin a process that is very important to your success in life: gaining control of your dreams. Before you shutdown for the night, focus on direct sensation and declutter your mind, as suggested in the Before Dreaming Protocol, by repeatedly scanning your body for its in-the-moment sensations, by keeping yourself from repeating negative and positive thoughts, and by maintaining the intention of dreaming without undue distraction. In your next day's journaling, write down how these activities influenced your dreams.

After a night of rest, move to the next waypoint: "Two Prerequisite Understandings." After you get there, be sure to make entries into your Heartwood Path Activity Journal, as instructed.

4

Two Prerequisite Understandings

SECURE A POSITIVE SELF-CONCEPT AND KNOW THE MAIN UNIVERSAL PRINCIPLES

To be successful along the Heartwood Path, which will help you to be successful in your life, one will have to commit to performing two chores. These actions are very important, which is why they are combined here at the outset of the Heartwood Path.

One of the required initial chores has to do with developing a positive self- concept. The other, knowing the main universal principles.

Doing only one of these chores will not be enough. Doing them later risks losing your way in the beginning, which is never a recommended way to do anything important.

In the next activity you will be asked to do some soul-searching. One simply has to put one's inner world in proper order by developing a positive self-concept. Without doing so, one cannot be truly happy nor can one make a difference in restoring sustainability to the diverse and beautiful natural world.

While doing these tasks keep the following postulate in mind:

The inner world of individuals underlies the world's ecological predicament.

For this reason, most of what we will be doing along the Heartwood Path will be working on awakening yourself to the riches of your own inner world, beginning with how you feel about your self.

To best develop a positive self-concept, one will have to do the things necessary to be able to answer "yes" to the five questions you are asked to answer in the activity that follows.

Do not worry if you cannot honestly answer "yes" to each of these questions at this time. The Heartwood Path, especially if you sign up for guidance, will help you to put your inner house in order. Along with a positive self-concept, one's life is also affected in substantial ways by powerful, pervasive, and enduring forces.

Certain universal principles have the biggest impacts on your life.

As important as a positive self-concept is to the development and continuation of one's happiness and a fruitful environment, living in accordance with eight important universal principles will prevent one from a life of difficulty and disorder.

Do not worry about totally understanding or accepting these principles now. You will learn more about them in a subsequent Heartwood Path book. In the activity that follows, just do your best to answer the questions the best you can.

These questions and the actions associated with the universal principles are presented in the following activity to kick-start your learning and to enable you to later be able look back to see how much you have learned.

To Develop A Positive Self-concept And To No Longer Swimming Upstream In Life…

HumaNatureConnect Activity

Start-up Protocol

If this is not a day when you prefer to spend time in nature without an agenda, do the Heartwood Path Start-up Protocol found in the Appendix. Then return here to do the remaining portion of this activity:

Developing A Positive Self-concept And Learning About Universal Principles In Nature

This is a very important two-part activity. One's best hope for developing into a person of merit is to work inwardly to develop a positive Self-concept and to work outwardly to go with the flow created by universal principles.

First, ask yourself the four questions that lead to the development of a positive self-concept as a person of merit:

1. Do I accept criticism?

> If you don't you will not have an opportunity to grow. If you do, you can benefit from the input of others. Criticism that is helpful rather than demeaning leads to a positive self-concept.

2. Do I obtain goals?

> Setting, and more specifically, writing down goals, leads to success. Without goals, you will engage in actions that do not lead to where you want to go. Your positive

self-concept will grow as you meet and celebrate the achievement of measurable objectives that let you know that you have achieve unmeasurable goals.

3. Am I willing to take risks?

No growth occurs in the Comfort Zone, that place where you are free of stress because you are avoiding uncomfortable stressors. Likewise, no growth occurs in the Panic Zone, where stressors are large enough to give you an urgent feeling to fight or flee rather than to apply yourself to personal growth. By being neither complacent nor in a state of panic you can enter the Growth Zone where you can take risks because you have appropriate safety nets in case you falter. In this way taking risks develops a positive self-concept.

4. Do I try new experiences?

Continuously retrying what has not worked before is not as good of a strategy for personal growth as seeking out new experiences. Saying "yes" to new approaches and events is not only exhilarating, it is also a worthy strategy for creating a positive self concept.

If your answers to the above questions are not "yes" you will know where you need to take corrective actions.

Second, to help you stop swimming against any of the big, pervasive, and enduring currents of life, do some awareness-building tasks aimed at helping you take the first steps toward consciously experiencing the main universal principles:

1. Everything is mental. Do not focus on nature as a separate physical entity nor as an unrelated figment of your imagination but on your awareness—your impressions—of attractive beings and landscapes.

2. As above, so below. Look for ways that you or other beings are microcosms of the larger universe or how you function the same way the universe functions.

3. All is in vibration. Pay attention to comings and goings, repeated patterns and sounds, and the rise and fall of your own feelings.

4. Rhythm compensates. Note the "beat" and the "space" between the beats, as in breathing in, delay, and breathing out; or the onset of morning bird sounds, then relative quiet at night, followed by the return to morning chatter.

5. Everything is dual. Note examples that show, for example, how for every beginning there is an end.

6. Every cause has its effect and every effect has its cause. Notice how, for example, compassionate acts are both a means and an end, or how happiness is both a means and an end.

7. Everything has masculine and feminine characteristics. Look for how females can exhibit the masculine characteristics of strength and aggression just as males can exhibit the feminine characteristics of relaxing, rejoicing, intuiting, receiving, and feeling. And

8. One needs to become the change one seeks in the world. Think about what you want to see occur in the world and how you will have to be, both inwardly and outwardly, to evoke your improved image of a better world.

Pick an aspect of your chosen natural being or its natural surroundings that illustrates any one of the universal principles just mentioned. Write down in your journal how both you and your natural being or its surroundings are benefitted by heeding this universal principle. Explain what you think might happen to your chosen attractive being if it was not in line with this universal principle. Lastly, write down how your life is better by being in line with this universal principle. If you picked the "Everything is dual" universal principle, for example, you may note that if the leaves don't wither and fall there will be no soil to support new life. And that by shedding some old pattern of behavior that is no longer useful you are making it problems to begin new, more useful patterns of behavior.

Follow-up Protocol

For best results, write down your impressions of this activity in your journal using the Heartwood Path Follow-up Protocol found in the Appendix. Afterwards, consider sharing your interpretations with others.

Heartwood Path Axioms

Key Assertions From Waypoint 1.4

1.4.1.

Know how to develop and sustain a positive self-concept and know the main universal principles.

1.4.2.

The inner world of individuals underlies the world's ecological predicament.

1.4.3.

Keep a record of your dreams, for they are one way nature provides guidance.

Nocturnal Pilgrimage 1.4

For best results, write down your impressions of each night's dreams in your journal using the Heartwood Path Dreaming Time Protocols found in the Appendix. Afterwards, consider sharing your Dream Tending with others.

Sleep. Dream. Pay attention to your dreams. Keep a record of them in a dream journal.

When ready, move to the next waypoint: "Fortitude."

5

Fortitude

IDENTIFY YOUR BEST STRENGTHS

There is a type of uncommon fulfillment that you can achieve that will be both good for you and good for the environment. What you have to do to achieve this abundant, authentic and abiding form of satisfaction is awaken to the nature of happiness. By this, I mean, that a primary source of your happiness is not within you as a separate being but stems from your unyielding but largely forgotten connection to Nature.

This series of books and courses will take you to a very special place where your own happiness meets the world's great need for ecological sustainability. You can do this for your own pleasure and for the sake of the environment. Either way, you will be happier in your endeavors if you make good use of your best personal strengths.

For the next activity, make a list of what Martin E.P. Seligman (2011) calls "signature strengths." Such strengths are best suited to helping you obtain Triple A Happiness. They are the aspects of your character that allow you to say: "This is the real me." These aspects of your character make you feel excited while displaying them. They provide a sense of ease in learning how to apply them. They give a sense of yearning for how to use them. They provide a sense that your application of them is inevitable. They make you feel invigorated rather than exhausted. They give you the desire to undertake related personal projects. Lastly, they provide a sense of joy and enthusiasm.

To Personal Happiness...

HumaNatureConnect Activity

Start-up Protocol

If this is not a day when you prefer to spend time in nature without an agenda, do the Heartwood Path Start-up Protocol found in the Appendix. Then return here to do the remaining portion of this activity:

Identifying Your Best Strengths

With previously mentioned parameters in mind, pick your top three signature strengths from the following list:

1. Love of learning
2. Bravery
3. Vitality
4. Leadership
5. Appreciation of beauty and excellence
6. Humor
7. Creativity
8. Curiosity
9. Open-mindedness
10. Perspective or wisdom
11. Persistence
12. Integrity
13. Love
14. Kindness

15. Social intelligence
16. Fairness
17. Gratitude
18. Hope
19. Spirituality
20. Forgiveness and mercy
21. Self-regulation
22. Citizenship
23. Humility/Modesty
24. Prudence

My three are 1) appreciation of beauty and excellence, 2) curiosity, and 3) integrity. By developing this series of books and courses aimed at helping others preserve the beauty and excellence (sustainability) of the environment, by being a guide for the Heartwood Path, which requires me to use my curiosity about the participants to help them with their own personal growth, and by making the Heartwood Path very holistic and thus suitable to my strength of integrity, I feel that my life is well-suited to my personal strengths—a factor that accounts for my general sense of happiness.

Once you determine your "signature strengths," write down why you made your choices, whether you are happier because your life is aligned to take advantage of your strengths, and, if not, what changes you need to make to best apply your "signature strengths" in your life. If you feel you need help with this assignment, call 618-632-5600 for Guidance.

Follow-up Protocol

For best results, write down your impressions of this activity in your journal using the Heartwood Path Follow-up Protocol found in the Appendix. Afterwards, consider sharing your interpretations with others.

Heartwood Path Axioms

Key Assertions From Waypoint 1.5

1.5.1.

Under the positive influence of a chosen natural being and its surrounding natural environment, work to identify your strengths.

1.5.2.

Working on one's strengths is more fruitful than trying to improve one's weaknesses.

1.5.3.

Pay particular attention to aspects of your character that provide a sense of excitement and enthusiasm, that provide a sense of ease in learning, that provide a sense of yearning for how to use one's strengths, that provide a sense that one's application of a particular strength is inevitable, and that make you feel invigorated, desirous, and joyful.

Nocturnal Pilgrimage 1.5

For best results, write down your impressions of each night's dreams in your journal using the Heartwood Path Dreaming Time Protocols found in the Appendix. Afterwards, consider sharing your Dream Tending with others.

Tonight as you dream, and while dreaming for the next several nights, look for examples of what may be your signature strengths in your dreams. There may be numerous examples, easily forgotten if you do not do the component of the Before Dreaming Protocol titled "Journal Ready," which has to do with placing your dream journal in or near your bed so you can write in it without moving upon waking after your dream.

After the customary period of overnight reflection, proceed to the next waypoint: "Well-being." Be sure to note what went well for you during your most recent day. This is a nice habit to adopt.

6

Well-being

NOTE WHAT WENT WELL TODAY

Best-selling author and Positive Psychologist Martin E. P. Seligman believes "that well-being can be robustly raised" (2011, p. 32). Part of the technique for raising one's well-being has to do with focusing more on personal strengths than on weaknesses. Another is to focus on the positive, including affirmative skills that come from goodwill towards others and lead to virtue, and goodness—all aspects of our next topic.

To Change Your Own Well-being...

HumaNatureConnect Activity

Start-up Protocol

If this is not a day when you prefer to spend time in nature without an agenda, do the Heartwood Path Start-up Protocol found in the Appendix. Then return here to do the remaining portion of this activity:

Noting What Went Well Today

For this activity, write down a list of five things that went well to-day. After each item on your "went well" list, write down how and why you feel this aspect of your life turned out to be positive.

Follow-up Protocol

For best results, write down your impressions of this activity in your journal using the Heartwood Path Follow-up Protocol found in the Appendix. Afterwards, consider sharing your interpretations with others.

Heartwood Path Axioms

Key Assertions From Waypoint 1.6

1.6.1.

One's state of well-being can be raised.

1.6.2.

Positive true stories about yourself make you feel good.

1.6.3.

Note what went well today.

1.6.4.

To boost well-being, commune with nature, find the goodness and virtue that comes from goodwill towards others, and note what goes well each day.

Nocturnal Pilgrimage 1.6

For best results, write down your impressions of each night's dreams in your journal using the Heartwood Path Dreaming Time Protocols found in the Appendix. Afterwards, consider sharing your Dream Tending with others.

Now is an opportune time to wrap together the theme of this waypoint (one's state of well-being can be raised) with the benefit that comes from the Dreaming Time Protocol having to do with looking to your dreams for what you need to remember. In this instance, your task was to remember what went well today. If you are doing this remembering while you are indoors and you are not satisfied with the results, try going back outdoors and do your recollections in the presence of an attractive natural being. Compare your results. You may be pleasantly surprised with what is revealed. With your good fortunes listed in your journal, consider and record how each of your personal strengths led to each of your positive outcomes. Having done this, take your self-assessment one step further. Develop the intention to dream about how your strengths are improving your specific outcomes and, generally, raising your overall level of wellbeing, and repeat this intention to yourself over and over again until you fall asleep. As you dream, look for examples of the impact of your strengths on your wellbeing. If no examples appear, keep trying until you feel satisfied with what you are able to record in your dream journal. Compare your waking time recollections to your dreaming time recollections. How, if at all, did spending time in nature and tending to your dreams reveal anything new?

You are moving through this book nicely. After recording your overnight dreams, move to the next waypoint, entitled "Ethos." While you are there, come to an understanding of what "ethos" means and then write a positive true personal story, one that makes you feel good about yourself.

7

Ethos

DEVELOP YOUR PRACTICAL SKILLS, WISDOM, VIRTUE, GOODNESS, AND GOODWILL TOWARDS OTHERS

For our purposes here "ethos" means "an accustomed place where customs and habits mark the starting point or appearance of the disposition of individual and collective character" marked in three ways: 1) practical skills and wisdom; 2) virtue and goodness; and 3) goodwill towards others (Webster's Online Dictionary).

The Ecological Need For Ethos

There is not an ample supply of skills, wisdom, virtue, goodness, and goodwill for others to overcome overpopulation, hunger, poverty, species loss, habitat destruction, and climate change. The world is facing unprecedented problems, partly because there are so many people with the means to consume, pollute, and use harmful technologies. These are troubles in the outer world that do not stop there.

The Psychological Need For Ethos

At its root, the planetary pickle we face—overpopulation, hunger, poverty, species loss, habitat destruction, and climate change—is caused, largely, by a deficiency in the inner world. Speaking of climate change, we all know that former U.S. Senator Al Gore won the Nobel Prize for his work on how mankind's heat-producing industrial processes are adversely affecting the environment. As a result of his work, many people now realize that we need a new formula for living sustainably on this planet. I propose we base this formula on a new "Algorhythm." Doing so along the lines suggested in the Heartwood Path series of books would not only improve our environment, but also our character.

Too many humans are ignorant of the true inner nature they share with others and the true inner nature that makes them unique. We have a crisis of mind and spirit and this malady manifests itself not only in the human mind as mental illnesses but also throughout the world's environment. We as a species need to become what the earth needs for its own survival. To achieve this transformation for the sake of the earth and ourselves we will need to overcome some serious psychological challenges caused, in part, by being in less contact with the *wild*.

We need to overcome our own be*wild*erment. This will require a conversion, person by person, from a psychological acceptance of being reduced to cogs the our culture's economic machine to being instead whole people living in harmony with nature. Until this happens, humanity will live in a bewildering state of inner turmoil that causes many of our outer world problems.

This inner confusion is multifaceted. It is the lack of understanding about how everything is relative. It is the lack of understanding about how nothing is self-sufficient. It is the lack of understanding about how everything is the result of a run of causes and conditions. The inner confusion is the failure to grasp how everything is interdependent. Important for our purposes here, the inner confusion stems from the failure to recognize that our modern culture is no longer doing what is needed to produce the kind of elders required to promote the genuine solving of our biggest challenges. Failure to understand such things has resulted in mental illnesses, war, poverty, disharmony, and environmental destruction.

Our be*wild*erment leads to behaviors that are accompanied by attitudes and beliefs that make the normal course of our daily lives "seem sensible, even though business as usual is jeopardizing future survival" (Winter and Koger, 2004, p. 2). By business as usual, Winter and Koger are referring to, among other things, the modern emphasis on individualism with its sense of freedom and mobility (p. 6).

Beyond the determination of technological answers, we humans will have to change the way we behave, change the way we see ourselves, and change the way we perceive our relationship to nature. We need to rethink our excessive individualism. It promotes self-indulgence and a lack of concern for others.

We have big global problems, the biggest of which is perhaps the dismantling of the earth's life support systems—most of which occurring during my own more than half century of life. These problems are causing people to worry that their lives will be changed in unwelcome ways. Even our survivability as a species is called into question.

Over-consumption "is not delivering the goods," at least not psychologically. Empirical studies of people's happiness shows that it is not how much stuff people own but the condition of their social relations, their work, and their leisure time that determines how much fulfillment people experience (Winter and Koger, 2004, p. 22).

Despite any grim assessments, take heart, for at least one aspect of the "boom-ster" perspective rings true: as always, big solutions arise from big catastrophes. That is what is happening now. People are beginning to see the scope of the global dilemma and, here and there, fitfully, the real cause of all of it is beginning to be recognized—a first step towards finding out what it will take to make positive advancements towards real solutions. That first positive step is the realization that humans are not separate from nature. We all know that Americans will eventually do the right thing, after trying everything else.

To Your Favorable Autobiography…

HumaNatureConnect Activity

Start-up Protocol

If this is not a day when you prefer to spend time in nature without an agenda, do the Heartwood Path Start-up Protocol found in the Appendix. Then return here to do the remaining portion of this activity:

Writing A Positive Story About Yourself

For this activity, note any strengths of character you notice in your environment. These may include the strength of a tree trunk, the flexibility of grass, or the apparent cheerfulness of a bird. Make correlations between such strengths in the environment with your own strengths of character. Then write down a positive one-page story that illustrates your best character strengths.

Follow-up Protocol

For best results, write down your impressions of this activity in your journal using the Heartwood Path Follow-up Protocol found in the Appendix. Afterwards, consider sharing your interpretations with others.

Heartwood Path Axioms

Key Assertions From Waypoint 1.7

1.7.1.

Good will toward others, virtue and goodness, and practical skills and wisdom form an individuals or a community's "ethos."

1.7.2.

There is not an ample supply of skills, wisdom, virtue, goodness, and goodwill towards others to overcome overpopulation, hunger, poverty, species loss, habitat destruction, and climate change.

1.7.3.

The world needs a new blueprint that honors the former ally to environmentalists in the U.S. Senate, a new "Algorhythm" that converts each person from a state of psychological acceptance of being reduced to a cog in the culture's economic machine to being instead a whole person living in harmony with nature.

1.7.4.

Achieving environmental sustainability requires the ending of our bewilderment; that is, the end of excessive individualism, self-indulgence, lack of concern for others, over-consumption, and the beginning of finding the big solution imbedded in the big problem.

Nocturnal Pilgrimage 1.7

For best results, write down your impressions of each night's dreams in your journal using the Heartwood Path Dreaming Time

Protocols found in the Appendix. Afterwards, consider sharing your Dream Tending with others.

Having some experience with both the Heartwood Path approach to communing with nature and the Heartwood Path approach to tending to your dreams, you are ready now to notice the parallels between the two. Go out and commune with nature before you fall asleep tonight. Do this again even if you have already done an Heartwood Path activity today. Set an intention that in your next dream you want to identify the Dream Character that appears in your dream as an attractive natural being. This image may or may not be the same as one of the most recent attractive natural beings chosen by you in recent Heartwood Path Activities. It may not even be an attractive natural being, especially at first. Take what may be your first jab at communing with such a Dream Character in the same way you commune with natural attractive beings during your waking time. Your attempts to notice similarities (if any) between attractive natural beings and attractive natural Dream Characters may occur while you are dreaming, if you are able to dream lucidly. Or, you may pay attention to the similarities and differences as they occur in your memory after you dream. As you would your attractive natural beings, remain with your attractive natural Dream Character long enough to verify, through your continued attraction, the giving of consent to participate in your connection experience. Apply the components of our HumaNatureConnect Activity Start Up Protocol to your connection experience with your Dream Character. In your dream journal, list both the similarities and the differences, not only between your specific connection experience partners but also between your impression of waking time attractive natural beings and attractive dreaming time natural beings, in general. In doing so, you are developing the way for guidance from attractive natural beings to be delivered, and perhaps clarified, through the Dream Characters in your dreams. For this reason, learning to attend to Dream Characters, especially dreaming time images of attractive natural beings, is an important skill for you to develop as you proceed along the Heartwood Path.

Do not be concerned if you have difficulty with this assignment. Do whatever you can, recognizing that you are a beginner. You will have more chances later. Your abilities will improve with practice, so make your comparisons as often as you like. Help will follow.

If you have slept and recorded a new dream in your journal, it is time to move to the next waypoint, entitled "Holistic Growth." Prepare to put your strengths to work for you.

8

Holistic Growth

BECOME MORE ECO-CENTRIC

Underlying all of our big outer world problems is a largely unrecognized inner world epidemic: the widespread and growing failure to grow in depth on the inside as we grow up on the outside. Most of us humans are not maturing as much as we can and certainly not as much as we ought to do considering the problems we face.

Given the problems of poverty, racism, environmental destruction, hunger and the like, we no longer have the luxury of merely growing up into the kind of adults our culture is currently producing. Almost all of us are maturing physically but we are not maturing psychologically or spiritually. Along with merely growing into physical maturity—the kind of old age we can visibly see in the outer world—we need to also grow and develop within the invisible inner world; that is, we need to become comprehensively mature (both inside and out) to the point that will be necessary if a person is to become a true eco-centric volunteer or life coach capable of helping others with their comprehensive development.

To A Strong Coming-of-age...

HumaNatureConnect Activity

Start-up Protocol

If this is not a day when you prefer to spend time in nature without an agenda, do the Heartwood Path Start-up Protocol found in the Appendix. Then return here to do the remaining portion of this activity:

Applying Personal Strengths To Situations And Using Personal Strengths To Become More Comprehensively Mature

For this activity, look over your personal strengths list and story (from the previous activity) and write down ways that your strengths can be applied to at least three current situations in your life. Then write down how using your strengths on these situations helps to make you more comprehensively mature (by which I mean mature in ways other than merely growing older, such as the ability to handle conflict with grace, or the ability to see opportunities in negative events, or remembering that your own problems are small when compared to the problems facing the whole earth).

Follow-up Protocol

For best results, write down your impressions of this activity in your journal using the Heartwood Path Follow-up Protocol found in the Appendix. Afterwards, consider sharing your interpretations with others.

Heartwood Path Axioms

Key Assertions From Waypoint 1.8

1.8.1.

Underlying all of our big outer world problems is a largely un-recognized inner world epidemic: the widespread and growing failure to grow in depth on the inside as we grow up on the outside.

1.8.2.

Along with merely growing into physical maturity—the kind of old age we can visibly see in the outer world—we need to also grow and develop within the invisible inner world; that is, we need to become comprehensively mature (both inside and out) to the point that will be necessary if a person is to become a useful elder, or, more specifically an eco-centric volunteer or life coach.

1.8.3.

One good way to work on being a useful elder is to write down how using one's strengths in three different life situations helps to make one more comprehensively mature (by which I mean the ability to handle conflict with grace, the ability to see opportunities in negative events, or remembering that one's own problems are small when compared to the problems facing the whole world).

Nocturnal Pilgrimage 1.8

For best results, write down your impressions of each night's dreams in your journal using the Heartwood Path Dreaming Time Protocols found in the Appendix. Afterwards, consider sharing your Dream Tending with others.

Just as it is never unproductive to wander in nature without an agenda, it is likewise often a welcome diversion to just let your dreams work their magic on you without prompts or pre-set intentions. Go ahead. Whenever you like, get a little lost in the wilderness of the back woods. Go for an aimless moonlit hike tonight. When you return, keep any yearnings to control what happens at bay, psychologically step off the beaten path that has become overused in your mind, and linger for a spell in the untamed regions of the dream world.

Having slept and recorded your unrestricted dreams, it is time to step up your intimacy with nature. Move to the next waypoint, labeled "Nature Intimacy." Be sure to count your blessings and record them in your journal.

9

Nature Intimacy

DRAW CLOSE TO NATURE AND
COUNT YOUR BLESSINGS

This series of books and courses presents a way for people to develop and put to use a specific type of necessary but uncommon maturity. For the sake of finding solutions to our serious problems and for the sake of the happiness of humans we need to move people beyond the more typical arrested state of psycho-spiritual development—a condition I will describe subsequently. We need to instead return to "our species' original intimacy with the natural world" (Plotkin, 2010, p. 11-12). As we shall see, Dr. Cohen's methodology will be very helpful in this regard.

Becoming significantly reacquainted with the natural world will help create not only eco-centric elders but also a human/earth partnership. The mutuality that is implied by the forward slash in the previous sentence can only occur if we determine a way to ripen people, to teach them how to grow up fully, to allow them to become, not only old, but also wise. Simply put: we need more people concerned about others and respected for having skills that help people grow into responsible adults.

To deserve this respect, elders will need an appreciation for the natural world—for that is where the blueprint of human development lies; they will have to have valued traits; they will need to be able to see what is needed for the present and the future; and they will need to be willing and even driven to stand up persistently to injustice, not just for their own benefit, but also for the welfare of others. Respect for such elders ought not be based on their chronological age, their place in society, their physical development, nor their mental abilities. Respect for elders ought to flow naturally to those who do the psychological and spiritual tasks associated with each stage of human development (as described subsequently). Respect and gratitude ought to flow to those who persevere in their efforts to transform the world for the benefit of all.

Such eco-centric elders—whether they be volunteers or professional life coaches—by their words and actions, show us that there is no survival in isolation. Eco-centric elders demonstrate that our species will simply have to start showing more concern for others, and not just human others.

Humanity's tumultuous troubles—including, hunger, resource depletion, wars, climate change, and species loss—have finally awakened a few people to the need for a paradigm shift. This alone is a good start, but it is not enough.

Only when there are enough vociferous voters, guided by ecologically-minded elders and clamoring for change, will governments react and enact the necessary changes. This required movement of people will only happen if someone or some group makes it happen. It will occur as a result of a significant conversion of humanity towards valued values, treasured traits, prized priorities, esteemed ethics, and beneficial spiritual beliefs.

Such subjects—morals, ethics, mores, beliefs, and collective values—in short, "ethos"—will be presented in detail in Heartwood Path Book/Course # 5: Connecting with Valued Traits. As we will see, these are critically important topics. More so than politics, economics, or technology, ethos will ultimately be the root cause of humanity's and the earth's pursuit of salvation.

Unless we ponder, discuss, and hone an ecological ethos, I feel the other instruments of change will not be enough. We do not need more religiously imposed moralistic restrictions. We need a moral or spiritual heading.

It will take the development of eco-centric elders (volunteers and coaches) to spread this way of being amongst us. And someone or some group will have to train the trainers of the eco-centric life coaches. That is where you, a participant in this series of books, one of a cadre of so-called "eartHearts," can serve a vital role.

There is not only an ecological crisis in the outer world. There is also a spiritual crisis in the inner world. Together, these crises are hitting us hard and just in time to wake us up so we can avoid answering T.S. Elliot's question about which sound would accompany the end—a "whimper" or a "bang."

Despite the seriousness of these crises, there remains a continuous array of blessings for you to appreciate. While remembering that serious issues confront us all, let us begin our journey to Gladandgreen Junction by developing the useful habit of focusing on the positive.

To Cataloging Your Windfalls...

HumaNatureConnect Activity

Start-up Protocol

If this is not a day when you prefer to spend time in nature without an agenda, do the Heartwood Path Start-up Protocol found in the Appendix. Then return here to do the remaining portion of this activity:

Cataloging Your Blessing

For this activity, go through the following seven ways to catalogue your blessings:

1. Write down three to five sentences about what makes you feel grateful each time you open your blessings journal.
2. Every day add slips of paper, each commemorating one of your blessings, to a gratitude jar or box, decorated to your liking. Read your gratitude slips at least once per year.
3. Stack up rocks into a cairn that commemorates your blessings. Do not leave such a disturbance in a wilderness area.
4. To overcome the inevitable periods of "the blues," read over your answers to questions that serve as your gratitude prompts. Questions to answer include: What/who made me smile today? When I think about the person I am today, I am proud of these things: Who are the people who make my world joyful? These are some things that inspired me today: What is the experience I feel most touched by today? Who/ What brought positivity into my life in the last couple of days? Who helped me solve an emotional/ work-related problem today? What did I receive in the last couple of days that made me happy? Which part of my body did the most work today? What/Who entered my world unexpectedly today? What opportunities presented themselves to me lately? What motivated me in the last couple of days to move forward with my life? To prompt yourself to remember more blessings, finish the following sentences: I'm grateful for three things I hear:... I'm grateful for three things I see... I'm grateful for three things I smell... I'm grateful for three things I touch/ feel... I'm grateful for these three things I taste... I'm grateful for these three blue things... I'm grateful for these three animals/ birds... I'm grateful for these three friends... I'm grateful for these three teachers... I'm grateful for these three family members... I'm grateful for these three things in my home... I'm grateful for these three people who hired me...

5. Write and send a letter of gratitude.

6. Make a collage of your blessings.

7. Modify your calendar to make it a reminder of your blessings.

Follow-up Protocol

For best results, write down your impressions of this activity in your journal using the Heartwood Path Follow-up Protocol found in the Appendix. Afterwards, consider sharing your interpretations with others.

Heartwood Path Axioms

Key Assertions From Waypoint 1.9

1.9.1.

We need to return to "our species' original intimacy with the natural world, we need to become significantly reacquainted with the natural world, we need more people concerned about others, and we need to deserve to be respected for having skills that help people grow into responsible adults.

1.9.2.

To deserve respect, elders will need an appreciation for the natural world—for that is where the blueprint of human development lies; they will have to have valued traits; they will need to be able to see what is needed for the present and the future; and they will need to be willing and even driven to stand up persistently to injustice, not just for their own benefit, but also for the welfare of others.

1.9.3.

Unless we ponder, discuss, and hone an ecological ethos, the other instruments of change will not be enough, for instead of more religiously imposed moralistic restrictions, we need a moral or spiritual heading.

1.9.4.

Despite the seriousness of the world's crises, there remains a continuous array of blessings for one to appreciate.

Nocturnal Pilgrimage 1.9

For best results, write down your impressions of each night's dreams in your journal using the Heartwood Path Dreaming Time Protocols found in the Appendix. Afterwards, consider sharing your Dream Tending with others.

Let me now begin what will be a series of tips for how to learn what your dreams may be telling you. I offer this information because you will be encouraged to dream and record your dreams before you start each new waypoint. Much of what I will be saying about awakening to the power of dreams to transform your life will come from Stephen Aizenstat, Ph.D., author of the book **Dream Tending** (2009). Strange as it may sound, at first, "dream tending," as Aizenstat calls it, is the nighttime version of connecting with a natural being, for he claims that dreams are a "present living reality that you can engage with and learn from in your daily life" (2009, back cover). I see dreaming and keeping a dream journal as a way to interpret the "vibes" and feelings you glean from, not only your dreams, but also from connecting with your chosen attractive natural beings. More information about how to make the figures in your dreams helpful mentors will unfold, along with the reminders to record your dreams, at each of the Nocturnal Pilgrimages in this book.

Although the Dreaming Protocol was written to help you witness and interact with your dreams so that you can best tend to them later, the advice given (be receptive, fluid, interactive, and grounded) is also helpful as you go outside to commune with attractive natural beings in nature. Prior to your journalling always engage actively, openly, and gratefully.

To find a useful template for how you can keep a record of your impressions as you continue down the Heartwood Path see the guide for the "EartHeart Chronicles—" (found at www.heartwoodpath.com/eartheart-chronicles-guide.html) which includes a Waking Time Journal, a Heartwood Path Activity Journal, and a Dream Journal. You can copy this template and use it as it is or modify it according to your own needs and attractions. For now, in your own journal, simply jot down your impressions of your dreams from the night before, then continue down the Heartwood Path by moving to the next waypoint, titled "Serviceable Bitterness." You will get better at dream tending in a step-by-step fashion throughout this series of books.

10

Serviceable Bitterness

PUT YOUR ANGER TO GOOD USE

Despite the criticisms of doomsday rhetoric, despite how poorly such words are taken by the political elite, by technologists, and by the academic establishment, our global situation demands that we recognize the scope of our problem and no longer turn solely to technology alone, or science alone, or religion alone, for the fix. We need to develop the people who can give us the best sort of ethos to guide us, even if we use technology, science, and religion as part of the solution. Unless "we better understand our own behavior and how to change it, we will not use sophisticated technological solutions when and if they become available" (Winter and Koger, 2004, p. 21).

A recognition of this need leads naturally to three questions: What sort of eco-centric elders do we need? How do we produce more of them? What is the sort of ethos that is required for human happiness and ecological sustainability? By the end of the Heartwood Path you will be able to answer each of these questions.

For now, learn what it takes to make a major step towards being a part of the solution rather than a part of the problem. This step has to do with finding the light side rather than just the dark side of anger.

Looking back at the successes I contributed to in my conservation career, it was the love of certain natural places plus the proper channeling of anger over their potential devastation that, over and over, propelled us through difficult times to eventual positive end results. The thought of the long-operating Mullen Farm going under water as a result of the proposed Meramec Dam on one of my favorite canoeing streams, for example, made me livid. And it was the bitterness I felt about the audacity of planning the desecration the finest forest cathedral in Missouri—the Irish Wilderness—that provided the impetus I needed to sustain me over the years of effort that largely ended when that wild place—so precious to me—was added to the National Wilderness Preservation System.

Hindsight reveals that when I was angry over the thought of some impending destruction of a beloved natural place I worked on the issue; and when I wasn't, I work less or not at all. At the time, I didn't know that I, along with the other leaders, were appropriately channeling our anger in ways that ended in conservation successes. We were just muddling through. We focused almost solely on the outer world resources. We essentially never focused on our own inner world motivations, resilience, or clarity. Thanks to what is presented next, you do not have to repeat this more difficult and unimaginative approach.

Given what I now know, I cannot imagine ever justifying the diminishment of anger. Temper your anger. Don't extinguish it.

Five Steps Toward Making Your Anger Useful

The importance of the next five steps you take down the Heartwood Path cannot be overstated:

Step One. *Decide if your anger is worth expressing.* Rather than fuming out loud to others about grievances that have no solutions, save your outbursts for issues that can be corrected. Any imagined solution, regardless of its difficulty to achieve, will do for this step. Imagine it is solved and it will be solved, especially if you do not listen to experienced predecessors who may claim that the work will be too difficult or that the desired outcome is unlikely. Get mad at anyone who demoralizes the key players in the environmental movement—the naive amateurs—who, while often not knowing it, have within themselves the ability to do the impossible.

Step Two. *Apologize for your imperfect expressions of your anger in advance.* Do not apologize for your anger, for it gives you energy and conveys importance. Just tell others that your expressions may be less than ideal because your anger keeps you from always communicating clearly. Admitting your anger-driven discomfort will make your audience more empathetic.

Step Three. *Slow down.* Rather than engaging in a rapid-fire monologue, take a break, and be silent for however long it takes for you to regain your composure. These breaks will likely add to the impact of your presentation.

Step Four. *Monitor your anger as you proceed.* Make sure your anger continues to give you energy and is helping you to convey your message. The goal of this monitoring is to make sure that you are using your anger in ways they convey urgency—the need for rapid participation, the need for greater involvement now, the grave need to protect some being, or the need to act earnestly to do something that adds to someone's happiness. Also, check on the impacts of your anger on others.

Step Five. *Set limits on the severity of your expressed anger.* If your anger is too much for you or your audience, or if your anger is a distraction, cool it down. A walk through a natural setting is one of the best ways to bring your anger down to an acceptable level. If your anger is not sufficient to give you the energy you require, or if your expressed anger is not imparting enough urgency, heat up the expression of your anger. To do so, imagine the negative impact of a proposal on a loved one and express with greater vehemence (perhaps with pounding fists, fire in the eyes, or stronger language) your displeasure about the prospect and your determination to do something significant to right the wrong.

To Practice Putting Anger To Good Use...

HumaNatureConnect Activity

Start-up Protocol

If this is not a day when you prefer to spend time in nature without an agenda, do the Heartwood Path Start-up Protocol found in the Appendix. Then return here to do the remaining portion of this activity:

Noting What Angers You And How That Makes You Feel

For this activity, be thankful for the way anger provides you with energy and conveys urgency about some public issue, imagine yourself apologizing in advance for your less-than-perfect expressions of anger, imagine monitoring your anger as you proceed with your efforts on a social or environmental cause, and imagine putting upper and lower limits on your anger, noting how too little robs you of energy, and how too much is a distraction.

Follow-up Protocol

For best results, write down your impressions of this activity in your journal using the Heartwood Path Follow-up Protocol found in the Appendix. Afterwards, consider sharing your interpretations with others.

Heartwood Path Axioms

Key Assertions From Waypoint 1.10

1.10.1.

Determine what makes you angry, how that feels, and how to put your anger to good use.

1.10.2.

We need to develop the people who can give us the best sort of ethos to guide us, even if we use technology, science, and religion as part of the solution.

1.10.3.

The five ways to put anger—which has the positive effect of providing energy and conveying urgency—to good use are: 1) deciding if your anger is worth expressing, 2) apologizing for your imperfect expressions of your anger in advance, 3) slowing down through the effective use of emotion-resetting pauses, 4) monitoring the impact of anger on yourself and others, and 5) setting both upper and lower limits on the severity of your expressed anger.

1.10.4.

Tuning into the meaning and significance of dreams in a way that offers guidance happens over time and in stages through the use of association, amplification, and animation (each explained in the following Nocturnal Pilgrimage section).

1.10.5.

Like living animals, dreams have presence, place, and body.

Nocturnal Pilgrimage 1.10

For best results, write down your impressions of each night's dreams in your journal using the Heartwood Path Dreaming Time Protocols found in the Appendix. Afterwards, consider sharing your Dream Tending with others.

Consider the notion that "dream images not only live within us, but they exist all around us, in every animal, plant, and object of this world" (Aizenstat, 2009, p. 8). Tuning into the meaning and significance of dreams in a way that offers guidance happens over time and through various means. Aizenstat mentions three major approaches:

1. From Sigmund Freud, there is association—wherein dreams help us with our infantile rage, latent wishes, and repressed aggressive sexual drives, which are often too upsetting for the conscious mind to process. (Aizenstat, 2009, p. 15).

2. From Carl Jung, there is amplification—wherein dreams originate in the collective human psyche and can represent universal archetypes, similar to themes and characters found in literature. Amplified dreams tell us something of the grand story in which we live. In Jung's technique, "we expand (amplify) the (dream) image to its full stature as an archetype and then see how that archetypal motif is currently active in our lives" (Aizenstat, 2009, p. 12-19)

3. From James Hillman, there is animation—wherein dreams are "more than signs pointing to some answer, as Freud said, or symbols representing a meaning, like Jung said. According to Hillman, dreams are also "phenomenal, like living animals, and have presence, place, and body" (Aizenstat, 2009, pp. 12-19).

Of these three approaches, we in this series of books/courses will be using animation the most, but not at first. You are encouraged to look at tonight's dreams (and the next several night's dreams as well) as signs of repressed drives. Look for how your dreams may be revealing yearnings, thoughts, memories, or feelings that you may be hiding from yourself by burying them in your subconscious mind. You may be driven to things, actions, relationships or thoughts that, if they were revealed, would be unsettled or embarrassing. Dreams bring such repressed drives into your awareness in ways that are psychologically manageable or, if necessary, jolting. Once revealed you can deal with your repressed baggage simply by bringing them to light; by mulling them over yourself; by discussing them with trusted friends or family; or by bringing them to the attention of a counselor, social worker, life coach, Heartwood Path guide, or psychologist. Any time you reveal a repressed drive you have the fortunate opportunity to reach important understandings, make appropriate changes, and, free yourself from a burden that was holding you back, even if it was operating beneath your awareness.

After recording your impressions of your repressed drives in your dream journal (assuming you have revealed one or more) move to the next waypoint: "Life Coaches."

11

Life Coaches

WRITE A LETTER OF FORGIVENESS

Human happiness and environmental sustainability are supported or thwarted largely by the maturity level of human society. A mature society fosters both gladness and the preservation of nature, while an immature society diminishes both. A "more mature human society requires more mature human individuals" (Plotkin, 2010, p.13). Eco-centric elders, both the volunteers and the life coaches, are such mature individuals. Eco-centric elders work to transform others into whole, mature, and effective individuals.

The kind of eco-centric elders we seek to develop in this series of books is not those that know best how to extract wealth from the environment or how to teach children to "work the system." Rather, they know how to foster both human happiness and environmental sustainability. To be able to do this, they will first need to be made "whole, one life stage at a time, by embracing nature and the soul as (their) wisest and most trustworthy guides" (Plotkin, 2010, p.13).

Dr. Cohen's methodologies and Bill Plotkin's Wheel of Life will certainly be helpful for this first step. Additional steps include the organizing methods David Brower used to create the world's environmental movement and the development of eco-self help groups throughout the country (and world).

Through these steps, the eco-centric elders I call "eartHearts" will focus first and most on selfless assistance; second on glory or respect in the community; and lastly, if at all, and if they are professional life coaches, on remuneration. What is needed is a cultural transformation, one that changes materialistic, anthropocentric (human-centered), competition-based, violence-prone, unsustainable, and class-stratified so-called "egocentric" societies into "imaginative, eco-centric, cooperation-based, just, compassionate and sustainable" so-called "soul-centric" societies (Plotkin, 2010, p. 13). Along with this need, our modern society would benefit from a human development approach that is based not on biological development, or on mental abilities, or on social roles, or on chronological age but rather on a progression that is "spurred by the individual's progress with the specific psychological and spiritual tasks encountered at each stage" of life (Plotkin, 2010, p. 13).

Given how most of us humans in modern society have not developed spiritually up to our own species' capabilities, we do not only need more average or typical people. We also do not need only those who would be recognized for their hard work and for their ability to satisfy their practical responsibilities. Instead, we also need a particular sort of human development approach wherein people mature into good examples of what I call "eartHearts" or "eco-secular saints"—that is, visionary people who have the following characteristics:

1. They are wise.
2. They have a broad and deep perspective.
3. They know how to show their gratitude.
4. They are working to obtain a high level of spiritual development.
5. They see what needs to be done at both personal and ecological levels.
6. They stand up to injustice. And
7. They are easily driven to help others.

We need more people who have developed a mystical relationship with nature. For this relationship to develop, we need a methodology (Dr. Cohen's for example) that is used along a purposeful path (the Heartwood Path, for example) and occurs over the course of one's psychological development that may span over a period of decades (Bill Plotkin's Wheel of Life, for example). The use of these and other tools are blended in this series of books in such a way that it will not take the participants decades but rather months to reach a satisfactory level of maturity.

All the tools used in this series of books—including mine, Cohen's, and Plotkin's—will be more helpful to you if you relieve yourself of the burden of the negative emotion of holding a grudge, holding on to anger, or retaining feelings of bitterness. To clear up the psychic space needed to become an effective eco-centric elder (volunteer or paid nature-centered life coach) or to further your journey towards the well-being that is found at Gladandgreen Junction, be sure to, at a minimum, be extra kind to a person you have privately forgiven or, better yet, actually voice your forgiveness. If such an action is daunting, do the following activity.

To Forgiveness...

HumaNatureConnect Activity

Start-up Protocol

If this is not a day when you prefer to spend time in nature without an agenda, do the Heartwood Path Start-up Protocol found in the Appendix. Then return here to do the remaining portion of this activity:

Writing A Letter Of Forgiveness

Once you are in the natural setting of your chosen attractive natural being, look around for examples of grudge-holding, of lack of forgiveness, or of bitterness and anger. Note how well nature works without such negativities. Note how swiftly, decisively, and automatically things that you label as impingements are apparently effortlessly and intelligently reacted to by other entities in nature in ways that do not generate long-held anger, bitterness, the holding of grudges, or any lack of forgiveness. While pondering the peacefulness, intelligence and utility of the apparent absence of such psychological burdens in the wild, get more in tune with nature's intelligence by writing (and not necessarily sending) a letter of forgiveness. In this letter, describe the transgression, pledge to forgive the transgressor, and note how you feel after making such a pledge. Then write down whether holding on to grudges or nature's lack of grudges is more loving, intelligent, attractive, and focused on the present. Learn from this activity. Lastly, use what you have learned to behave in ways that are most useful to yourself and others.

Follow-up Protocol

For best results, write down your impressions of this activity in your journal using the Heartwood Path Follow-up Protocol found in the Appendix. Afterwards, consider sharing your interpretations with others.

Heartwood Path Axioms

Key Assertions From Waypoint 1.11

1.11.1.

Human happiness and environmental sustainability are supported or thwarted largely by the maturity level of human society.

1.11.2.

A mature society fosters both gladness and the preservation of nature, while an immature society diminishes both.

1.11.3.

There is a need for a cultural transformation, one that changes materialistic, anthropocentric (human-centered), competition-based, violence-prone, unsustainable, and class-stratified so-called "ego-centric" societies into "imaginative, eco-centric, cooperation-based, just, compassionate, and sustainable" so-called "soul-centric" societies.

1.11.4.

There is a need for a particular sort of human development wherein people acquire the following characteristics: wisdom, a broad and deep perspective, a propensity to show their gratitude, a high level of spiritual development, a drive to stand up to injustice, and an easy willingness to help others.

1.11.5.

To clear up the psychic space needed to become an effective eco-centric elder or to further one's journey towards well-being it will be helpful to be extra kind to a person one has privately forgiven or, better yet, write and send a letter of forgiveness.

Nocturnal Pilgrimage 1.11

For best results, write down your impressions of each night's dreams in your journal using the Heartwood Path Dreaming Time

Protocols found in the Appendix. Afterwards, consider sharing your Dream Tending with others.

As you did last night, look at your dreams as signs of repressed aggression or rage, or as signs of latent wishes, or as anything that you may not want to think about.

Record your impressions in your dream journal, then move to the next waypoint, titled "Visioning," to continue your participation along the Heartwood Path by writing a letter or thankfulness.

12

Visioning

WRITE AN ECO-ETHICAL VISION STATEMENT

A worthy eco-ethic has to take into account equity, fairness, and sustainability for not only present and future generations of humans but also for present and future generations of non-humans. This eco-ethic will need to focus on the appropriateness of business action but, even more importantly, it will also have to help us develop and share a global ethos that serves as a set of guiding beliefs that would "shift human behavior in ways that would protect the biospheric life support system and make better use of natural capital" (Cairns, 2001, p. 1).

According to biologist John Cairns, Jr., an "ethos based on fairness and equity regarding human society's behavior within its own and other species seems to be the only possible unifying theme for sustainable use of the planet" (2001, p. 2). An ethos with such a plank does not require a significant disregard for individual rights.

In the United States, "individual 'rights' are proclaimed much more frequently than individual responsibility for the greater or universal good" (Cairns, 2001, p. 3). Surely honoring and respecting the uniqueness of each individual can be achieved without endorsing uncivil, disruptive behavior.

One approach that guides this writing comes from my best answer to the question: What is more important in making progress towards solving the global environmental predicament than greener technology, more sensitive science, a safety net of environmental laws, and religion becoming an advocate for a sustainable environment? My answer is an eco-psychology that brings out the best in people so that they can, if they choose as I hope they will, trade Band-Aid solutions for remedies that go to the root of the problem. That root is the human mind. Fix it and you fix the planet. As Dudjom Rinpoche says: "The nature of mind is the nature of everything" (George, 1995, p. 54).

It is, therefore, critical that the premier step towards securing the happiness that comes from preserving natural beauty and establishing environmental sustainability is to make changes in the inner world, for if we do not, all attempted improvements in the outer world will be sabotaged by our psychological demons. I am not talking about the need to force intellectual conclusions. Rather, I am talking about the development of optimal mental-emotional-spiritual functioning so that people are in the best shape psychologically to create good ideas in their heads that are tempered by their hearts.

Inner world improvements alone will not be adequate if people do not find a way to better link what is in their heads with what is in their hearts. Such links come from direct experience, which is why in this series of books the reader finds simple yet profound ways to experience nature and to glean its heart and wisdom. Such experiences will be helpful because they will help us with, as Einstein says, "widening our circle of compassion to embrace all living creatures and the world of nature in its beauty" (George, 1995, p. 54). As an important precursor to the development of more compassion towards others, do the following activity. It is about visioning, which is an important first step in goal setting. We will be asking you to write a personal vision statement, one that paints a clear picture of how you want to be after you have transformed yourself along the Heartwood Path. You will be asked to include in your word-picture many of the eco-ethical component previously mentioned in this waypoint.

To Your Heartwood Path Goals...

HumaNatureConnect Activity

Start-up Protocol

If this is not a day when you prefer to spend time in nature without an agenda, do the Heartwood Path Start-up Protocol found in the Appendix. Then return here to do the remaining portion of this activity:

Writing An Eco-ethical Vision Statement

For this activity, write down in your journal how you would like to be and what you would like to be doing after you have transformed yourself along the Heartwood Path. You can write this statement any way you like. We will, however, offer some suggestions. The goal here is to write down the picture you are forming in your mind regarding your role in the Great Work!, which will need to be an immense project that increases human happiness by making people more effective in preserving the beauty of nature and more effective in securing environmental sustainability. In this word-picture, write in the present tense. Describe as vividly as possible how you are flourishing in whatever ways you describe. Begin this vision statement with the statement "I see myself..." being someone or doing something that best demonstrates your happiness in being an advocate for environmental protection. Write so that others can really see such happiness in you. Mention how you are or what you are doing as a result of fairness, equity, and sustainability. Talk about what you are doing to overcome the conflict between individual rights and collective responsibility. Talk about how you maintain your optimal emotional, mental, physical, and spiritual functioning. Paint in the readers mind a picture of you communing with nature, working on a cause or causes, growing as a result of journaling about your Heartwood Path Activities, and being abundantly, authentically, and abidingly happy. Do not attempting to write a perfect or conclusive vision statement. As it is, refer to it often. And rewrite it whenever you like.

Follow-up Protocol

For best results, write down your impressions of this activity in your journal using the Heartwood Path Follow-up Protocol found in the Appendix. Afterwards, consider sharing your interpretations with others.

Heartwood Path Axioms

Key Assertions From Waypoint 1.12

1.12.1.

It is critical that we make changes in the inner world, for if we do not, all attempted improvements in the outer world will be sabotaged by our psychological demons.

1.12.2.

We need the development of optimal mental-emotional-spiritual functioning so that people are in the best shape psychologically to create good ideas in their heads that are tempered by their hearts.

Nocturnal Pilgrimage 1.12

For best results, write down your impressions of each night's dreams in your journal using the Heartwood Path Dreaming Time

Protocols found in the Appendix. Afterwards, consider sharing your Dream Tending with others.

Again tonight, examine your dreams as signs of repressed sexual drives or infantile rage. Be sure to jot down your dreams immediately upon waking. Otherwise, dreams are too easy to forget.

After recording your dream impressions, continue on your way down the Heartwood Path by moving to the next waypoint: "Optimism." By doing so, you will learn how to maximize qualities or be satisfied with quantities.

13

Optimism

MAXIMIZE QUALITIES AND BE SATISFIED WITH QUANTITIES

There are reasons for optimism. Our history shows that we as a species can do the work suggested by Einstein: "widening our circle of compassion." The shift to live according to a new ecological paradigm is not significantly more daunting than our other previous massive shifts. We as a species, for example, made the leap from hunters and gathers to living in agricultural communities. Then, called again to face big cultural changes, we again made another big leap, this time from living in agricultural communities with simple technology to living mostly in cities and suburbs with complex, modern technology. James George points out that we are "endowed with some degree of freewill, and therefore with contradictory capacities for both self-destructive behavior and for extraordinary breakthroughs of creative energy and intelligence" (George, 1995, p. 105). I, for one, think that we will, after trying everything else, eventually make the right choices.

If we can make the shift from being hunters and gatherers to being agriculturalists and if we can make the shift from living in agricultural communities with simple technologies to living in urban and suburban communities with complex technologies, which required huge shifts in perspectives and behaviors, it stands to reason that we can also shift from a state of lower well-being that comes from always demanding but never quite gathering up more and more stuff to a higher state of well-being that goes with being satisfied with having enough stuff.

To Become A Maximizer...

HumaNatureConnect Activity

Start-up Protocol

If this is not a day when you prefer to spend time in nature without an agenda, do the Heartwood Path Start-up Protocol found in the Appendix. Then return here to do the remaining portion of this activity:

"Maximizing" Vs. "Satisficing"

For this activity, look for ways that nature maximizes qualities (examples: adds diversity, displays beauty) and seems to be "satisfied" with quantities (examples: hermit crabs do not fill their houses with stuff nor do they attempt to have more than one house, black rhinoceros browse on shrubs and, therefore, do not compete for food with white rhinoceros that graze on grass). Write down at least three specific examples that you can perceive during this activity of nature both maximizing qualities and being "satisfied" with quantities. Then make a plan for how, in five different ways, you can become a maximizer of qualities and a "satisficer" of quantities.

Follow-up Protocol

For best results, write down your impressions of this activity in your journal using the Heartwood Path Follow-up Protocol found in the Appendix. Afterwards, consider sharing your interpretations with others.

Heartwood Path Axioms

Key Assertions From Waypoint 1.13

1.13.1.

Given other huge shifts in human perspective, it stands to reason that we can also shift from a state of lower well-being that comes from always demanding but never quite gathering up more and more stuff to a higher state of well being that goes with being satisfied with having enough stuff.

1.13.2.

Become a maximizer of qualities and a "satisficer" of quantities.

1.13.3.

For help with life's big changes, look for ways your dreams may be signs of latent wishes or repressed anger.

Nocturnal Pilgrimage 1.13

For best results, write down your impressions of each night's dreams in your journal using the Heartwood Path Dreaming Time Protocols found in the Appendix. Afterwards, consider sharing your Dream Tending with others.

Work on making Freudian associations with your dreams by looking for ways they may be signs of latent wishes or repressed anger. Here's a few tips to help you with this important analytical tool:

1. Choose an image that really gets your attention in your dreams.
2. Look for characters, people, creatures, a natural scene, or a natural being. And
3. Pick images in your dreams that seem to linger into your waking life. As accurately as you can, write a detailed description of the Dream Character. Look for ways to connect this character to ideas, feelings, and events from your life. Do not bother trying to find the one right answer. Instead, observe where free associations take you (Aizenstat, 2009, p. 21).

After writing your description, continue on your way down the Heartwood Path by looking for examples of optimism and pessimism in nature after you move to the next waypoint: "Self-absorption."

14

Self-absorption

LOOK FOR EXAMPLES OF OPTIMISM AND PESSIMISM IN NATURE

We will discuss our individual Will and our collective Will in future Heartwood Path books and courses. Here, we are focusing on an introduction to the ethos that is needed to guide both our individual and our collective Wills to the development of both human happiness and a sustainable environment upon which we all depend. To serve us well, this ethos will have to be based on the truth as apprehended and comprehended directly in the moment. This comprehension cannot be the constrained kind of truth that comes from the mind alone. According to James George, we will need to use knowing through reason (mind), sensation (body) and intuition (feeling) to find the truth. The inner work of individual transformation has to precede the "the outer work of helping nature" (George, 1995, p. 113).

In the previous waypoint we discussed how one type of preoccupation, incessant pessimism, is particularly distracting, unproductive, and harmful. The next activity addresses this all-too-common preoccupation.

To Become Optimistic…

HumaNatureConnect Activity

Start-up Protocol

If this is not a day when you prefer to spend time in nature without an agenda, do the Heartwood Path Start-up Protocol found in the Appendix. Then return here to do the remaining portion of this activity:

Looking For Examples Of Pessimism Vs. Optimism

For this activity, look around your outdoor setting for examples of pessimism. These may be hard to find without stretching for obscure metaphors. Despite this hardship, if you see any examples of pessimism be sure to write them down. Look for ways, if any, that nature closes the door on future opportunities. Then, look for examples of optimism in nature. These may include the early buds on flowers when snow is still present or the great blue heron that lands along a river bank, "optimistic" that it will find a fish to eat. After developing your list of "closed doors" that indicate pessimism in nature and "open doors" that show optimism in nature, turn your attention inward to yourself. List at least five ways you are closing doors with your pessimism and at least five ways that you are opening doors to optimism.

Follow-up Protocol

For best results, write down your impressions of this activity in your journal using the Heartwood Path Follow-up Protocol found in the Appendix. Afterwards, consider sharing your interpretations with others.

Heartwood Path Axioms

Key Assertions From Waypoint 1.14

1.14.1.

To serve one well, an ethos will have to be based on the truth as apprehended and comprehended directly in the moment, not the constrained kind of truth that comes from the mind alone.

1.14.2.

One needs to free oneself from the self-centered preoccupations that keep one unaware.

1.14.3.

To help rid yourself of unwanted preoccupations or to learn other things about yourself amplify your dreams so that instead of just being a sign of something repressed they also (or instead) mean something that is regal, noble, fierce, or big-hearted in your nature.

Nocturnal Pilgrimage 1.14

For best results, write down your impressions of each night's dreams in your journal using the Heartwood Path Dreaming Time Protocols found in the Appendix. Afterwards, consider sharing your Dream Tending with others.

Continue to look on dream associations, as you have in previous waypoints, but begin working on also amplifying your dreams. You can take any previous images from your dreams or one from your next dream and "amplify" it so that instead of just being a sign of something repressed it also (or instead) means something that is regal, noble, fierce, or big-hearted in your nature. When applying your dreams, one does not subject a Dream Image to a cut and dried intellectual translation. Instead of forcing the image of a dog to mean one repressed thing, such as "I have a hidden issue with subservience," (as you might do with dream association) the dream tender doing dream amplification might ask "What is a dog?," or "What does a dog do?," or "What does a dog remind me of?," or "What do I like or dislike about a dog?." With questions such as these the dream tender can become more familiar with the Dream Image. Write down your answers to such amplification questions in your journal. Continue to "amplify" the Dream Image until you are confident that someone who previously knew nothing about dogs, for example, would have a very good idea of what the dog in your dream represents. Keep the amplifying positive, enough so that the Dream Images become like positive universal archetypes, such as "The Loyal Friend" or the "The Devoted Servant." Continue to work on amplification for the next several nights.

After your next dream entry in your journal, continue on your way down the Heartwood Path by moving to the next waypoint: "Unhealthy Dependence."

15

Unhealthy Dependence

SHED YOURSELF OF
MISINTERPRETATIONS

Beware of any teacher, course, religion, or path that does not have an exit strategy. One can benefit from most teachings, but dependence on any one path, especially those that claim exclusive authority or correctness, is unhealthy.

This series of books, is, among other things, a users guide that has a set of activities and explanatory text that helps the reader/pilgrim replace any dependence on this and other paths with love, openness, awareness, and sweetness.

The Heartwood Path is also a "tattvopadesha" in that it is a sequential, logically connected presentation. Part One of the Heartwood Path (the first three books), is designed to be completed in about 14.5 months. After that, you are free to do nothing, you are free to enroll in other upcoming courses, or you are free to become even further involved in the Heartwood Path by becoming a Great Work! associate, which means you would be certified to become a Heartwood Path Guide, a Heartwood Path public speaker, or Heartwood Path researcher, or any other Heartwood Path paid professional.

The present book will help you explore the sweetness of being in love with awareness itself. This book will help you be drawn beyond any path to the truth of your being and the nature of the world. Furthermore, this book will help you apply knowledge (which is love refined by coherent clearness) and love (which is knowledge infused by pleasantness) for the betterment of the Greater Self which includes (but is not limited to) your individual self.

By the end of the Heartwood Path, after reading many savory concepts and doing many fragrant activities, you will have an open heart and a broadness of love. Wrong identifications will have fallen away. Your inquiry here will cause the object of your love to expand to include everything. Your beloved will no longer be found in one direction. Everywhere you turn you will find sweetness. This broadness of love, which is sometimes called "liberation," will be made easier to accomplish if you begin working on freeing yourself from the five afflictions or "kleshas" identified in numerous classical scriptures, most notably Patanjali's Yoga Sutra. (Cope, 1999, p. 64).

The five kleshas—the obstacles to the experience of oneness and liberation—include ignorance, egoism, attachments to people or things, aversion to transformation, and clinging to life. Ignorance is considered a psychological poison when one mistakes the impermanent for the permanent, when one mistakes the impure or the pure, when one mistakes pain for pleasure, and when one mistakes the non self (your outer identities, such as those that come from your job, for example) with the Self. Egoism is considered a psychological poison because it causes one to minimize oneself to judgmental labels one sticks onto oneself (examples would include superiority over others and entitlement). Attachment is a psychological poison when one's healthy attractions (like to natural beings or loved ones, for example) do not result in the usual happiness, inspiration, or lightness, but instead cause suffering. Aversion to transformation is a psychological poison when it causes one to remain in one's comfort zone, thus averting any discomforts or unpleasantness that sometimes occur when one pushes oneself to grow. Clinging to life is a psychological poison when the fear of loss keeps one from making daily lists of priorities, from overcoming the delusion of immortality (especially during the first half of one's life) or, when one thinks there is an eternity of time remaining for saying "I love you," "I am sorry," "I forgive you," or "thank you." More can be learned about the pertinence of these kleshas in your life by answering thoughtfully the questions in the following activity.

To Shed Yourself Of Misinterpretations...

HumaNatureConnect Activity

Start-up Protocol

If this is not a day when you prefer to spend time in nature without an agenda, do the Heartwood Path Start-up Protocol found in the Appendix. Then return here to do the remaining portion of this activity:

Loosening Yourself From The Illusion Of Separateness

Go beyond your present understanding of what may be preventing the onset of greater happiness in your life by considering carefully the answers to the following questions, each associated with a different klesha:

The Affliction Of Ignorance:

What five topics most display your ignorance and, at the same time, are topics you would like to learn more about?

I, for example, know practically nothing about music theory, but would love to know more.

The Affliction Of The Ego:

How would you describe, if possible, your lesser individual self and your Greater, More-Than-Individual-Self?

One's individual self is that which makes one unique among people, one's Greater Self is all that is, one's individual self integrated into the whole.

The Affliction Of Attachment:

How, if at all, do you completely identify or keep from identifying with your attractions?

I, for example, identify with natural beings that seem to display human characteristics, such as shaking when nervous or the drive to eat and drink, and I keep from identifying with my attractions by adopting the ever-common delusion of separation.

The Affliction Of Aversion To Transformation:

In many of the activities that follow you will be asked to find a natural attraction and use it for your own guidance, healing, or information. Why, if at all, do you think it would be advisable not to completely identify with these attractions but to instead use them as merely transitional or transformative objects (things that help you grow, heal, or become informed)?

I, for example, feel one with all beings but also recognize that each one has its own agency, its own recognizable identity, its own different perspective and purpose.

The Affliction Of Clinging To Permanence And Solidity In One's Life:

In what ways, if at all, do you feel small, neat, permanent, and solid?

In ways, if at all, do you feel vast, incomprehensible, impermanent, and discontinuous?

I, for example, feel small when I walk along a beach next to the ocean, not neat enough when I am in someone's house who is obsessively cleanly, permanent when I consider the longevity of my written words, solid when I hit my toe on the foot of a table, vast when I recall the diversity of my thinking, incomprehensible when I, in vain, try to write about the ineffable, impermanent when I feel my heart flutter, and discontinuous when I see aspects of nature behaving in ways that I do not.

How, if at all, does thinking of your self in these ways feel like remembering your true self?

I, for example, feel that such questions cause me to look at myself in atypical ways, ways that help to reveal the More-Than-Individual-Self that sometimes hides behind my illusions of separateness.

Follow-up Protocol

For best results, write down your impressions of this activity in your journal using the Heartwood Path Follow-up Protocol found in the Appendix. Afterwards, consider sharing your interpretations with others.

Heartwood Path Axioms

Key Assertions From Waypoint 1.15

1.15.1.

One can benefit from most teachings, but dependence on any one path, especially those that claim exclusive authority or correctness, is unhealthy.

1.15.2.

Along with freeing yourself from any dependence on any controlling pathway of growth rid yourself of the five afflictions: ignorance, ego, attachment, aversion, and clinging to permanence and solidity in one's life.

Nocturnal Pilgrimage 1.15

For best results, write down your impressions of each night's dreams in your journal using the Heartwood Path Dreaming Time Protocols found in the Appendix. Afterwards, consider sharing your Dream Tending with others.

There are all sorts of important questions for you to answer at this waypoint. I bet you have not totally done so yet. Perhaps you are wondering when you will ever have time. I suggest you work on these self-revealing questions by engaging in the component of the Dreaming Protocol titled "Wake-Back-To-Bed." This component offers the suggestion to get back to spending your nights the way nature intended; namely to sleep for four hours or so and then, for twenty minutes or so (more if you desire), wake up, get out of bed and attended to your private thoughts, quandaries, and sensations before sleeping again until morning.

Had our sleeping patterns not been usurped by controls imposed on us by our workaday pressures, we would nightly be two-time sleepers. I suggest that, at first, you use the middle-of-the-night so-called "Watch" period to finish up unfinished or neglected activities, such as answering the questions associated with the previously-mentioned five kleshas. Once you finish your assignments, make it a habit to continue doing whatever you want during that peaceful time of night when nobody will disturb you, when you can devote yourself to private pursuits, and when you can hasten your development as an eco-centric elder. Starting this habit may be difficult at first. But, I assure you, it will be well worth it.

Slow to become a regular habit, the so called "Watch" has become my favorite time of day. I devote over an hour to it every night.

Sleep for a few hours. Wake up and "take care of business" for an hour or so. Go back to sleep, dream, and amplify your dreams (turning dream characters into positive universal symbols).

Record your amplifications in your journal. Then, move to the next waypoint: "Meditation And Action." Commit to bring the benefits of the "Watch" into your life.

16

Meditation And Action

COMMEMORATE THE GOOD WORK OF OTHERS

Inner work, often done on meditation cushions, is the first step but it cannot be the last. Those "who think that the world will take care of itself if only they sit well on their cushions are as lopsided as those who are so obsessed with practical actions to save the environment that they have no time for inner work" (George, 1995, p. 113). I would add that those who only seek to appreciate their attractions in nature and who do not take practical actions on behalf of nature are likewise lopsided.

We sometimes hear that our suffering is due to our clinging on to our status or to our reputation. We are told that meditation is a way to free ourselves from such attachments.

We all know that meditation is a good way to do nothing and still be respectable. Meditation cushions are always dirty because the meditators, especially those who have become free of attachments, no longer have the parts they need for vacuum cleaning.

Here's one way to act positively, even if it is not you that is doing the acting.

To Celebrate Others...

HumaNatureConnect Activity

Start-up Protocol

If this is not a day when you prefer to spend time in nature without an agenda, do the Heartwood Path Start-up Protocol found in the Appendix. Then return here to do the remaining portion of this activity:

Commemorating The Work Of Others

For this activity, look around your natural scene, be it backwoods or backyard, and list five ways one entity there is acting on behalf of another. Examples would include the tree that provides the squirrel with a place to build a nest and the twigs that provide the squirrel with materials for its nest. After you list and reflect on nature's endless gift giving, plan a way for you to celebrate someone's gift or to give a gift to someone or something else. After you complete this celebration, write in your journal how organizing such an event boosted your happiness and/or affected your own self-esteem.

Follow-up Protocol

For best results, write down your impressions of this activity in your journal using the Heartwood Path Follow-up Protocol found in the Appendix. Afterwards, consider sharing your interpretations with others.

Heartwood Path Axioms

Key Assertions From Waypoint 1.16

1.16.1.

Inner work, often done on meditation cushions, is the first step but it cannot be the last.

1.16.2.

Those who believe that the world will take care of itself if only they sit and meditate on their cushions are as lopsided as those who spend all their time doing practical actions to save the environment and claim to have no time for inner work.

1.16.3.

Those who only seek to appreciate their attractions in nature and who do not take practical actions on behalf of nature are lopsided.

1.16.4.

To overcome self/other imbalances, plan a way for you to celebrate someone's gift or to give a gift to someone or something else.

Nocturnal Pilgrimage 1.16

For best results, write down your impressions of each night's dreams in your journal using the Heartwood Path Dreaming Time Protocols found in the Appendix. Afterwards, consider sharing your Dream Tending with others.

For tonight's nocturnal pilgrimage, compare your present way of being with some ideal universal role model. Set a high standard for what you will become and plot ways to embody your Ideal Future You.

Imagining yourself as an archetype is a key step in becoming a happy person in a sustainable and beautiful world.

Here's an example of what such an identification can do for you. My revered former boss unknowingly or unknowingly embodied the Archetype of the DragonSlayer, sort of like little David who killed mighty Goliath. After years of living up to this clear image for himself, David Brower's lifetime of doing monumental conservation actions earned him the reputation of Patriarch of the Environmental Movement (which, in itself, is good example of the ideal universal role model I am asking you to privately now develop for yourself).

The universal positive role model you pick for yourself is not to be bragged about. It is rather something you keep to yourself but strive to embody in such a fashion that others will be able to state what you have become.

In your self-assessment, you may determine that some serious personal changes are required. To this end, follow the advice given in the component of the Dreaming Protocol titled "Shape-Shifters," presented with each waypoint. List in your journal the kinds of changes you need to make so that your chosen Archetypal Self can be recognizable to others.

It may help you become the dream you set for yourself if you search for a suitable role model and celebrate that person in some way. Having birthday parties for famous deceased conservationists was my own way to honor the work and Archetypal Majesty of my own role models.

If you are a meditator whose involvement is confined to your meditation cushion, for example, examining the life of your chosen Archetypal Role Model may encourage you to balance your meditating with some form of regular physical actions. Conversely, if you are an activist who pays little attention to inner world workings, you may want to look at the spiritual pursuits of the people you admire and adopt similar devotions for yourself.

Like the last two nocturnal pilgrimages, record your amplifications of your dream. Expand the image of the dream to its full stature as an archetype. Determine how your dream offers an archetypal motif that relates to something in your life. After doing so, move to the next waypoint, titled "Gratefulness."

17

Gratefulness

RESPOND TO YOUR INDEBTEDNESS

We as a species seem driven by an insatiable need to improve upon things. This inner yearning leaves us with an unquenchable thirst for control. Propelled by this yearning, we do things that fractures our natural wholeness. This break hurts, deeply. Yet, we have largely become accustomed to this pain. We have devised many veils of illusion to make us lulled into a stupor of acceptance regarding our separation from the grace of the wild. This book/course is for the few who seek to give heart to the job of removing the veils of separation, each described subsequently.

Taking off these veils makes one feel less secure; and that is how it ought to be, for the veils of illusion are a false security. Without them, one can look both beyond and within. These are the two directions of perception one needs to fathom whom one really is—both individual and united. The reward for removing the veils is a return to love: the return of the feeling of the love of the feminine, the feeling of the love of nature, and the feeling of the love of the mediated presence of the Absolute that is one's true home. Perceiving clearly allows one to become wonderfully responsive to one's place, to be bowled over by the beauty of aliveness, to be inspired by the beauty of the day, and to be awed by the beauty of the night.

Take off those veils! Hear what the cicadas sing. Hear the wooing of the whip-or-wills. Catch the blowing of dolphins and whales. Listen to everything. In whatever language, it is the same call: "Be here now, be here now."

Stop trying to control. When you look at a tree, for example, resist the urge to name it. I think a tree's slow movements are its resistance to being labelled. Stop naming and be welcome and welcoming. One has to do more than simply feel kindly towards nature. One has to participate in the healing of the world. This cannot happen effectively, however, unless one stops perceiving Nature as something different from one's self.

Make constant gratitude towards Nature a given. Come together in your abiding place. Accept your scientific reckoning but do not mask your primal being.

Become the experience. You and whatever you perceive are together nothing but awareness.

Make nothing of it. It just is. Be grateful for it.

You do not have to become a backpacker to be an eartHeart. The "everywhereness of wilderness" makes it possible to show your gratitude in the back country and the back yard.

A precursor of gratitude is appreciation. Without appreciation there is nothing in one's awareness that merits gratitude.

Throughout this book, you will be asked to go to a natural place, to find a natural being that you appreciate—a plant, animal, mineral, or setting that you admire, treasure, value, respect, and/or hold in high regard. These responses are the result of the natural being's attractiveness to you. Before we talk about attraction, let's discuss the merits of appreciation.

Most people struggle with demands at work, demands at home, and many other assorted irritations. Appreciation works wonders to counter such difficulties. "Appreciation is the simple act of noticing the good in your life" (Luskin and Pelletier, 2005, p. 76.) Going to an attractive natural being, as you will when you do the practices in this book series, gives you ample opportunities to develop and practice appreciation. "Learn to focus your attention on things that are beautiful" (Luskin and Pelletier, 2005, p. 85.) "Appreciating other people, the beauty of nature, and the joys of everyday life may be the simplest and most immediate way to create health and happiness" (Luskin and Pelletier, 2005, p. 89.) Doing so will give you a warm feeling inside, help you to feel more peaceful and less stressed, and improve your relationships (Luskin and Pelletier, 2005, p. 87). It will also bring you into the state of mind necessary to do the HumaNatureConnect Activities for this book/course.

Appreciation often turns into gratitude. When, for example, those who engage in the HumaNatureConnect Activities described later appreciate natural attractions a natural compulsion towards thankfulness arises, a felt requirement for gratefulness presents itself, or an informal sense of duty to serve naturally emerges.

Appreciation is neutral in that it does not demand compensation. Gratitude, however, has embedded within it a self-imposed obligation —weak or strong—to offer some form of repayment.

There is no common phrase "debt of appreciation" but commonly there are "debts of gratitude." Nature can be regarded as both a benefactor and as a recipient of your gratitude.

As perhaps the ultimate benefactor, Nature gives freely. Her gifts are gratis. Sunshine, rain, and the beauty of birds, for example, come without financial payment. Yet, when we feel grateful for these gifts we often feel we are in debt to nature and ought to make some form of compensation. Our gratitude frequently makes us feel a sense of duty, a desire to dutifully give something back for the gifts we have received.

This duty of benevolence fuels the environmental movement. It certainly is the basis for this series of books.

Since nature gives us so much, there is a natural sense of indebtedness to it, an indebtedness that leads to empathy, concern, and/or attachment. Showing gratitude to nature is perhaps the response of a person who knows that the benefactor—in this case, nature—is offering something of value (breathable air, for example). Perhaps the recipient does not think that the benevolence was done solely for nature's benefit but was, somehow, done for the benefit of people. Perhaps the recipient is being grateful in order to insure the recognition, establishment, maintenance, or continuance of a two-way moral community that includes both nature and people. Perhaps the gratitude is a way to show respect for the benevolence of nature.

In any of these scenarios, showing gratitude is an act that displays one's regard for nature. The gratitude may be the result of the recognition that the benevolence is somehow beyond an automatic give and take. The gratitude may be the result of an attempt to show the mutuality of the relationship. Lastly, the gratitude may be a way to be appropriate in a moral community.

Many of those who consciously seek to show gratitude for the benevolence of nature do so in ways that cost them time, in ways that are inconvenient, or in ways that involve the saying of words or the doing of actions. Typically, gratitude towards nature does not involve the offering of a return in kind—partly because this would likely be impossible (people cannot give nature the support of a solid earth, for example) but also because such a return would possibly be considered an inappropriate undercutting of the apparent magnanimity of nature's offerings (nature gives to everyone, even the ungrateful).

There are pathological forms of gratitude to nature. These include giving back too much to nature in an attempt to make it in one's debt, giving a show of gratitude as a way to justify one's own incessant demands on nature, or being exuberantly grateful as a way to improve one's reputation or to increase one's own status over others.

Beyond these missteps, appropriate gratitude to nature is a time-tested way to induce the positive thinking that is a natural check against sadness. Positive forms of gratitude to nature include sunrise ceremonies, making small non-lethal sacrificial offerings (as is the custom of many Native American tribes, sprinkling a small amount of tobacco on the forest floor, for example), celebrating astronomical or seasonal events such as the Winter Solstice, and maintaining a reverential attitude while engaging in earth-friendly buying choices and while engaging in recycling.

Such forms of gratitude may, to our modern technological way of thinking, seem trite, falsely magical, or misguided. Despite such protestations, participating in events such as those mentioned above does create a nature-supportive frame of mind and this condition in the person often yields benefits to the planet. Towards this end, we have work to do in both the inner world and the outer world. Writes George:

> "What happens in the world and what happens in us are in constant relationship, whether we are aware of it or not. The microcosm and the macrocosm differ only in scale, and they are never separate" (1995, p.133).

One way to show this lack of separation is to consider who or what you owe a debt of gratitude. The following activity will illustrate the inseparability of all that surrounds you.

To Begin Responding To Your Indebtedness...

HumaNatureConnect Activity

Start-up Protocol

If this is not a day when you prefer to spend time in nature without an agenda, do the Heartwood Path Start-up Protocol found in the Appendix. Then return here to do the remaining portion of this activity:

Examining The Tree Of Gratitude

For this activity, look for ten acts of giving in the natural scene and record them in your journal. Then draw a simple tree and place your name on the trunk of the tree. Above that trunk are big branches.

Label each of these tree parts with a debt of gratitude that you feel you owe to someone or something. Above the larger branches are smaller branches. Each giver that is labelled on the big branches receives benefits from some givers that can be listed on the smaller branches. In this way, one continues to label the tree parts with gratitudes until the last branch has a giver that receives from the sky. The same progression occurs with the big roots, smaller roots, and soil. Once you see throughout your drawn tree that each giver is also a receiver, you can perceive the causes for one's own never-ending, expansive set of debts of gratitude. After you come to understand how much is given, directly and indirectly, for your own benefit, write down how being supported in so many different ways makes you feel.

Follow-up Protocol

For best results, write down your impressions of this activity in your journal using the Heartwood Path Follow-up Protocol found in the Appendix. Afterwards, consider sharing your interpretations with others.

Heartwood Path Axioms

Key Assertions From Waypoint 1.17

1.17.1.

We as a species seem driven by an insatiable need to improve upon things, an unquenchable thirst for control that, at great psychic pain, fractures our natural wholeness.

1.17.2.

We humans, having devised many veils of illusion to make us lulled into a stupor of acceptance regarding our separation

from the grace of the wild, eventually receive rewards of love for removing these veils: the feeling of love of the feminine, the feeling of love of nature, and the feeling of love of the mediated presence of the Absolute that is one's true home.

1.17.3.

When those who engage in the Heartwood Path's HumaNature-Connect Activities regularly appreciate natural attractions a natural compulsion towards thankfulness arises, a felt requirement for gratefulness presents itself, and an informal sense of duty to serve naturally emerges.

1.17.4.

Many of those who consciously seek to show gratitude for the benevolence of nature do so in ways that cost them time, in ways that are inconvenient, or in ways that involve the saying of words or the doing of actions.

1.17.5.

Nature can be regarded as both a benefactor and as a recipient of your gratitude.

Nocturnal Pilgrimage 1.17

For best results, write down your impressions of each night's dreams in your journal using the Heartwood Path Dreaming Time Protocols found in the Appendix. Afterwards, consider sharing your Dream Tending with others.

Amplify your night time dream again. If you are having questions or difficulties, try correlating the Dream Images to universal themes that show up in many forms of cultural expression, including symbols, mythological figures, archetypes, literature, and theater (Aizenstat, 2009, p. 22). Continue to make associations and to amplify your dreams before starting each of the next several waypoints.

Write your impressions in your journal, then move to the next waypoint: "Follow Your Attraction." Enjoy your time with your chosen natural beings as you continue this book/course.

18

Follow Your Attraction

MEET REGULARLY WITH
ATTRACTIVE NATURAL BEINGS

We will recommend repeatedly that you go outside to places that are not artificial. You will be asked to do this to make sure that you are moving away from your everyday life that is, more than likely, conducted mostly indoors.

For the same reason there are retreats, you will be asked to move to unconventional spaces, places where an attractive natural being is located, so that you can conduct spiritual practices with a fresh and open perspective. Speaking of spiritual practices, Jesus was not significantly inspired by sitting inside. Instead, he spent forty days in the wilderness. Buddha did not gain enlightenment contemplating a house plant. He chose to sit outdoors for many days under the Bodhi Tree. Moses did not have his direct conversation with God next to an indoor fireplace. He communicated with God by way of a burning bush outside.

I, like many others, feel something I need is lacking when I spend too much time indoors. So I tend to spend a lot of time outdoors, often near moving water and almost every night as I sleep beneath the stars. I feel best in certain dynamic places outdoors: on immense rivers, in sparkling streams, in ocean waves, and under waterfalls (both above and below ground), for example.

It turns out that one of the things that may be giving me a boost in such places is the preponderance of negative ions that occurs when moving or falling water breaks up into droplets. When this happens, negative ions (electrically charges atoms)—and, specifically, negatively charged electrons—"are knocked loose from the water molecules then combine with oxygen atoms in the air to create negative ions" (MacGregor, 2010, pp. 147-148). In each sugar cube-size bit of air in most outdoor places there are 1,200 to 4,000 negative ions (MacGregor, 2010, p. 148). This number can peak to 2000 for country air, 50,000 for mountain air, and to over 100,000 negative ions where ocean waves or waterfalls interact with the land. Compare these relatively high numbers to the following relatively low numbers of negative ions indoors: in smoky indoor air, 0-100; in sealed office buildings, 0-250; and in normal indoor air with the windows open, 250-500 (TotalWellnessWorldwide Website). You may be wondering why these numbers are so important.

> "Once released into the atmosphere, negative air ions are easily inhaled into the lungs and absorbed into the bloodstream. There, negative ions can have a significant positive effect on health. Negative ions have been found to alleviate depression and stress, and to boost energy. They also produce biochemical reactions that increase levels of serotonin, creating feelings of elation and high spirits" (MacGregor, 2010, p. 148).

Indoor air that is surrounded by a grounded steel structure (like a typical modern skyscraper) draws off any negative ions. Central heating and air conditioning strips the air of negative ions. Synthetic carpets, upholstery, and curtains absorb negative ions. These are some of the reasons why germs and viruses flourish in indoor dead air.

It is best to sleep, work, and live in outdoor country air. Mountain air is invigorating. At concentrations of 50,000 negative ions per cubic centimeter, the air is both stimulating and relaxing. Such concentrations also kill germs.

For these reasons alone, it is a good idea to regularly sit by an outdoor being—as we will be suggesting you to do during your time along the Heartwood Path. Here are some other reasons:

Richard Louv, author of **Last Child in the Woods** and **The Nature Principle** identifies why you will be encouraged to commune with a natural being repeatedly in this series of books and courses. He speaks of "the transformative powers of nature," how it "can reshape our lives now and in the future," and lists several reasons for the "re-naturing" of everyday life, including:

1. To help balance for our high-tech lives.
2. To increase our intelligence, creative thinking, and productivity.
3. Make nature as important as human history.
4. Conserve and create natural habitat (Louv, 2012, p. 5).

Writes Louv:

"Simply living and working in a natural or re-natured environment... can have a profound impact on our mental health...

Nature-guided therapy is entering mainstream psychology as the combination of urban pressures and loss of natural habitat create psychological problems that other forms of treatment seem inadequate to fully address...

The great work of the twenty-first century will be to reconnect to the natural world as a source of meaning..." (Louv, 2012, pp. 66-246).

I am an eartHeart—formerly known as "environmentalist"—formerly known as a "conservationist." That means I care as much about our relationship to place as I do about the place itself. I support a spiritual/political movement that delivers what the heart has always needed: a meaningful relationship to the diversity of life. With such a movement, we can go beyond sustainability. I, for one, would not want only a sustainable environment any more than I would want only a sustainable intimate partnership. The place, the people, and the relationship needs to be sustainable, but it also needs to grow and transcend. Not fearful of the future, I want to be a good ancestor—one that has banished prejudice, not only between the races, but also between people and the land, and between the generations. There ought to be not only a botanical garden in every city but also a sustainable and creative town in every botanical garden. The Ecozoic Era the eartHearts of the Heartwood Path seek to promote is a time in the not-so-distant future when humans will enhance the earth rather than destroy its species. This Era can only dawn within the hearts of people, within those who are made more expansively loving through nature experiences. It will be a time of not only appropriate technology but also of green people, made verdant by systematic experiences with attractive natural objects, which are really beings who serve as emissaries from nature, beings who are intelligent, beings who can send us smart signals, if only we learn to listen.

We will need to make new things and approaches expected and normal. Louv (2012) writes about the three aspects of a proposed expanded environmental movement: the First Ring of traditionally funded, direct-service, nonprofit, and conservation organizations; the Second Ring of individual docents and other volunteers; and a Third Ring of networked individuals, families, associations and communities using social networking to connect people to nature and each other. This Third Ring could help find the people the other Rings find too difficult to reach. The Third Ring could also expand political clout. Help add the Third Ring to the environmental movement by spreading the word about the Heartwood Path.

What is needed is an international network of HumaNature teachers and life coaches, people who understand the importance of nature experiences. I propose to call these Third Ring teachers and life coaches, at least the ones that go down the Heartwood Path, "eartHearts." They will need to gain power, honor, connectivity, and identity. For these purposes, we offer the Heartwood Path and its website.

EartHearts will need to develop their approach, complete with adequate theory, suggested activities, and well-stocked tool kits. They will need to raise funds. They will need to be able to articulate the benefits they will provide, the efficiencies they will put into place, and the specific problems they will address. They ought to talk not only about outer world global climate change, for example, but also about inner heart climate change.

The environmental movement needs to move, and this is the direction I see it needing to go: toward the Third Ring of social networking that encourages people to regularly get up from their computers, leave their mobile devices at home or turned off, immerse themselves in the informed, intelligent vibrations of attractive natural beings, and make sure there are and always will be enough beings and places for this immersion. In this effort, I encourage eartHearts to remember that degraded habitats will produce degraded people and vice versa.

Along with the three "rings," the environmental movement has three messages. Each has its benefits. Despite these blessings (discussed next), participating in all rings and delivering all messages can be dissipative.

EartHearts will not focus much on environmental movement's First Message: the earth is facing an eco-catastrophe. We all know that by now. The doom-sayers gave us a way to kick-start a much-needed movement, but claiming that the earth is or soon will be beyond re-naturing is depressing. True, untrue, or waiting to be proven, gloom and doom is not capturing the public's imagination.

EartHearts will also not focus much on the environmental movement's Second Message: green economic benefits. If we all buy natural shampoos and the like a lot of natural plants and many natural places will be pulverized. The main thing that will be saved is the Aveda Corporation. The corporate hijacking of the consumer's ecological sensibilities has left the public too placated. This corporate hijacking has left consumers too brainwashed into thinking that buying green products is the only needed remedy. And this corporate hijacking has left the public too jaded by the false claims of corporate green-washing.

If the Second Message of green economic benefits is all that is needed then there would not be so many graduates of college environmental programs unemployed or looking so long for decent jobs. First Message claims of impending catastrophe and Second Message claims of green economic benefits, while both are true, are also both partial. They are not the whole story.

Another message, the one eartHearts will focus on, is, therefore, very much needed. The Third Message of the environmental movement is about the importance of the natural world to our health, to our learning process, to our happiness, to our spirit. As Louv (2012, p. 285) points out: "exposure to natural settings reduces stress, stimulates creativity and cognitive development, and tunes in all the senses." This Message has with it a new, ever-emerging call to action. Begin by continuing to move from waypoint to waypoint down the Heartwood Path, and by enjoying your time with your chosen natural beings and their attractive natural surroundings. If finding such places nearby is difficult, you have identified another action step.

We need not only equal protection from the bad stuff of society but also equal access to the good stuff. Some of this good stuff is green space and green jobs but some of it is also green rights that include access to nature. Additionally, we need green ethics and green philosophies that inform us of our inseparability from nature. We cannot allow nature to be plundered nor can we allow too much of it to be placed under protective house arrest. We need to pursue more open access to the wild. We also need more happiness—a grand gladness that comes from being made "whole" (known in the Bible as being made "perfect") through the kinds of conversion experiences outlined in this series of books.

To A Response To Your Attractions...

HumaNatureConnect Activity

Start-up Protocol

If this is not a day when you prefer to spend time in nature without an agenda, do the Heartwood Path Start-up Protocol found in the Appendix. Then return here to do the remaining portion of this activity:

Following Your Attractions

For this activity, use your relaxed, improved state of concentration, which you gained by communing with nature, to think about two gloomy reports about some impending environmental catastrophe (these are reports from the First Message of the environmental movement, as mentioned above). In your Activity Journal, write down how you feel about learning of this peril. Then, think of two environmental organizations and determine how you can support them (thus, participating in the First Ring of the environmental movement). Include your plans in your Activity Journal . Next, move to another natural being, focus on its attractiveness rather than on your own worries for at least ten seconds, and use the calmness and optimal functioning that results from your attraction to consider the Second Message of the environmental movement (by considering two changes in your purchasing to make your lifestyle more "green,"such as using reusable grocery bags and walking instead of using your car) and the Second Ring of the environmental movement (by considering how you can volunteer in some way to help wildlife or the environment). Enter a record of your impressions about the Second Message and the Second Ring in your Activity Log. Lastly, move to another natural being, focus on its attractiveness rather than your common-place hassles and use the resulting improved functioning to consider the Third Message of the environmental movement (by recollecting the importance of a specific natural being or a specific part of the natural world to your health, to your ability to learn, to your happiness, and to your spirit) and the Third Ring (by determining how you can network with like minded environmentalists or eartHearts). Write down your notes about the Third Message and Third Ring in your Activity Journal.

Follow-up Protocol

For best results, write down your impressions of this activity in your journal using the Heartwood Path Follow-up Protocol found in the Appendix. Afterwards, consider sharing your interpretations with others.

Heartwood Path Axioms

Key Assertions From Waypoint 1.18

1.18.1.

For the same reason there are retreats, you will be asked to move to unconventional spaces, places where an attractive natural being is located, so that you can conduct spiritual practices with a fresh and open perspective.

1.18.2.

I am an eartHeart-formerly known as environmentalist formerly known as a conservationist, meaning that I care as much about our relationship to place as I do about the place itself.

1.18.3.

To reduce stress, stimulate creativity, develop cognitively, improve all the senses, and expose yourself to a natural setting.

1.18.4.

Transcend to the Third Environmental Message and the Third Environmental Ring by thinking about First Message gloomy reports of some impending environmental catastrophe and how you will support First Ring environmental organizations; then consider the Second Message of the environmental movement by considering two changes in your purchasing to make your lifestyle more "green" and, in accordance with the Second Ring, consider how you can volunteer in some way to help the environment; but rest on the Third Message of the environmental movement by recollecting the importance of a specific natural being or a specific part of the natural world to your health, to your ability to learn, to your happiness, and to your spirit and rest on the Third Ring by determining how you can network with like minded environmentalists or eartHearts.

Nocturnal Pilgrimage 1.18

For best results, write down your impressions of each night's dreams in your journal using the Heartwood Path Dreaming Time Protocols found in the Appendix. Afterwards, consider sharing your Dream Tending with others.

You can't get the most from the Heartwood Path by remaining in your favorite chair. Go outside and follow your attractions. And then watch for them to recur in your dreams. If you do not think that you are dreaming about your natural attractions perhaps you are having difficulty remembering your dreams. A solution to this problem is listed subsequently. As stated in the component of our After Dreaming Protocol titled "First-Off," remain in your sleeping position as you wake up. Doing so will give you a chance to revisit your dreams. Lying motionless in your sleeping position with your dream journal close by will help you to determine what can be learned from your dreams, including what guidance you can receive from your chosen attractive natural beings.

With your dream journal in or next to your bed, sleep. Dream about good things. To get to all these good things in your waking time will require the adoption of some sort of spiritual endeavor.

Finding a sense of the whole is the topic of the next waypoint for this book/course: "Spiritual Practice." You are making great progress. Keep going.

19

Spiritual Practice

UNDERTAKE PRACTICES THAT
LEAD TO A SENSE OF THE WHOLE

Spiritual practice begins in awareness—a self-sensing of objective reality—and leads to consciousness—the "very substratum of all existence" (Paul, 2004, p. 214). Awareness pin-points an object, bringing it into one's perception. Consciousness

> "is complete and inclusive; it is a sense of the whole . . . Spiritual practice (ought to) always be undertaken on behalf of the whole. That is why the systemic development of consciousness is essential to spirituality" (Paul, 2004, pp. 214-215).

Doing spiritual practices in the midst of everyday life is too full of distractions. That is one reason why we will be asking you to find an attractive natural being and, even better, an attractive natural being surrounded by an attractive landscape or seascape, free of unsettling artificial distractions. This finding will reveal that your deepest roots are in nature.

Connecting with your natural roots satisfies essential needs. Fulfilling these needs are reason enough to search for and connect with a natural being and its nourishing realm, as you will be directed to do over and over again along the Heartwood Path. "Whether you're aware of it or not," writes Charles Cook, "you still have a vital need for regular, meaningful contact with this nourishing realm" (2001, p. vii).

Do not miss an opportunity to actually visit a natural being as you conduct Heartwood Path activities. Do not try to save time by being an armchair course participant. And do not try to avoid the tribulations of being exposed to nature.

Remember that the tragedy of your life will not be about what makes you pass out. The big mishap of your life will be about what you pass up. Don't let nature be among these.

> " . . . it's difficult to stay stressed out or maintain a negative mood while quietly focusing or meditating on nature. . . troubles shrink to more manageable sizes while you are away, and you can later view them 'through fresh eyes' from a more balanced perspective affected by your experiences in nature. . . (Cook, 2001, pp. viii-xv).

For these reasons and more, the Heartwood Path will help you develop a meaningful and lasting personal relationship with nearby natural beings and their natural surroundings.

> "When you begin weaving more of nature into your everyday existence. . . your sense of life may open up to encompass the much richer, more complex, more communal, and more timeless universe that you're actually part of. . . What we have to gain from our efforts is no less than the preservation of life on this remarkable planet" (Cook, 2001, pp.255-258).

Armed with these motives, the following activity offers some tips you can use for tracking down an attractive natural being.

To Your Activity Partner...

HumaNatureConnect Activity

Start-up Protocol

If this is not a day when you prefer to spend time in nature without an agenda, do the Heartwood Path Start-up Protocol found in the Appendix. Then return here to do the remaining portion of this activity:

Tracking Down An Attractive Natural Being

For this activity, do the following: Find an attractive non-human partner for this activity. Use what you learn here for future activities, as well. Clear your mind. Forget time while looking for a natural being. Linger where you feel comfortable. Let go of worries. Be quiet while in nature. Do not try, just be. Forget identifying or naming the things you encounter. If you choose to write about them, describe them without naming them. Look for uniqueness, without analyzing. Follow your heart into the wild. Do not worry what others may think. Like myself as a child, immerse yourself. Jump into the swamp, stand chest deep in murky water, look at the snake eye-to-eye, and lie down with the turtle. Or climb the tree, secure yourself in a safe spot, and meditate. To find animals: look where they would find food, water, cover. Search in areas where the terrain or vegetation changes. Consider the seasons and the time of day. To see nature: look at unfamiliar places, adopt the point of view of various animals, look wide but also up close, frame your viewing as a photographer would do. To hear nature: open your ears and close your eyes, cup your ears with your hands, and listen in concentric rings away from you. To smell nature: get down on all fours, pick up and view things while holding them close to your nose, close your eyes. To taste nature: sample the paw-paws and pick blackberries. To experience nature, combine all of the activities mentioned above.

Follow-up Protocol

For best results, write down your impressions of this activity in your journal using the Heartwood Path Follow-up Protocol found in the Appendix. Afterwards, consider sharing your interpretations with others.

Heartwood Path Axioms

Key Assertions From Waypoint 1.19

1.19.1.

Spiritual practice begins in awareness—a self-sensing of objective reality—and leads to consciousness—the "very substratum of all existence."

1.19.2.

Connecting with your natural roots satisfies essential needs.

1.19.3.

Remember that the tragedy of your life will not be about what makes you pass out but it will be about what you pass up.

Nocturnal Pilgrimage 1.19

For best results, write down your impressions of each night's dreams in your journal using the Heartwood Path Dreaming Time Protocols found in the Appendix. Afterwards, consider sharing your Dream Tending with others.

Sleep. Dream. Look for guidance in your dreams. Your connection experiences in your waking life may leave you with bits and pieces of signs and symbols in your dreams.

Prepare yourself for receiving guidance, information, and healing from your chosen attractive natural beings by moving to the next waypoint: "Now What."

20

Now What

PREPARE TO RECEIVE GUIDANCE, INFORMATION, OR HEALING FROM AN ATTRACTIVE NATURAL BEING

You are encouraged to keep your attractive natural beings and your chosen attractive natural landscapes secret. The beings will become your private friends. The landscapes will become you secret gardens. These will become places where you can both be free of expectations and be free to desire nothing except for your own happiness and the health of yourself and your surroundings.

Absorb the Earth's vibrations any way you like. Ways will be described later. And make your appreciations and show your gratitude anytime and anyplace. Such random feelings are good, better than the feelings of stress. But they are like a mere sixty-watt lightbulb that puts only a dim glow on everything.

To turn your appreciations and gratitude into a power tool like a laser beam I suggest you do two things. First. Be sincere. Second. Choose an attractive natural being to help you find guidance, information, and health.

Sincerity

Nature designs core heart feelings to be amplified by sincerity. One's heart knows the difference between the light bulb of random appreciation and the laser beam of sincere thoughtfulness (such as asking for consent) and gratitude. Sincere appreciation in the form of heart-felt attraction puts your nervous system into balance.

So does avoiding gossip. We all know that the only things that travel faster than the speed of light are bad checks and rumors. Put more of the light of your attention on appreciation.

"Appreciation has a way of smoothing out life's lumps and bumps. It puts things into perspective, reducing the heaviness and density of stressful thoughts and feelings. In a moment of sincere appreciation, your day no longer feels like the burden it used to be. You're free to see and acknowledge the good things in life for a change" (Childre and Martin, 1999, p. 23).

Opening your heart to an attractive natural being and its surroundings is like putting an adjustable lens on the camera of your perception. You can focus on details of the being or, expanding your view outward, the nearby natural scene.

"When you are in a state of appreciation, your energy is more buoyant and spirited. You feel better mentally, emotionally, and physically (Childre and Martin, 1999, p. 106).

Feeling better in these ways is enough excuse to appreciate anything. Still, if you want to amplify the feelings and secure that they come from or go to more than just your individual self, continue down the Heartwood Path and learn how to conduct your absorptions (what you take in from nature experientially) and demonstrations of appreciation (what you give back to nature) in proximity to an attractive natural being. That way you can entrain to the good vibrations of a being honed by a force of immense immediacy, intelligence, attractiveness, and love. Always be sincerely respectful, appreciative, thankful, and grateful for the opportunity to make such a connection.

"Just feel grateful for something, anything, in that moment . . . This act of appreciating . . . will help you resolve your challenging situation much more quickly and will increase your energy assets . . . If you're forever wanting and longing for more without first appreciating things the way they are, you'll stay in discord (Childre and Martin, 1999, p. 109-111).

Engage With An Attractive Natural Object

If things are bleak in your life, and it is difficult for you to appreciate anything at the moment, there is always an attractive natural object for you to go to, a being you can show your gratitude to, a fellow Earthling to ask for its consent to have a connection experience, and a natural place where you can immerse yourself with heartfelt sincerity in the good vibrations you feel when close to nature. After connecting with nature in this way and having a night's sleep, you will likely have answers to your questions. You may very well have a new course to follow. The Heartwood Path is charted to make you glad, happy enough to have the reserves needed take care of yourself, to take care of other people, and to work to protect the planet, perhaps that part for which you feel a new sense of gratitude.

Preparations Before Your Contact With A Chosen Attractive Natural Being

Some further preparations may be useful before you visit and appreciate your attractive natural beings or places. These include ceremoniously showering beforehand as a way to purify yourself; wearing loose, simple, natural clothing; bringing earphones capable of blocking out unwanted noises; bringing matches and incense (such as non-endangered wild sage) to purify the space and remove unwanted smells; bringing flowers, petals or leaves as offerings; bringing water to ceremoniously purify the being or its surroundings; facing the traditionally powerful directions of east or the north when visiting your chosen beings; establishing set times for your visits; visiting your natural emissaries of the Absolute Spirit before you eat so that you are not lethargic during your visit; remembering the mantras and postures you will learn subsequently; keeping your eyes on the attractiveness of nature while in the presence of your chosen natural being; seeking solitude; bringing a pen and a notebook; making offerings of gratitude (not just pronouncements of appreciation); and remembering to pause and reflect in silence.

How To Be With Your Chosen Attractive Natural Being

You may be wondering what you do after you pick an attractive natural being. I suggest that, for starters, you move close to it and assume one of the three most basic yoga postures. The purposes of these postures, besides giving you something to do when in proximity to your chosen natural being, is to restore balance and facilitate healing. Use the following three-part activity to help you do this balancing and restoring. Do it for yourself, for the emissary of nature you are visiting, and for the surrounding natural environment.

To Proper Posture While Visiting An Attractive Emissary Of Nature…

HumaNatureConnect Activity

Start-up Protocol

If this is not a day when you prefer to spend time in nature without an agenda, do the Heartwood Path Start-up Protocol found in the Appendix. Then return here to do the remaining portion of this activity:

Using Three Asanas While In The Presence Of Your Chosen Natural Being

For this activity, try out each of these three postures (asanas):

Lying Down

This posture facilitates deep surrender and profound healing. When prone, we feel received by the Mother Earth's bosom. Her forces of gravity will merge with your own energy. Use this posture if you feel the need to return to the ground of your being, to relinquish personal agendas and to become open to new experiences.

The method is as follows: Lie flat on your back. Stretch out your legs in front of you. Align your feet to become symmetrical but then let them relax. Place your arms beside you with your hands slightly away from your body. Relax and allow your energy to sink into the ground. Move nothing but your abdomen as you breath. Focus your attention on the in and out of your abdomen. Once you have achieved focus on your relaxed body and moving abdomen, say "so" on the inhalation and "ham" on the exhalation. This will further unify you to the ground of all existence. (Paul, 2004, pp. 154-155).

While in this lying down position, take advantage of the opportunity to renew yourself energetically and spiritually, to see your way through complex problems, and then return to your life with renewed confidence. The following addition to the lying down activity will bring forth acute listening, feeling, and receptivity. It will help you learn to hear and feel the vibrations of the body, even the Greater Body of the Earth, not just with the ears but also with the intuition and the deep sensitivity of the soul.

The following practice is called "yoga nidra." It needs to be practiced in a private space outdoors because it works best when you wear nothing but loose-fitting clothing or nothing but the sky. Once nude, or nearly nude, in a private space, bring your awareness to your head, eyes, nose, mouth, ears, cheeks. As you do so, refrain from judgment or commentary. Focus on the appearance of mental images, colors, shapes or patterns. Pay attention also to sounds, rhythms, and vibratory textures. Notice the flow of air through your throat by making your breathing audible, as previously described ("so" and "ham"). Focus on the flow of air in your chest, all the way inside to the heart. Listen to the pulsing of the heartbeat. Pay attention to the rise and fall of the abdomen as you breath. Inhale deeply and hold the breath momentarily. Release the air slowly. Relax the body, and focus on the genitals. Stay aware of the effects of deliberate breathing on the genitals, paying close attention to throbbing, pulsations, and changes in size, hardness, or wetness. Move your awareness to the anal opening. Gently contract or release your anal opening. Work this contracting in with the rhythm of your breathing. Stop the anal contractions and move your attention to your legs, beginning with your thighs and moving down to the ankles, toes, and soles of your feet. Focus next on the weight of your entire body on the ground. Extend the sense of your body to include the air in your lungs and the Earth under your body. Perceive any vibrations in your Greater Self that includes your individual body, the air that sustains it, and the Earth that supports it.

Standing

This posture can be practiced near almost any chosen natural being. It too balances your energy and, beyond that, it helps you relieve tension. Place your palms together in namaste gesture which means you finger tips are touching, your hands are pointed upward and slightly outward, and your palms are slightly apart. Close your eyes, relax your face, and breathe evenly. Relax your shoulders and the rest of your body, section by section. Pay attention to the subtle shifts in your feet needed to maintain balance. This will stimulate the two main channels of subtle energy running up each side of your spine. Keeping your mouth closed, focus your attention on your heart and your breathing process in your chest. As you exhale slowly say, the best you can with your mouth closed "aah." Make this sound soothing, as if the sound of a soothing wave. As you inhale, move your palms so that they touch the area of your heart and lungs, as if compacting your breath. Think of the in and out of your hands as creating space and depth in your heart.

Sitting Cross-legged

This iconic pose has been proven by yogis to be most conducive to the flow of life force. The straightness of the spine and the knees pressing on the ground forms a sort of holy triangle that naturally collects and concentrates body energies. The interlocking of the legs corresponds to the harmony of all pairs of opposites—female and male, intuitive and rational, hot and cold. We will not be suggesting that you do a full lotus pose. We will instead offer you a choice of three relaxed and easy cross-legged poses.

The methods are as follows:

For the Easy Posture: sit with your buttocks on a cushion or directly on the ground; place your legs on the ground, crossed comfortably; keep your back erect; and keep your hips higher than your knees.

For the Stable Posture: sit on a cushion or directly on the ground; pull your left foot close to your pelvis; pull your right foot as close as you can to the front of your left shin; press your ankles against the ground; make sure you do not place your feet one on top the other; press your knees against the ground; and avoid leaning forward.

For the Half-lotus Posture: pull your left foot close to your pelvis with your left ankle pressing against the ground; pull your right foot onto your left thigh, as close as possible to your pelvic area; if this is too difficult, rest your ankle on the opposing calf or ankle; if your right knee is off the ground, place a cushion under your buttocks so that you can lower your right knee to the ground. To change your position, place your right leg under the left.

Try each of these postures. Record your impressions in your journal.

Follow-up Protocol

For best results, write down your impressions of this activity in your journal using the Heartwood Path Follow-up Protocol found in the Appendix. Afterwards, consider sharing your interpretations with others.

Heartwood Path Axioms

Key Assertions From Waypoint 1.20

1.20.1.

Always be sincerely appreciative, thankful, and grateful for the opportunity to entrain to the good vibrations of a being honed by a force of immense immediacy, intelligence, attractiveness, and love.

1.20.2.

If things are bleak in your life, and it is difficult for you to appreciate anything at the moment, there is always an attractive natural being for you to go to, a being you can show your gratitude to, a fellow Earthling to ask for its consent to have a connection experience, and a natural place where you can immerse yourself with heartfelt sincerity in the good vibrations you feel when close to nature.

1.20.3.

**After connecting with nature and having a night's sleep, you
will likely have answers to your questions, you may very well
have a new sense of purpose, you will be happy enough to have
the reserves needed take care of yourself, to take care of other
people, and to work to protect the planet.**

Nocturnal Pilgrimage 1.20

For best results, write down your impressions of each night's
dreams in your journal using the Heartwood Path Dreaming Time
Protocols found in the Appendix. Afterwards, consider sharing your
Dream Tending with others.

After a night of sleep, after making more dream associations, after
amplifying your dreams, and after recording your dream impressions
in your journal, you are ready to move on.

The next waypoint, entitled "Higher Consciousness," is about developing a state of consciousness suitable for the demands of completing
this series of books and becoming an effective eartHeart or nature-
oriented life coach.

21

Higher Consciousness

DEVELOP THE STATE OF MIND NEEDED TO BECOME AN EFFECTIVE ELDER

Ethics demands that humanity develop a state of consciousness that is energetically higher than ordinary and, therefore, enables the people of the world to perceive and respond to the plight of the planet. We need, for example, to be able to do what Thick Nhat Hanh says we ought to do: "to hear within ourselves the sounds of the earth crying" (George, 1995, p.16). We also need to reverse, in the words of the Dalai Lama, "the gradual breakdown of the fragile ecosystems that support us" (George, 1995, p.16).

Without such a collective purpose to deepen our consciousness, humanity will end up "tinkering with symptoms endlessly" (George, 1995, p.21). Unless we develop a higher collective consciousness, humanity will focus too much on technological solutions because it will not be able perceive that technology is part of the problem. We need a spawning of a wide and deep interest in inner personal work because it is within the inner world of humans—the birthplace of greed, addiction, and confusion—that our outer planetary problems begin.

Writes George: "If the earth is as it is because we are as we are, then nothing less than the transformation of human beings on this planet will begin to correct (the ecological problem)" (George, 1995, p.21). "Until this distorted dream of a technological paradise," writes George, "is replaced by a more viable dream of a mutually enhancing human presence within an integral Earth Community, no effective healing will take place, for the dream drives the action. In the larger cultural context the dream becomes the myth that both guides and drives the action" (1995, p.160).

Important as a viable dream is, equally important is a rarely used but well known and respected approach to the seeking of higher consciousness. That important technique is living often in the present. Being in the present is sometimes referred to as experiencing "flow"—a psychological state that allows one to ignore hunger, discomfort, and fatigue as one seems to flow along in an engrossing experience. This "complete absorption in what one does" as Mihaly Csikszentmilhali is quoted to say (Lyubomirsky, 2007, p. 181), is fulfilling, pleasurable, and "provides a natural high that, unlike artificial highs or pure hedonistic pleasures, is a positive, productive, and controllable experience that does not cause guilt, shame, or other damage to self or the society at large" (2007, p. 182).

Given the benefits of experiencing flow, it is acceptable to set your goals high, as long as you enjoy the struggle of achieving them. The next activity will help you enter into this beneficial state of "flow." Keep the techniques in mind as you read about the origin of the Heartwood Path. I unwittingly entered into this state of flow frequently during the years I spent researching, writing, and experiencing the activities presented here.

The Heartwood Path stands as a testament to the benefits of flow. Here's how to increase some for yourself:

To Get Into The Swing Of Things…

HumaNatureConnect Activity

Start-up Protocol

If this is not a day when you prefer to spend time in nature without an agenda, do the Heartwood Path Start-up Protocol found in the Appendix. Then return here to do the remaining portion of this activity:

Increasing Flow

Think about and then write down ways to bring more flow into you life. If you have difficulty, assume the essence of your attractive natural being, and, as it, perceive and communicate ways to get out of your "ruts," if any, and ways to keep your flow experiences from becoming addictive. Perhaps a personal example will help you with this activity: I can recall a time when I sat near a large palm tree on the beach and I imagined that it was telling me to spend more time quietly listening to the soft sounds in nature as a way to enter into flow, to restore myself, and to improve my creativity. I imagined that this palm tree was reminding me to practice a sort of yoga of sound in wild places but to be careful not to overdo it because doing so would make the harsher sounds of the city too irritating.

Follow-up Protocol

For best results, write down your impressions of this activity in your journal using the Heartwood Path Follow-up Protocol found in the Appendix. Afterwards, consider sharing your interpretations with others.

Heartwood Path Axioms

Key Assertions From Waypoint 1.21

1.21.1.

Ethics demands that humanity develop a state of consciousness that is energetically higher than ordinary and, therefore, enables the people of the world to perceive and respond to the plight of the planet.

1.21.2.

Unless we develop a higher collective consciousness, humanity will focus too much on technological solutions because it will not be able perceive that technology is part of the problem.

1.21.3.

We need a spawning of a wide and deep interest in inner personal work because it is within the inner world of humans —the birthplace of greed, addiction, and confusion—that our outer planetary problems begin.

1.21.4.

Being in the present is sometimes referred to as experiencing "flow"—a psychological state that allows one to ignore hunger, discomfort, and fatigue as one seems to flow along in an engrossing experience.

Nocturnal Pilgrimage 1.21

For best results, write down your impressions of each night's dreams in your journal using the Heartwood Path Dreaming Time Protocols found in the Appendix. Afterwards, consider sharing your Dream Tending with others.

Sleep before you engage in the next waypoint in this book. Make dream associations and amplify your dreams, as previously instructed.

Move to the next waypoint, "The Origin Of The Heartwood Path," to learn more about the curative aspects of nature. The next two waypoints are unusually long so be prepared by setting aside enough time.

22

The Origin Of The Heartwood Path

UNDERSTAND THE CURATIVE ASPECT OF NATURE

For thirty years my main professional focus was outer world environmental action. I established conservation goals, worked hard, and, by 1983, met my goals. Although I was a successful conservationist, my intuition told me that I needed to hunt for something more.

The Heartwood Path Began As A Burnout Cure

This hunt started as a charge to find a cure for "burnout" in environmental activists. From this narrow bud, a flower emerged that is much more universally significant.

The Heartwood Path Blossomed Into A Cure Of Personal, Social, And Environmental Ills

When this small but special bud blossomed its petals revealed a map showing a path for how to make the world better. In following my newly blossoming course, I found sweet nectar. Pulled to drink this elixir, I found a magical cure for personal, social, and environmental ills.

A Remedy To Personal And Environmental Ills Is Current

The invisible cure for personal, social, and environmental ills I discovered while preparing these books is a remedy that comes in two forms of *current*—that is, both 1) *current* as presence and 2) *current* as flow. It is, metaphorically speaking, a nameless enduring stream. Its power comes like the flow of water in the main channel of a powerful but largely forgotten river. Like the ever-present air we breathe, the enduring stream is, without the viewer receiving special guidance, too pervasive to be seen, too invisible to be appreciated, and too amorphous to be used. And so, we resort to scrounging benefits from its smaller, familiar, but less fruitful seemingly detached remnants.

For most of my life, I lived on the banks of the Father of Waters, the Mississippi River. Like the Enduring Stream, this main artery in the system of rivers in North America flows endlessly, it is rich in symbolic meanings, and despite the construction of levees, dams, dikes, the destructive practice of dredging and other monumentally misguided efforts, it refuses to be contained either physically within the government's navigation channel or within the imagination of those who are fortunate enough to witness its magical might. Due to its nature of meandering so extensively that it has historically altered its course, parts of the enduring Mississippi River have occasionally been abandoned as u-shaped lakes called "oxbows." Now that the main flowway of the Mississippi has taken a more opportune route, one such remnant of the river nearby my hometown is Horseshoe Lake. Though huge, unlike the main channel of the river which cannot be seen in its entirety, Horseshoe Lake can be captured by the eye and contained within its banks. Having lost the self-scouring power of the main flow of the Mississippi, Horseshoe is stagnant, shallow, and less attractive.

The flow has stopped and topsoil from near-bye farm fields threatens to fill-in this lake so important to migratory birds. There are signs that this body of water was once a section of its abandoning parent, but the magical symbolism of the Mighty Mississippi flows elsewhere. Unlike the Mississippi which sensually comes from some distant place upstream and flows to some out-of-sight place downstream, all the edges of Horseshoe Lake are within sight, measurable, namable, and suitable for the construction of the Granite City steel mill and other industrial developments nearby. For these reasons, the abandoned channel of the greater river is diminished in its symbolic meaning.

Though diminished of the vast metaphorical power it had when it was part of the main river, some benefits can be gleaned in the abandoned lakes and solid crusts left aside at edges of the lake. Trees, for example, become timber. Chemicals become medicines. Plants and animals become classified, dissected, studied, and used. In the abandoned pools left behind by the flowing Father of Waters, the water is shallow and calm enough for a grandfather to hook fish, give the pole to his grandson, and then marvel at how many fish the little lad can catch. It was from Horseshoe Lake that I, at age four, along with my grandfather at age fifty-four brought home my first remembered bucket of bluegill for dinner. The lake and the bucket were in my awareness. There are no such memories regarding the parent stream, which seems too vast, too dangerous, and too mysterious to be plucked out by a single family's memories. Not threatened by the wrath of the churning waters in the main channel of the river, a little boy's self-esteem and confidence grew, a steel mill belched out salmon-colored "pay-dirt," and the human culture around the lake became bigger, louder, and brighter, but also more destructive.

I did not include this description of a river and an oxbow because of some need for you to understand hydrology. The important lesson here comes at the end of the next section.

Hard To Swallow

The realization of the curative powers of the enduring stream was a bit of a rude awakening for me. I was happy in my acute awareness but troubled when that awareness broadened into a more expansive consciousness.

I spent thirty years stopping dams, power plants, mines, highways, and other rude aspects of civilization. It is a bit hard to come to the realization that during all of the time I was working save the earth from (metaphorically speaking) the ax of civilization when really it is the madman wielding the ax that ought to have been changed. It took an understanding of the Enduring Stream for me to come to that conclusion, which would not have been possible without the study of Natural Attraction Ecology and a form of eco-psychology offered by Dr. Cohen at Project NatureConnect. Dr. Cohen enabled me to, among other things, make rich distinctions between the Mississippi River (broader consciousness) and its abandoned oxbows (limited awareness). The Heartwood Path is not about the stagnant oxbow of limited awareness. It is about the enduring stream of broader and higher consciousness.

The Discovery Of The Path

The man who saved the Grand Canyon and essentially invented the modern environmental movement once asked me to "write a piece" about how to prevent "burnout" in environmentalists. My first response to his call to action was to ask: "why me?" My second response, kept to myself, was to wonder what I would have to say in such a "piece."

David Brower's (1912-2000) call for me to write happened in 1986. It did not take me numerous decades to become articulate about the subject of perseverance. It has, however, taken me that long to be able to produce what I believe to be the real benefit of Brower's request. In looking for ways to keep environmentalists active I also discovered ways that personal growth is good for the planet, ways the planet can aid in helping people add to their development, and ways nature can lead us to find happiness. These ways come from the Enduring Stream itself, but, to reap its rewards, one has to first uncover the Enduring Stream, for it is largely hidden from the bulk of humanity, especially those of us who live the bulk of our lives indoors, detached from nature, where "the enfolding earth is filtered through a dense panoply of technology" (Abram, 2010, p. 263).

The initial uncovering of the Enduring Stream can begin for you in a number of ways, including:

1. by participating in the activities in my Heartwood Path series of books,
2. by attending our "Better You/Better Earth" multi-day presentations or retreats,
3. by watching to one of our "Enduring Stream" podcasts,
4. by attending my forty minute "Let's Make It All Better" multimedia presentations, and
5. by living your life according to a helpful but unrestrictive basic assumption I call "The PIERCE Principle" which, in its shortest version is: "transforming the planet requires transforming the person."

While this principle will be described subsequently, the basis for it has been discussed by other authors. Nordhaus and Shellenber (2010), for example, demonstrate the need for such a principle when they state "The (environmental) problem is so great that before answering What is to be done? We (have to) first ask, What kind of beings are we? and What can we become?" (p. 8).

Since the nature of something is often best revealed in its origins, I will explain here how Brower's charge to help fight "burnout" in environmentalists led to something that is good for everyone. Like a prophet, Brower arose to the occasion, knew what was needed, and knew how to, at least, get it started.

Given the alarming dropout rate for volunteer and professional environmentalists, given my passion to protect nature, and given my undying admiration for David Brower, I would eventually become excited about my new assignment. Not at first, however. Here's how it went down:

David Brower, the man a book-writer name Stephen Fox called the "most prominent conservationist of the post-war period," wanted me, then a seasoned regional representative for one of Brower's organizations, (Friends of the Earth), to figure out how to help my eco-comrades persevere. Although that was for me quite an honor; it was also daunting, to say the least.

"Why do you want me to write it?" I asked. "After all," I said, "who better than you to pen such a 'piece?' You have four more decades of experience than I, and nobody has a better history of successes."

His answer began curiously: " You live in the Midwest." I suppose for him the Bible Belt section of the Midwest was the American equivalent to living in Siberia.

"And with practically no support" he continued, "you stick to it, year after year, winning scores of conservation battles on a limited budget." Then came the part he knew would make me rise to the challenge, just to prove a point:

"And, despite the low pay and isolation, you never give up." There, he said it: "isolation. " He knew that would be the clincher. Dave knew how I felt about being regarded as an "isolated, out of touch, hick from the sticks." He meant that, except for periodic lobbying trips to the nation's capital and trips to the West Coast because I had become a Friends of the Earth board member, I was largely isolated from San Francisco or Washington D.C—the nation's two power centers for environmentalism.

Looking like he realized his statement demonstrated a prejudice against the Heartland, he wryly asked with a self-knowing chuckle: "How do you keep the fight going year after year after year?" I was flattered.

Then it hit me. Despite my history of attempting to overcome "Midwest-ism" by attempting to be a good example of an articulate, dedicated, mover-and-shaker, I had no answer for the one man I admired most professionally. I did not know what I did to keep myself from "burning out" so how was I going to write a piece about perseverance in environmentalists?

This realization sent me on a quest, and in the process of attempting to present "burnout" remedies for activists, my own and those proposed by others, I discovered something that can be good for everyone, especially those who seek to make a difference in the world without crashing. Eventually, I would put all I learned into this series of books that I continuously see as being beneficial to both individual participants and the planet as a whole.

The Discovery Of Applied Eco-psychology

Along the way to present this "piece" I discovered applied ecopsychology. With that and a host of other practices, I believe I am helping to develop a new arm of the environmental movement. So fruitful do I believe this approach to be, I am now personally doing what I never imagined I would do: I am transcending the approach I learned from Brower and others in the environmental movement: I am presenting a new, softer approach to the old mildly militant one from my days working at Friends of the Earth and elsewhere.

This is not a change, for that would imply giving up the old approach. I believe Brower's approach is still valid: fervently and legally use the political system to demonstrate, though media attention, local demonstrations, and letter-writing campaigns to governmental officials, that one's will to protect wild places is greater than the collective will of everyone hell-bent to destroy such places.

This approach is well suited to winning conservation battles, but I fear in the years to come that it, by itself, will not be enough to win, using the jargon of my fellow eco-warriors, the overall "war to protect the environment." While saving individual wild places is a valid endeavor, saving natural places alone will prove to be an insufficient solution to the global environmental predicament because during the fray to save a place (or a species, for that matter) little is done to correct the root cause of the global environmental predicament.

To be truly successful, the environmental movement needs to add to its agenda changing the collective human mindset that is now leading to environmental destruction. The magnitude of the job of reversing the psychological underpinning that promotes the ecological destructiveness of modern civilization understandably causes much of the burnout amongst environmentalists Brower was asking me to address. Changing the minds of the masses seems too overwhelming for even a legion of environmentalists to take on.

Indeed, lack of motivation occurs when one sees a huge job but does not have the tools necessary to do the work effectively. So the question arises: "What sort of manageable "fulcrum" can be used to tip the big, collective mindset of humanity towards a consciousness that promotes ecological sustainability?"

Given that we in the United States are blessed to live with a political structure that allows citizens to affect change, I am not advocating throwing out what works well on targeted campaigns. I am, however, about to propose an additional tool, a sort of fulcrum, one that is an adjunct to both traditional psychotherapy and the traditional environmental advocacy approach. The new approach I am about to present, therefore, is not a change but a transcendence.

I am proposing that those who care about the environment add to their time-tested targeted tactics a new approach that will have a broad and deep impact. I make this suggestion because I have found that when environmental advocacy is combined with helping people work to regain their psycho-spiritual sense of wholeness with nature, the total is greater than the sum of the parts—especially when the work is laid out along an understandable and doable pathway.

Luckily, the work of two men—David Brower and Dr. Michael Cohen—served as a guide for my proposed deeper, two-tier approach to environment protection: 1) engage in targeted battles to save specific aspects of nature and 2) show those who care about the environment how to add to their personal growth, expand their world view, and become both more effective and happy sustainably.

The path I will describe here is for one's personal growth. This path is where the perseverance Brower wanted me to write about comes about. Beyond the attainment of perseverance, this path is also where one can find an amazing source of guidance, information, and the healing—all necessary for personal happiness, improved relationships, and a protected environment.

Brower, more than anyone else, taught me how to "save the earth, one place at a time." As I have said, I have used his approach to fight dams, nuclear power plants, lumber barons, and huge mining companies, with considerable success. Along with these positive results, I have also seen the ill-effects of such battles on my cohorts.

For their own personal and private reasons, most of the activists that have worked with me in conservation are not still participating actively in the movement. Brower recognized this problem throughout the world and requested that I present a "burnout" cure.

His charge made it possible for me to add "saving the earth, one person at a time" to my suggested approach to environmentalism. My proposed approach requires the following of the practices developed by eco-psychologists such as Michael Cohen along a path that I will describe here.

I have already summarized Brower's way of saving the environment. Now, since you will be repeatedly asked to spend time outdoors appreciating nature in the activities that follow, it is useful here at the outset to switch for the moment from saving the environment to savoring the environment and, specifically, to savoring in ways that engender greater Triple A Happiness.

A good anchor for your own happiness is the source of your calling. The following activity will help you recall the origins of your passion.

To Recall The Source Of Your Calling…

HumaNatureConnect Activity

Start-up Protocol

If this is not a day when you prefer to spend time in nature without an agenda, do the Heartwood Path Start-up Protocol found in the Appendix. Then return here to do the remaining portion of this activity:

Revealing The Origin Of Your Passion

For this activity, look around the scene for natural aspects that jog your memory about what led you to become passionate about someone or something in your life. Write down what, if anything, in nature led to your calling or was a source of your passion. If possible, recall the moment or moments something in nature set you on a primary pathway of interest in your life. Write down a brief story about the natural origins of your major life interest or interests. The origin of my life's work, for example, came in an instant: the moment in 1963 that my boyhood friend Doug Roewe told me that a large leaf in our forest playground was a Sycamore, and that there were numerous other types of trees, thus starting a lifetime of nature study and conservation.

Follow-up Protocol

For best results, write down your impressions of this activity in your journal using the Heartwood Path Follow-up Protocol found in the Appendix. Afterwards, consider sharing your interpretations with others.

Heartwood Path Axioms

Key Assertions From Waypoint 1.22

1.22.1.

With awareness, a small part the Enduring Stream becomes measurable, understandable, and available.

1.22.2.

David Brower's approach to environmental protection is to fervently and legally use the political system to demonstrate, though media attention, local demonstrations, and letter-writing campaigns to governmental officials, that one's will to protect wild places is greater than the collective will of every-one hell-bent to destroy such places.

1.22.3.

To be more successful, the environmental movement needs to add to its agenda changing the collective human mindset that is now leading to environmental destruction.

1.22.4.

Here is the eartHeart's two-tier approach to environment protection: 1) show those who care about the environment (which is most people) how to add to their personal growth, expand their world view, become both more effective and happy by receiving guidance from nature, and return the favor by using their expanded consciousness and David Brower's approach to conservation; and 2) engage in targeted battles to save specific aspects of nature.

Nocturnal Pilgrimage 1.22

For best results, write down your impressions of each night's dreams in your journal using the Heartwood Path Dreaming Time Protocols found in the Appendix. Afterwards, consider sharing your Dream Tending with others.

Once you have recalled the beginnings of your own passion or life's work, as you did in the previous activity, bring these origins to mind immediately before going to sleep. It will likely help if you associate some natural being that was in or near the scene where your inspiration occurred. The same power that gave you your original motivation can also guide you toward important adjustments. To increase the chances that you will have dreams that offer origin-related images that you can use to make associations and amplifications that help you with your most important tasks, repeatedly give your appreciation with your inhalations and offer your gratitude with your exhalations (similar to what you do when following the component of our Start Up Protocol titled "Attractive Natural Being"). Having done this, develop the intention that you will look for ways in your dreams to further express your gratitude; for ways to improve upon your existing work; and for, quite possibly, images that propel you towards a different, more satisfying, line of work.

After once again recording your dream associations and amplifying your dreams in your journal, as previously instructed, practice delighting in your chosen attractive natural beings by moving to the next activity, "Savor," after a few helpful suggestions.

Read the next waypoint slowly and carefully. Bordering on the ineffable (incapable of being described in words) the next waypoint may seem ponderous. If the following waypoint is too dense, read it twice; if it is too mentally exhausting, read it slowly. If you still have difficulty grasping the critically important points, consider getting some helpful, individualized assistance from a Heartwood Path Guide. You are about to enter the heartwood of the heartwood, the core where the curative strength of Heartwood Path is revealed.

23

Savor

DELIGHT IN BEINGS OUTDOORS

I am happy that you are progressing this far in your odyssey towards your own happiness and towards environmental sustainability. Continuing on this path will be comprehensively curative—that is, it will help you mend not just your physical maladies but also your unhealthful points of view. This mending will occur best once you absorb a bit more about NNIAAL, elaborated in the following eight sections.

The Essence Of Nature

The cure found along the Heartwood Path comes largely from NNIAAL: the essence of nature—the ethereal quality of nature I call the "Enduring Stream." From an awareness of this spiritual aspect of nature comes education, healing, guidance, and growth.

Now—the First "N" in NNIAAL

One cannot see this remedy as a separate entity, Still, it is nearly everywhere, especially outdoors. It exists now, perpetually.

Whenever confusion occurs to you along this or any other pathway of growth, the first most fruitful remedy will likely be in remembering and taking to heart the Sanskrit phrase: "Tat Tvam asi" (Johnson, 1939, p.378). It means:

Thou art that.

This individual is that individual. Each is an aspect of the One Supreme. Until this notion is taken to heart the pilgrim will spend too much time in the earlier stages of growth—that of scattering (running after all sorts of objects), darkening (dullness, laziness, evilness), and gathering (overcoming scattering) before arriving at the final stage of concentration ("the one-pointed form of mental action"—that undisturbed state of mind that is free from all distractions and preoccupations—which can result in what we will call "samadhi" (Johnson, 1939, pp. 378-379).

Namelessness—the Second "N" in NNIAAL

Throughout this pilgrimage we will remind the sojourner of what is said in Vedic literature: "Ekam sat vipra bahunda vadanti" (Johnson, 1939, p.376-377). Translated in English:

That which exists is one: sages call it by various names.

We too will call it by various names; but during the meditative processes described along the Heartwood Path it is most accurate and best to allow it to be nameless. It can be experienced, but not through words or stories. Words are mere representations of it. Tales tell mere tiny tidbits of its constitution and technique.

One soon learns that great personal and social remedies stem from the Nameless One that is also intelligent. These remedies are hidden to most people because the Nameless One is, to them, invisible. Yet the invisible Nameless One is pervasive. Its therapeutic tonic is available for humans and nonhumans alike. This pervasive, hidden Nameless One is not only conscious, it is wise.

The pervasive, hidden Nameless One cures disorders and relieves symptoms in the most intelligent way. Without producing pollution, it creates a uni-verse of beauty and diversity.

That is one reason why the tonic offered by the Nameless One is so attractive. "Tat Tvam asi" (Thou art that): this intelligent, nameless, infinite, and perpetually present unseen one is the tonic that is aware-ness of attraction itself. Let me repeat, for this point is critical:

The remedial nectar found
along the Heartwood Path is
awareness of attraction itself.

The Nameless One offers a remedy that comes from the attractive-ness of the way it presents itself to us, in pleasing points in the stream of our awareness. Its flowing remedial nectar (inseparable from itself except in inaccurate perception and in language) is fascinating, en-grossing, and alluring. It is magnetism, it is erotic, it is the pull between lovers, it is the hold of gravity, and it is the draw of one's attention to attractions in nature. This current of Now's nameless, intelligent attraction, has yet another important aspect.

Intelligence—the "I" in NNIAAL

From "Vivek"—the right discrimination—that occurs in the gather-ing stage of the meditative process to "vairagya"—the mental detach-ment of oneself from the external world—that occurs in a later stage of the meditative process—we shall encourage Heartwood Path sojourners to go all the way to the first glimpse of the highest meditative plateau, gain the reward found there (mental detachment), then come back one step so the material world is still important. In doing so, the sojourner will discover the fantastic inherent intelligence of Nature, realize the fruits of being a *sage,* but work on behalf of all sentient beings in the real world as a *saint.*

Attraction—the First "A" in NNIAAL

Even when asked to identify and go to an attractive natural being or place (as you will be asked to do repeatedly along the Heartwood Path), love your attractive natural being as it loves you—without attachment and without desire. A mind full of such clinging sensual desires will enslave the soul and reduce the positive impact of the One's intelligent remedies. To remove any blocks in the flow of the One's healing nectar, continue to seek out your attractions in nature. Stifling such callings is counterproductive because negations such as "Thou shalt not" are ineffective. Better than stifling oneself is finding something better for oneself.

In this way you can remain fruitfully unattached by continuing to seek out natural beings of desire where the nectar of the One is most concentrated while, at the same time, perceiving and considering them as something that is greater than mere physical natural beings or outdoor places. Think of your attractions in nature not as desired things or places, for these things and places are impermanent and, at higher planes of your personal development, they will prove to be distracting and stultifying for you.

It is very important to think of the attractive beings as arisings in your awareness. Think of them, more specifically, as wonderful connection experiences. Consider these experiences as passages, audible in both the outer and inner worlds (which is all one), as parts of the healing, guiding, and informative symphony of the life stream.

Aliveness—the Second "A" in NNIALL

As one experiences nature in the Now, without imposing names, by paying attention to its intelligence, and by receiving helpful and healthful gifts from its attractive natural beings, one becomes embraced by nature's love. In nature's nurturing encirclement, one becomes quickened as one is enfolded by teeming vitality. Full of vim, activity, vigor, and current, nature is animated. She is both sentient and alive.

Love—the "L" in NNIAAL

Love is the affection for learning, the adoration of nature, the devotion to purpose, the caring for people, the affection for pets, and the keenness for whatever one finds irresistible. The remedy is found in the flow of affection, the torrent of passion, the current of interest, and the stream of enthusiasm. It is not a dammed up sort of love, full of stifling attachments.

It is a higher sort of love that, odd to many in the beginning of their pilgrimage, is loving but not possessive. There is love but there is no self-identification with the object of one's love. We can say that this is a higher form of love because one is better able to serve those whom one loves when one is not enslaved by clinging possessiveness and the expectation of receiving rewards from one's love objects.

The sun shines on all yet asks for nothing in return. Spread your love in a similar fashion.

Detached love is the ideal. The soul lives on and on by giving, not by receiving. You will get most by giving most.

The Enduring Stream

The curative nectar reveals itself as a current—both in the sense of being in the perpetual present but also in the sense that, despite its ever-changing presentation to the world, it always has the tendency to move freely without a break. It surges without interruption in the inner world of intentions and ethics. It flows endlessly in the manifested outer world of behaviors and things.

Designating And Exhibiting

Naming and manifestation only occurs when a human consciously perceives something apart, something at the drying edge of this metaphorical enduring stream. For example:

> "Take in the glowing crimson color (of a rose flower) and say to yourself, 'Without me, this flower would have no color . . .'" Realize that if you subtract yourself from a sensation—sight, sound, touch, taste, smell—the rose would be nothing but atoms vibrating in a void" (Chopra, 2004, p.30).

Despite all the gleanings that come from the *limited awareness* of the manifested stagnant pools left abandoned by the enduring stream, and despite the *limited awareness* of the persistence of personal, social and environmental ills, the *limited awareness* shows us that the underlying source of our problems does not lie in metaphorical isolated pools of named techniques or in the named things that we do not truly love. Essential cures to pervasive problems—problems that are personal and problems that are ecological—come from the *broader consciousness* of the powerful, silent, and invisible yet venerable Enduring Stream itself.

The Curative Powers Of Wholeness

While traveling a certain path along the Enduring Stream one discovers that the root of remedy cannot be detached from the whole. Now's ever-changeable, ever-present, intelligent, attractive, loving and lovable current that I call "The Enduring Stream™" is, unlike the previously mentioned Horseshoe Lake of my youth, too wide to be named and too deep to be fathomable. No man-made bridge, however grand, can span the unabridged flow of nature.

One Trail To Healing, Guiding, And Growth-producing Experiences Is Called The "Heartwood Path"

Too much for words, what I call The Enduring Stream™ is best perceived through experience; which, fortunately for participants, can be adequately described with a careful use of the alphabet. In this book/ course, I will describe the healing, guiding, and growth-producing experiences one can have while following a specific path propelled by the Enduring Stream.

The Heartwood Path is that specific trail. Powering those who traverse its informative sections is the Enduring Stream which is an aspect of the Absolute Spirit, the One. As such, along the Heartwood Path one engages in a divine-human collaboration aimed at helping sojourners find their deep gladness at the intersection of the world's deep hunger. It takes you and the Enduring Stream to find this place. The Absolute Spirit in the form of the Enduring Stream alone will not do the job. You without the Enduring Stream cannot do the job. As the Pope is to God, those who follow the Heartwood Path become the Absolute Spirit's vicegerents on Earth. As we all know, eartHearts used to be agnostics, but now they aren't sure.

The Enduring Stream Provides The Power,

The Heartwood Path Provides The Direction

The power of the Enduring Stream and the direction of the Heartwood Path lead to and put to use a love of nature that feeds one's spirit through the experience of the wild. Why is this important? "For unless we see it, smell it, or touch it, we tend to forget it, and our souls wither" (Maathai, 2010, p. 89).

R.D. Lang (Jensen, 2000) has some important things to say about the influence of experience on behavior: "Our behavior is a function of our experience. We act according to the way we see things. If our experience is destroyed, our behavior will be destructive. If our experience is destroyed, we have lost our own selves" (p. 1).

Despite the separating armor of technologies we use indoors, our "creaturely body, shaped in ongoing interaction with the outer bodies that compose the biosphere, remains poised and thirsting for a relatively unmediated exchange with reality in all its more-than-human multiplicity and weirdness" (Abram, 2010, p. 264). "We could never have survived, as a species, without our propensity for animistic engagement with every aspect of our earthly habitat. And yet this highly adaptive style of experience has lain mostly dormant in the modern era" (Abram, 2010. p. 266).

This series of books and courses addresses what happens when one uncovers the Enduring Stream while applying a few soon-to-be-discussed topics such as my own PIERCE Principle ("Being happy and saving the earth requires an achievable high level of spiritual maturity."), Dr. Cohen's Natural Systems Thinking Process, and Bill Plotkin's Wheel of Life. The results obtained along the Heartwood Path have variety because the Enduring Stream, the PIERCE Principle, the Natural Systems Thinking Process, and the Wheel of Life—each encountered along the Heartwood Path—do not lead to a narrowly defined, predetermined end. By not interfering with each participating individual's personal goals and needs and by the combined affects of all of these forces, assumptions, methodologies, developmental life-cycle models, and books I feel the outcomes will be both diverse and significant.

Onward To Savoring

You are encouraged to proceed but not by only reading this text. That would be like reading about Beethoven's Ninth Symphony and never hearing it. To get right to experiencing, I will include five ways to savor in the following activity. Remember these ways, for they will be useful throughout your journey down the Heartwood Path.

To The Five Ways To Increase Your Delight…

HumaNatureConnect Activity

Start-up Protocol

If this is not a day when you prefer to spend time in nature without an agenda, do the Heartwood Path Start-up Protocol found in the Appendix. Then return here to do the remaining portion of this activity:

Savoring

For this activity, focus with appreciation on that being. Apply the following five ways to savor and write down how each of them affect you: 1) focus completely on this one aspect of nature or on a specific part of one natural being and write down how sharpening your focus, if at all, led to positive feelings; 2) congratulate yourself on any of your abilities and write down how self-congratulation, if at all, makes you feel; 3) share your experience of your chosen natural being with other people, and write down how this sharing, if at all, led to positive feelings, 4) reminisce about the positive feelings that, if at all, arose from savoring the natural being and write down how building a memory makes you feel; and 5) invite one or more people to participate in your online sharing via the Heartwood Path Exchange about your experience of the natural being and write down how, if at all, such sharing with others leads to positive feelings.

Follow-up Protocol

For best results, write down your impressions of this activity in your journal using the Heartwood Path Follow-up Protocol found in the Appendix. Afterwards, consider sharing your interpretations with others.

Heartwood Path Axioms

Key Assertions From Waypoint 1.23

1.23.1.

Until the notion of "each is an aspect of the one" is taken to heart the pilgrim will spend too much time in the earlier stages of growth—marked by running after all sorts of objects, dullness, laziness, and evilness—before overcoming such scattering and darkening and arriving at "the one-pointed form of mental action"—that is free from all distractions and preoccupations.

1.23.2.

The sojourner will discover the fantastic inherent intelligence of Nature, realize the fruits of being a *sage,* but work on behalf of all sentient beings in the real world as a *saint.*

1.23.3.

Apply the following ways to savor: focus completely on one aspect of nature; congratulate yourself on any of your abilities; share your experience of your chosen natural being with other people; reminisce about the positive feelings that arise from savoring the natural being; and invite one or more people to share in your experience of the natural object.

Nocturnal Pilgrimage 1.23

For best results, write down your impressions of each night's dreams in your journal using the Heartwood Path Dreaming Time Protocols found in the Appendix. Afterwards, consider sharing your Dream Tending with others.

Sleep. Dream. Keep heading down the Heartwood Path. From a brief introduction to saving the environment and to savoring the environment we turn in the next waypoint to the topic of saving the earth one person at a time.

Along the Heartwood Path one engages in a divine-human collaboration aimed at helping sojourners find their deep gladness at the intersection of the world's deep hunger for deepening sustainability.

For now, we shall define "sustainability" as ecological diversity and health that is undiminished over time. By "deepening sustainability" I mean sustainability that is accompanied by the perpetual spiritual development of the mass of humans, a development that occurs in each individual, a development that creates the kind of sustainable integrity that stems from transcending to higher levels of personal growth, and a development wherein each added level gives greater and more enduring depth to one's character.

With these words, if you have already tended to your previous night's dreams, you are ready to move to the next waypoint, entitled for some very good reasons, "Permission." Keep up your good work.

24

Permission

UNDERSTAND THE VALUE OF CONSENT

One of the key lessons I learned from Dr. Michael Cohen is the value and purpose of gaining consent. Due to the benefits of seeking and gaining permission, —the most important for us here being the resultant development of a sense of equanimity between all participants, including between a natural being and its admiring human in the nature connection experience— I ask for your consent to be led down the Heartwood Path.

I ask for your consent because it is my experience that applying eco-psychology practices along the Heartwood Path is life-changing and one ought to not lead a person to life-changes without seeking consent. I recommend that you only give your consent to be led down the Heartwood Path if you are curious about it and eco-psychology or if you seek personal and environmental improvements. Your continuing to partake in this waypoint indicates your consent.

"The eco-psychologist Michael Cohen has made a life's work of re-connecting people with nature . . . (He) believes that one of the most important laws we have forgotten about the earth is the Law of

Attraction and Consent. For life to thrive—not merely hang on but thrive and expand—Cohen believes it needs the consent, or welcome, of its surroundings" (McElroy, 2006, p. 82).

Certainly one would be more attracted to people and places that are welcoming. "How does a place become welcoming?" you may ask. Plants and animals, according to Cohen, feel the sense of attraction and consent in numerous particular ways, through a host of natural senses mentioned previously. Each time you seek consent from your chosen attractive natural being, you will know you have the beneficial energy of consent when your hands and body feel comfortably warmer, when you feel uplifted, when you feel drawn to the being, when you feel more energized, when you experience greater clarity, or when you feel lighter. If I notice any of these things along with my attraction, I interpret them as a sign of consent or permission to continue with the HumaNatureConnect Activities.

If, however, you feel your hands starting to get colder; if you feel nauseous, saddened, repulsed, or confused; if you feel your energy dropping; or if you feel pushed away, it is best to just nod respectfully toward the being and move to a more welcoming partner. If I feel any of these negative responses, or if I notice myself moving in a counterclockwise direction, I know in my heart that I do not have consent or permission to continue with the present being for the current particular HumaNatureConnect Activity.

We live in a world where consideration has profound value. Before engaging with a natural being or with a setting to have a connection experience, as suggested repeatedly in this series of books and courses, ask for the consent of that being or setting before continuing to seek advice or guidance. Doing so, aloud or in your head, promotes welcoming warmth, relationship, and peace.

By asking for permission to have a connection experience wherein you seek guidance from a natural being or setting, and by gaining consent that comes in the form of continuing attraction, you as the "asker" no longer feel like a blundering intruder. Such attraction opens one up to the feeling of being welcomed and supported. Asking for permission to remain and feeling the consent through the continuing attraction makes the human in the person-to-natural being or person-to-natural setting relationship feel less domineering. This lack of domination helps the person become more sensitive.

Being sensitive is a requirement for the reception of guidance from nature. If one does not feel welcome and supported one won't be in a frame of mind that allows for the sensitivity to feel the advice carried on the subtle vibrations that resound in nature.

Consideration is done not just for the object but also for the subject; in other words, for the human and not just for the natural being. It is not just a matter of being polite to the natural object or its surroundings. That borders on being unrealistically anthropomorphic. The subject—the natural being—will not understand your words, and it may or may not be aware of your emotional state. The importance of seeking and maintaining consent is rather about the human being remaining emotionally available for his or her own wellbeing, being considerate for his or her own sake, being attuned to feelings more than to concepts, and, therefore, being open to non-worded advice. Waiting for consent and checking on the continuation of consent through the continuance of attraction leads to the consideration, to the compassion, to the altruism, to the thoughtfulness, and to the sensitivity needed to make the activities of the Heartwood Path work as they are intended.

Asking for consent is for the human more than for the natural being or it is for the human rather than for natural setting. I am not asking you to be like Dr. Doolittle, talking to the animals. I am suggesting that you often become attentive to your attractions and that you ask for consent so that you will be emotionally available to receive "vibes" from nature, and, in so doing, become inwardly prepared to receive advice from an intelligent, albeit non-human, source—a More-Than-Individual-Source that is not separate or distant from yourself.

With your continued consent, which can be shown by continuing to move from waypoint to waypoint, I will bring you through an introduction to the Heartwood Path. I will describe Michael Cohen's applied eco-psychology. More specifically, I will describe the basics of Cohen's "Natural Systems Thinking Process" and the basis for it—what Cohen calls "Natural Attraction Ecology."

Then, I will in the next waypoint:

1. demonstrate how Cohen's practices lead to optimal psychological, emotional, physical, and social functioning;
2. demonstrate how this improved readiness will allow one to find in nature models of valued personality traits; and
3. demonstrate through a provided nature-inspired valued personality trait checklist that can help the reader determine whether she is or is not (in the reader's own assessment) ethically prepared at this time to go into action in ways that provide both personal happiness and a protected environment.

To Get The Ball Rolling…

HumaNatureConnect Activity

Start-up Protocol

If this is not a day when you prefer to spend time in nature without an agenda, do the Heartwood Path Start-up Protocol found in the Appendix. Then return here to do the remaining portion of this activity:

Giving Your Consent To Traveling Down The Heartwood Path

Go to a place where you can be alone. Consider if you really want to experience the growth in your character that will occur as you move down the Heartwood Path. If the answer is yes, shout it out loud with vigor while waving your hands triumphantly. Feel that warmth as I again say to you: "Welcome to the Heartwood Path!"

Follow-up Protocol

For best results, write down your impressions of this activity in your journal using the Heartwood Path Follow-up Protocol found in the Appendix. Afterwards, consider sharing your interpretations with others.

Heartwood Path Axioms

Key Assertions From Waypoint 1.24

1.24.1.

Like plants and animals, we thrive best in welcoming environments.

1.24.2.

Every being thrives when there is consent given through the attraction to remain, to stay near, to have a connection experience.

1.24.3.

Become attentive to your attractions and ask for consent so that you will be emotionally available to receive "vibes" from nature, and, in so doing, become inwardly prepared to receive advice from an intelligent, albeit non-human, source—a More-Than-Individual-Source that is not separate or distant from yourself.

Nocturnal Pilgrimage 1.24

For best results, write down your impressions of each night's dreams in your journal using the Heartwood Path Dreaming Time Protocols found in the Appendix. Afterwards, consider sharing your Dream Tending with others.

Get a good night's sleep, dream, and record your dreams in your journal, as previously instructed.

Continue heading down the Heartwood Path by moving to the next waypoint: "Deepened Identity." At this learning station we will make preparations for uprooting any unhappiness you may be experiencing.

25

Deepened Identity

UPROOT YOUR UNHAPPINESS

Along the Heartwood Path, one can experience the kinds of changes in perspective that will enable one to reconnect with the "whole" or the "Greater Self" (a self that includes the whole environment, as opposed to just your more narrow individual self), to improve relationships, to foster happiness, and to help preserve the planet. These changes are essential to the future success of the environmental movement because to remake the world a significant number of people will need to upgrade (convert) their perspectives.

"Before you can have a change of heart, you (have to) step outside yourself to get a larger perspective. The Ego (by which I mean one's everyday conscious self or personality) tries to narrow every issue down to 'What will I get out of this?' When you reframe the question as . . . What will everyone get out of this?' your heart will immediately feel less confused and constricted" (Chopra, 2004, p. 221).

A better earth requires a better you. Said in a way that removes the onus on you alone—a way that also probably originates from my upbringing in the Bible Belt: For God's Nature to be respected human nature has to be perfected. Conversion from individual self alienation to Greater Self integrity has to precede successful global conservation.

How to do that has not been the apparent aim of biological psychiatry or clinical psychology. Practitioners in both of these fields, encouraged by insurance companies that tend to support only brief therapy, seem to have given up on curing ills, favoring instead dispensing cosmetic treatments and overseeing short-term crisis management. While such symptom relief is a valid way station on the road to a cure, it does not correct the problem at its source. You can get to Gladandgreen Junction—that state of Triple A happiness that comes, in part, from deepening environmental sustainability—by living an unhappy life year after year after year. It will just be much harder to get there. You can achieve your work goals and maintain good relationships while you are sad, depressed, anxious, or angry.

Getting to Gladandgreen Junction will be made easier if you achieve the kind of "presences" going down the Heartwood Path gives to you: the presence of positive emotions, the presence of good relationships, the presence of accomplishment, and the presence of meaning. Adults need these presences to prosper. Activists need a wellspring of well-being to fuel their continuing campaigns.

The focus of the mainstream mental health profession on symptom relief rather than on curing people is one reason why the Heartwood Path is needed. Anyone who is an activist or a parent knows that, pathology or not, life goes on. Beyond relieving pathology, something is needed that helps teach people the skills necessary to thrive. "Misery may love company, but company does not love misery, and the ensuing loneliness of pessimists may be a path to illness" (Seligman, 2011, p. 206). It is not enough to do the job, big as it is, of curing misery. Beyond keeping suffering to a minimum, something is need that develops both optimism (which seems to fight cancer and foster longevity (Seligman, 2011, p. 202-203) and well-being. The Heartwood Path is needed to uproot unhappiness at its source and to reinstate the root causes of well-being.

Since obtaining short-term symptom relief may be helpful, I am not attempting to deter people who are really suffering from seeking professional help. If it is a cure to unhappiness and an end to ecological degradation that you seek, I suggest that, if only as an adjunct to professional care, or without professional care, you make a pilgrimage down the Heartwood Path to Gladandgreen Junction. The next step in this direction is the following activity.

To Elevated Feelings...

HumaNatureConnect Activity

Start-up Protocol

If this is not a day when you prefer to spend time in nature without an agenda, do the Heartwood Path Start-up Protocol found in the Appendix. Then return here to do the remaining portion of this activity:

Responding Actively

For this activity, invite a friend who has had a positive event that he or she (I'll just use "she" from now on since usually the gender does not matter) can share with you to go together to an attractive natural area and, in a spirit of appreciation, both of you look around you to find something that is attractive. State that you want to come to the natural area because it was a suitable site (peaceful, few distractions, private, etc.) to recollect her fortunate event. The two of you need not appreciate the same attractive being. Once each of you find an aspect of nature that is attractive to both of you continuously for at least ten seconds, ask the person you invited to share her positive event with you orally or in writing. Encourage her to relive the event. The longer the recollection the better. Listen intently, without interrupting; but, when the time comes, be talkative, unreserved, and expansive in your verbal responses. Demonstrate your happiness in her good fortune. Repeat this activity with at least two other people. After you part company, write in your journal a description of the other person's positive event, your response to her recollection, and her response to your attentiveness and appreciation of her good fortune. Note whether, after listening and positively responding to other peoples' fortunate events, people begin to like you more; you feel more comfortable sharing intimate details; your positive, active responses improve; or you feel better about yourself.

Follow-up Protocol

For best results, write down your impressions of this activity in your journal using the Heartwood Path Follow-up Protocol found in the Appendix. Afterwards, consider sharing your interpretations with others.

Heartwood Path Axioms

Key Assertions From Waypoint 1.25

1.25.1.

A better earth requires a better you.

1.25.2.

For God's Nature to be respected human nature has to be perfected. Conversion from individual self alienation to Greater Self integrity has to precede successful global conservation.

1.25.3.

Anyone who is an activist or a parent knows that, pathology or not, life goes on.

Nocturnal Pilgrimage 1.25

For best results, write down your impressions of each night's dreams in your journal using the Heartwood Path Dreaming Time Protocols found in the Appendix. Afterwards, consider sharing your Dream Tending with others.

In the previous waypoint you were asked to obtain consent from your chosen attractive Natural Being. In much the same way, you are now asked to obtain consent from your Dream Characters. Tonight, more specifically, it is suggested that you seek the Dream Character that is most attractive to you and, after obtaining its consent by maintaining your attraction, seek its guidance regarding your goal of deepening your identity sufficiently for you to be happy in a transformed and sustainable world. Look for clues coming from the characters in your dreams about how you can transform yourself so that you can best transform the world.

Do not just seek such consent tonight. Make tonight's consent-seeking a practice that, with due diligence, can be applied to your Dream Tending. Modifying slightly the advice of the Start Up Protocol titled "Consent," always seek the permission of any Natural Being or Dream Character that you wish to use to obtain guidance.

We are not here trying to imitate Dr. Doolittle. Remember that this advice is not coming solely from the Natural Being or Dream Character, just as it is not coming solely from your own mind. It arises from the bridge of awareness you construct between your mind and the Natural Being or Dream Character. It and you are always present in the generation of the guidance, including the direction necessary to deepen your identify. It's all one—one bridge of awareness. It is, therefore, pointless along the Heartwood Path to regard separate entities (you or it) as the source of your guidance.

After a night's sleep, and after recording your dreams, which may be trying to tell you something from your previous reading and activities, continue your conversion from separateness to integrity by moving to the next waypoint: "Pursuit Of Perfection." This waypoint will give you some insights into the topic of seeking "perfection," which really means "wholeness." You will also find another approach that will help you process your Heartwood Path Activities.

26

Pursuit Of Perfection

TRULY GROW UP BY LEARNING TO PROCESS HEARTWOOD PATH ACTIVITIES

Before anyone gets all prickly about my references to God let me reference some of the well-stated distinctions United Nation's Messenger of Peace Wangari Maathai makes between the name "God" and the words "Source," "Nature," and the "Creator": The word "God" is "used to describe the monotheistic deity of the Abrahamic traditions" while the words "Source," "Nature," or the "Creator" is the entity of "all knowledge and awareness...the repository of all that we cannot explain" (Maathai, 2010, p. 21). To this list I will add and most often here use the words "The Absolute," by which I mean both "God" in the Abrahamic traditions and "the Source" in the spiritualists' tradition, leaving for others any debate about the differences. This is not pushing aside God. It is just including all religious perspectives. As we all know, exposure to God may prevent burning. Religious or not, the forbidden fruits often produce jams.

Before anyone gets all bent out of shape about "being perfected," let me define what I mean. It is more accurate to say "perfect-in-one" or, better yet, "awakened to your preexisting perfection."

Here, I am not speaking of a preordained measure of faultlessness, rightness, or flawlessness. "Perfect-in-one," what Jesus asked God to help us all obtain in his heart-wrenching prayer in Garden of Gethsemane, can be interpreted to mean "oneness."

For our purposes here, it is the seeking rather than the attainment of oneness (or perfection) that is the crucial factor. As we shall see, this sense of oneness arises most fully when one reaches high levels of spiritual maturity; and so, I will most often mean "seeking spiritual maturity" when I say seek to be "perfect" or work to become "perfect-in-one." What I am really talking about is simply a matter of "growing up," which many of us never really do, spiritually speaking. Work on your conversion to spiritual maturity without expecting to ever be finally converted, perfected, matured, or completed.

The Heartwood Path is not to be viewed as an only way to perfection or to salvation. It can, however, be viewed accurately as a way to truly grow up. It offers a route but along its course the individual is free to accept or reject any theory or practice. While I can attest to the accuracy and validity of what is found along the Path, the allowance for questioning, self-guidance, and self-determination plus the scope and significance of what is presented means that the results are both differing and substantial.

Healthy human psycho-spiritual development is marked by an ever-increasing sense of oneness. This state of resplendent wholeness is revealed naturally in stages that can happen suddenly or may span a lifetime.

The trouble with relying solely on any lifelong approach to oneness —which is so critical to the development of eco-centric life coaches— is two-fold: 1) it is so slow world problems will become too severe before enough people mature enough to adopt solutions, and 2) without guidance along a path of development, unassisted development has too great a chance to become unhealthy or repressed. These are reasons why it is so important to combine Bill Plotkin's Wheel of Life Model with Dr. Cohen's Project NatureConnect methodologies along the Heartwood Path. Having said this, it remains necessary to look at each

of the components of the recommended solution to human unhappiness and environmental destruction individually and then determine
how they can best be combined for the greatest possible benefit. It is
possible, if one follows a course such as the Heartwood Path to speed
up one's develop in such a way that it takes less than a lifetime to
become a saint, less than a lifetime to become an eco-centric life coach,
less than a lifetime to be happy, and less than a lifetime to reap the
benefits of feeling one with nature.

One of the best ways I discovered to seek oneness without having to
go through a lifetime of psycho-spiritual development, is Dr. Cohen's
applied eco-psychology. This approach is based on what he calls "Natural Attraction Ecology" and serves to reconnect its participants with
nature. A full explanation of Dr. Cohen's methodology is provided later
but, since experiencing the real world outside brings about more of a
sense of wholeness than does merely reading about the outdoors from
a chair indoors, I will present here an activity aimed at giving you a
taste for the sorts of activities to come and a brief glimpse (without any
explanations) of the ways we will process these activity. As before, in
most of the activities that follow, you will be asked to go outside, find
and attractive natural being, and begin an activity only after the natural
being retains its attractiveness after ten seconds or so. There is a very
good reason to perform your activities in this way—a reason that will
become clear to you as you progress through the experience of doing
the activities in the presence of an attractive aspect of nature. Your acts
in nature are facts that are self-evident to you. Doing them outdoors
will help you function optimally so that your processing of the events
in the activities can be most helpful to you. For now, simply focus on
your experience. All necessary elaborations will occur shortly.

To Ponder The Pursuit Of Perfection And Begin To Use A Way To
Process Your Heartwood Path Experiences...

HumaNatureConnect Activity

Start-up Protocol

If this is not a day when you prefer to spend time in nature without an agenda, do the Heartwood Path Start-up Protocol found in the Appendix. Then return here to do the remaining portion of this activity:

Using Your Senses Outside To Draw Closer To Perfection

For this activity, think about your views on perfection. The following questions are all weighty, and they are open to various interpretations. Ask yourself whether you believe anything that is indisputable is more perfect than anything that is disputable. Then, use any of your senses to perceive a natural being in nature. Is it perfect? Is your sense of it disputable? Are your sensual experiences perfect? Does sensing beings in nature make you feel more whole or less whole? Is it possible that your experiencing of nature is indisputable and that your experiences, therefore, foster a sense of wholeness that brings you closer to perfection?

Follow-up Protocol

For best results, write down your impressions of this activity in your journal using the Heartwood Path Follow-up Protocol found in the Appendix. Afterwards, consider sharing your interpretations with others.

Heartwood Path Axioms

Key Assertions From Waypoint 1.26

1.26.1.

For our purposes here, it is the seeking rather than the attainment of oneness (or perfection) that is the crucial factor.

1.26.2.

Work on your conversion to spiritual maturity without expecting to ever be finally converted, perfected, matured, or completed.

1.26.3.

Your acts in nature are facts that are self-evident to you.

Nocturnal Pilgrimage 1.26

For best results, write down your impressions of each night's dreams in your journal using the Heartwood Path Dreaming Time Protocols found in the Appendix. Afterwards, consider sharing your Dream Tending with others.

Sleep and dream before taking your next step down the Heartwood Path. Be sure to look over the Protocols. You do not have to do them all, but each one is proven to be helpful.

After sleeping and recording your dreams, move to the next waypoint, "Basis And Basics." In the next waypoint we begin to get into some of the nitty-gritty of what you will be doing along the Heartwood Path. By continuing to move forward you will be on your way to being happy in a more sustainable environment.

27

Basis And Basics

USE THE HEARTWOOD PATH TO QUICKEN AND HEIGHTEN YOUR OWN MATURITY

Dr. Michael J. Cohen reminds us that virtually all of us live most of our lives indoors, separate from nature. We, therefore, do not experience how the world works so beautifully, how it sustains itself without pollution, and how it works in balance by using fifty-four natural senses that we humans inherit but, due to our nature-separated lifestyle, do not typically use (except for the well-known five senses of hearing, sight, smell and so forth). The Natural Senses include the:

The Radiation Senses

- Sense of light and sight, including polarized light.
- Sense of seeing without eyes such as heliotropism or the sun sense of plants.
- Sense of color.
- Sense of moods and identities attached to colors.
- Sense of awareness of one's own visibility or invisibility and consequent camouflaging.

- Sensitivity to radiation other than visible light including radio waves, X rays, etc.
- Sense of temperature and temperature change.
- Sense of season including ability to insulate, hibernate, and winter sleep.
- Electromagnetic sense and polarity which includes the ability to generate current (as in the nervous system and brain waves) or other energies.

The Feeling Senses

- Hearing including resonance, vibrations, sonar, and ultrasonic frequencies.
- Awareness of pressure, particularly underground, underwater, and to wind and air.
- Sensitivity to gravity.
- The sense of excretion for waste elimination and protection from enemies.
- Feel, particularly touch on the skin.
- Sense of weight, gravity, and balance.
- Space or proximity sense.
- Coriolis sense or awareness of effects of the rotation of the Earth.
- Sense of motion, body movement sensations, and sense of mobility.

The Chemical Senses

- Smell with and beyond the nose.
- Taste with and beyond the tongue.
- Appetite or hunger for food, water, and air.
- Hunting, killing, or food obtaining urges.

- Humidity sense including thirst, evaporation control and the acumen to find water or evade a flood.
- Hormonal sense, as to pheromones and other chemical stimuli.

The Mental Senses

- Pain, external and internal.
- Mental or spiritual distress.
- Sense of fear, dread of injury, death or attack.
- Procreative urges including sex awareness, courting, love, mating, paternity and raising young.
- Sense of play, sport, humor, pleasure, and laughter.
- Sense of physical place, navigation senses including detailed awareness of land and seascapes, of the positions of the sun, moon, and stars.
- Sense of time.
- Sense of electromagnetic fields.
- Sense of weather changes.
- Sense of emotional place, of community, belonging, support, trust, and thankfulness.
- Sense of self including friendship, companionship, and power.
- Domineering and territorial sense.
- Colonizing sense including compassion and receptive awareness of one's fellow creatures, sometimes to the degree of being absorbed into a superorganism.
- Horticultural sense and the ability to cultivate crops, as is done by ants that grow fungus, by fungus who farm algae, or birds that leave food to attract their prey.
- Language and articulation sense, used to express feelings and convey information in every medium from the bees' dance to human literature.
- Sense of humility, appreciation, and ethics.

- Senses of form and design.
- Sense of reason, including memory and the capacity for logic and science.
- Sense of mind and consciousness.
- Intuition or subconscious deduction.
- Aesthetic sense, including creativity and appreciation of beauty, music, literature, form, design, and drama.
- Psychic capacity such as foreknowledge, clairvoyance, clairaudience, psychokinesis, astral projection, possibly certain animal instincts, and plant sensitivities.
- Sense of biological and astral time, awareness of past, present, and future events.
- The capacity to hypnotize other creatures.
- Relaxation and sleep including dreaming, meditation, and brain wave awareness.
- Sense of pupation including cocoon building and metamorphosis.
- Sense of excessive stress and capitulation.
- Sense of survival by joining a more established organism.
- Spiritual sense, including conscience, capacity for sublime love, ecstasy, a sense of sin, profound sorrow, and sacrifice.
- Sense of homeostatic unity, of *natural attraction* aliveness as the singular essence-diversity attraction dance of all our other senses (NNIAAL). (Cohen, website: http://www.ecopsych.com/insight53senses.html).

The Basis For NatureConnect Activities: Natural Attraction Ecology

The foundation of Dr. Cohen's methodology is called "Natural Attraction Ecology." It can be summarized as follows: Planet Earth is, or functions like, a living organism that has its own perfection.

Our living planet's global life community enjoys non-literate communication between all of its plant, animal, and mineral members, including the sensory parts of humanity. All natural things are held together in communion by "webstrings" of attraction.

Webstrings are what tie together all the aspects of nature in the "web of life." They are natural attractions.

According to Cohen, attraction is intelligent enough to be conscious of it being attracted and attractive. Humanity registers the world through the fifty-four natural senses previously mentioned.

Nature generates joy, purity, and balance because its essence is like an enduring stream of self-correcting natural attraction relationships that flow around, through, and in us. Natural attractions have the power to recycle and restore relationships, to create optimums of life, cooperation, diversity, and beauty throughout the web of life, including humanity.

Nature does not produce garbage or our runaway abusiveness, stress, pollution, isolation, and disorders. These afflictions are not attractive. They do not support life. The purpose of life is to support life.

By using Dr. Cohen's methods, participants feel one with nature and achieve a sense of integrity that is integrated with the natural functions of the Earth. It is evident to just about anyone spending some quiet time in a natural area that nature has a powerful renewing and restorative effect on our psyche, thoughts, and feelings.

We humans know contact with nature works wonders. We inherit from nature the ability to bond with nature.

We humans are part of nature and it is attracted to help us live in balance with it as part of its attraction to support/nurture/purify its own life and to grow. Time spent in a shopping mall rarely produces this effect.

Life would be better if we were thinking in a harmless nature-connected mode most of the time. Instead, we not only disconnect from nature, but we bury it under the nature exploitive stories of our society.

Irritated, our nature-deprived psyche demands more satisfactions continually and thus fuels our economy while producing pollutants. Learning to think in ways that help us make greater conscious sensory contact with nature, backyard to backcountry, has proven to help nature help us organically reverse the destructive and delusional story that we ordinarily march to. Cohen provides the means to accomplish an earth-preserving way of thinking by focusing on the forty-nine "natural attraction senses" in addition to the five traditional senses.

Our natural sense to breathe, by the way, is an example of human/ nature oneness.

"As breathing involves a continual oscillation between exhaling and inhaling, offering ourselves to the world at one moment and drawing the world into ourselves at the next . . .so sensory perception entails a like reciprocity" (Abram, 2010, p. 61).

We breathe, touch, and perceive the Earth and the Earth breathes, touches, and perceives us. This is a purifying setup that we naturally love, find attractive, and can easily recognize to be intelligent.

This and other earth-human relationships require no labels to function. Having participants emulate this last aspect of Natural Attraction Ecology—the lack of names or the lack of words in nature— is very important to the success of Dr. Cohen's methods. There are no words or names in nature and we open ourselves to the misconceptions of nature-dominating stories when we put them there. As Dr. Cohen says:

". . . there is no substitute for the real thing, if a person is not in conscious connection with webstring attractions, they are probably playing god in some way without the wisdom to do so" (Cohen, Ecopsych Website).

Worded stories are either outright fantasies or are mere representations of facts. For these reasons, the emphasis in Dr. Cohen's methodology is not on words or labels. Words are used in a limited way after the activities. It is then that participants report to others and attempt to achieve validation (as others validate that they too have had similar experiences or results). Otherwise the emphasis is on the direct experiences of actions. "Acts are facts," says Dr. Cohen. Another example from natural attraction ecology is one's sense of thirst. After doing Dr. Cohen's related activity, one accepts that one's thirst is as much a part of water as is wetness.

According to Natural Attraction Ecology, one's thirst leads to an attraction to water and there is an inseparable relationship between the water and one's attraction to it. One's experience of Greer Spring in Missouri, for example, is, according to Natural Attraction Ecology, as much a part of the local ecology as is the water's coolness. This realization and many more are discovered in Dr. Cohen's NatureConnect courses though direct experience which is routinely validated through words with others.

Once we add living in the "N"ow" and "A"liveness to the "N"ameless, "I"ntelligent, "A"ttractive, "L"ove previously mentioned regarding the components of earth-human relationships, we are listing all of the ingredients of a particular form of psychological consciousness we humans naturally sense and enjoy; namely, a consciousness Cohen calls "NNIAAL" (Cohen, Ecopsych/Ecopsychology Journal Website). Reconnecting with "NNIAAL" is a vital component of Natural Attraction Ecology. It is also an encoded way to identify the Enduring Stream, mentioned previously. As you will discover in the next section, using the Natural Systems Thinking Process to reconnect with NNIAAL (or the Enduring Stream) is psychologically replenishing. I say "reconnect" because earlier in our history, more than one hundred years ago, we were still healthfully attached to the breast of nature and were, therefore, physically and psychologically nurtured. We as a species weaned ourselves from our mother's bosom prematurely. This collective form of self-neglect damaged the shared fitness of our thinking. "The wellness of our thinking determines our health, relationships and destiny" (Cohen, 1987, p viii). Reconnecting with the psychological embrace that occurs at Mother Nature's breast—a metaphorical way to say "communing with NNIAAL" or "bonding with the Enduring Stream," is also a way to persevere. The Natural Systems Thinking Process "helps you restore and enjoy the rewarding benefits of the way nature works to produce its balanced perfection" (Cohen, 1987, p 9).

Although the following section may seem redundant, read it anyway. The next section contains both repeated and new information that all eartHearts need to understand. Repetition is the sire of excellence.

The Basics Of The Natural Systems Thinking Process

Each of Dr. Cohen's activities put the participants through the same basic sequence:

First. Find an attraction in nature (backyard or backcountry). If you are attracted to a being because of its beauty, do not just use your eyes but also perceive its beauty in terms of its resonance, its ability to move you, to make you see and do things differently, to make you bow, cry, or give thanks, to make you want more and to become softer to get it, and to make you respond to its call for engagement.

Second. Make a sensory contact with this attraction, using any of one's fifty-four natural attraction senses (which include the radiation senses such as the sense of temperature, the feeling senses such as sensitivity to gravity, the chemical senses such as the sense of appetite, and the mental senses such as the sense of humility and appreciation).

Third. Obtain consent from the attraction to use it for your educational, counseling, or healing purposes (your continued attraction to the object (being) is your consent to continue and your un-attraction—perhaps as the noticing of ugliness or a feeling of lack of safety—marks a lack of consent and is a call to move elsewhere).

Fourth. Be thankful when you note how your natural attraction feels good.

Fifth. Trust your thoughts and your feelings arising from the contact.

Sixth. Psychologically assume the perspective of the attraction and wait for it to provide information, guidance, or healing. Doing so is a psychological technique that allows one the freedom to momentarily step out of one's limited identity and to forge new ways of perceiving the world. From the new vantage point of an attractive natural being, one has a better chance of seeing with fresh eyes and one can state what needs to be said but could not be said until one is beside one's Self. What may seem like a little psychological trick will be given much more merit as one assumes the perspective of the attraction and witnesses what unfolds. When one sheds one's own persona, so full of of one's own self-imposed mystique and so limited by forced, imbedded, hard-to-shed desires for consistency, one can be released from the shackles of selfhood and glean from one's temporary new perspective what one's awareness of Oak Tree tells, or what one's awareness of Rattlesnake says, or what one's awareness of Prairie Dog prescribes. This technique may seem to some to be a mind game; but, as long as the perspective is that of one's awareness of a real and attractive natural being (as encountered during the Natural Systems Thinking Process), as long as the gleanings (the resultant healing, information or guidance) are not totally self-generated within the mind of the practitioner, and as long as the gleanings come from the bridge of awareness between the human practitioner and the chosen, attractive natural being, the assumption of the perspective of an attractive natural being is a worthy part of the practice of eco-psychology along the Heartwood Path.

Seventh. Look for ways that your contacted being improves relationships.

Eighth. Validate your experiences by writing down your experiences; and, after reading your journal notes aloud to yourself, share your written words with others. "Doing the activities and sharing their results" writes Dr. Cohen (1987), "provides irreplaceable empirical knowledge, evidence, and energy for change" (p.vi).

It is worth repeating: asking a natural being or place to give its consent may seem dubious to those who do not realize that the consent does not come through words spoken by animal spirits, trees, or places in the style of Dr. Dolittle (who, in a beloved fairy tale, could talk with the animals). Instead, the consent comes from a person's continued reactions to his or her attraction to the natural being or place. This attainment of consent is a critically important step in Cohen's methodologies, as it creates within the participant a psychological state-of-mind that is non-domineering and suitable for the functioning of the fifty-four natural attraction senses and the resulting attainment of guidance, information, or healing.

According to Cohen, those who are attracted to a more nature-centered life and who recognize the negative impacts of our way of life, can unbury nature's way of living that has been covered over by living according the modern industrial society's stories and labels that betray an undeclared war on nature. This half-asleep way of living precludes us from using the natural attraction senses that enable us to participate in the beautiful way nature works. It is, therefore, one of the chief causes of "burnout."

Living according to nature-disconnected stories, which range from the children's tale of Little Red Riding Hood to the meta-story of the "American Dream," is one of the main underlying causes for most personal and planetary dilemmas. Nature-disconnected stories, prevalent through modern industrial cultures, tend to make people want, and to attempt to satisfy yearnings for connection with nature or a Higher Power with substitutes such as material objects, work, drugs, alcohol, or promiscuous sex.

All of these substitutes inevitably fail to compensate for a lack of connection with the Whole and leave people with palpable holes in their souls. When heard or read repeatedly in one's culture, a person begins to believe in nature-disconnected stories even when they lead to unsustainable actions and dire consequences.

Cohen's methods redress these root causes of most maladies and help to give people and the planet a healthful future by enabling participants to find oneness with the real thing, not with the words that represent the real thing. Using words only to receive guidance from nature is, using Cohen's humorous terminology, "like experiencing the gobble without the turkey" (Cohen, Thesis Quote Website).

Living "half-vast," which is Dr. Cohen's way of saying living according to nature-disconnected stories, is both ecologically disastrous and personally a burden that fosters burnout and other personal and planetary dilemmas. The remedy, according Dr. Cohen, is what he calls the "Natural Systems Thinking Process" (Cohen, Ecopsych/Lifeweb Website). This tool can be used to heal any person from an array of lifestyle stresses that lead to burnout, depression, anxiety, and addictions. It can be used to reverse challenging global and personal problems caused by nature separation that, in turn, causes abnormal wants that propel us into irresponsible relationships.

The Natural Systems Thinking Process promotes education, counseling, and healing with nature. This process is based on the principles of Natural Attraction Ecology, which identifies the strands in the web of life and indicates that they function according attractions.

According to Natural Attraction Ecology, all relationships are held together in the web of life because they are attracted to do so. These attractions do not appear in our consciousness with any regularity because regrettably we live much of our lives indoors. As a result, there is within us an organic void that feels like an uncomfortable psychological emptiness in our thoughts and lives.

Psychotherapist and author Chellis Glendinning (2007) maintains "that the traumatized state is not merely the domain of the Vietnam veteran or the survivor of childhood abuse, it is the underlying condition of the domesticated people" because "of the built-in displacement of our lives from the Earth" (p. xiii.).

Attempting to fill this void, we want, emotionally and materially; and, as we want, there is never enough. Greed, stress, and recklessness become pervasive, at great peril to oneself, to other people, and to the Earth. "The destruction of the environment is driven by an insatiable craving for more" (Maathai, 2010, P.43).

The nature-reconnecting activities of the Natural Systems Thinking Process brings natural sensory attraction relationships, called "webstrings," back into our lives. Their presence fights both the craving for more and the activists' burnout by reinstating forgotten but nevertheless reinvigorating personal and environmental relationships.

Maathai writes that the idea of " . . . enough is enough is a matter of monumental discipline. This will not occur unless it's linked to the raising of consciousness that is essential to healing the earth" (p. 40). The task of healing the wounds of the earth "is to find a balance between the perspectives...between knowledge based on measurement and data and knowledge that draws on older forms of wisdom and experience" (Maathai, 2010, p. 76).

After doing nearly one hundred of Dr. Cohen's activities and after discussing the results of these activities with dozens of fellow participants, I can attest to the fact that Cohen's methodologies help people overcome their nature-disconnected patterns of thinking and doing—a valuable metamorphosis (conversion) that relieves stress, reduces wanting, and increases participants' general satisfaction with life. While these benefits lead to the optimal functioning that is so critical to the development of people capable of helping others find happiness and environmental sustainability, by themselves Dr. Cohen's nature-connect activities are not designed to develop and then organize environmental activities. They do not, more specifically, lead all the way to the development of a cadre of eco-centric life coaches. For the specific purpose of helping activists better themselves and to persevere in their environmental participation, a "bettermorphosis" would occur if one would apply Dr. Cohen's excellent methodologies along a pointed course of study such as the Heartwood Path developed by myself as a way to answer Brower's 1986 call to write.

As a way to help you determine how, if at all, the Heartwood Path (when combined with Dr. Cohen's methodologies) does provide for a "bettermorphosis"—one that does cause greater gladness and environmental sustainability—I ask you to begin the habitual pattern described in the following activity.

To Keep A Record Of Your "Bettermorphosis"...

HumaNatureConnect Activity

Start-up Protocol

If this is not a day when you prefer to spend time in nature without an agenda, do the Heartwood Path Start-up Protocol found in the Appendix. Then return here to do the remaining portion of this activity:

Writing Down Three Good Things

For this activity, write down three good things that happened to you today. Write down why each of these events occurred and what each of these events mean to you.

Follow-up Protocol

For best results, write down your impressions of this activity in your journal using the Heartwood Path Follow-up Protocol found in the Appendix. Afterwards, consider sharing your interpretations with others.

Heartwood Path Axioms

Key Assertions From Waypoint 1.27

1.27.1.

Spending most of our lives indoors, separate from nature, keeps us from experiencing how the world works so beautifully, how it sustains itself without pollution, and how it works in balance by using fifty-four natural senses that we humans

inherit but, due to our nature-separated lifestyle, do not typically use.

1.27.2.

Living according to nature-disconnected stories, which range from the children's tale of Little Red Riding Hood to the meta-story of the "American Dream," is one of the main underlying causes for most personal and planetary dilemmas.

1.27.3.

Nature-disconnected stories, prevalent through modern industrial cultures, tend to make people want, and to attempt to satisfy yearnings for connection with nature or a Higher Power with substitutes such as material objects, work, drugs, alcohol, or promiscuous sex.

1.27.4.

Attempting to fill the void created by being separated from nature causes us to want, both emotionally and materially; and, as we want, there is never enough so greed, stress, and reckless-ness become pervasive, at great peril to oneself, other people, and the Earth.

Nocturnal Pilgrimage 1.27

For best results, write down your impressions of each night's dreams in your journal using the Heartwood Path Dreaming Time Protocols found in the Appendix. Afterwards, consider sharing your Dream Tending with others.

Much of what is said in this waypoint about communing with Natural Beings also, it seems to me, applies to your communing or, as we have been saying, "tending" to your dreams. Here are examples of how Dream Tending is similar to the Basics of the Natural System Thinking Process. The "Find an attraction in nature (backyard or backcountry)" of my wording of the Natural System Thinking Process could read "Find an attraction in your dream" in our Dream Tending approach. The "Obtain consent from the attraction" borrowed from my summary of the Natural System Thinking Process could read "Obtain consent from your Chosen Attractive Dream Character" in our version of Dream Tending. The "Be thankful when you note how your natural attraction feels good" statement pertaining to the Natural System Thinking Process would be "Be thankful when you note how your attraction to your Dream Character feels good" in our Dream Tending approach. The statements to "Trust your thoughts and your feelings arising from the contact" and "Trust your thoughts and your feelings arising from the contact" could apply to either the Natural System Thinking Process or our borrowed approach to Dream Tending. The statement to "Psychologically assume the perspective of the attraction and wait for it to provide information, guidance, or healing" would only need to be modified to read "Psychologically assume the perspective of the Dream Character and wait for it to provide information, guidance, or healing" to make it suitable for inclusion as one of our Dream Tending suggestions. The suggestion to "Look for ways that your contacted being improves relationships" in the Natural Systems Thinking Process would only need to be changed to "Look for ways that your selected Dream Character improves relationships" for it to be included as one of our Dream Tending suggestions. And, lastly, both the Natural Systems Thinking Process and our version of Dream Tending could share the following suggestion: "Validate your experiences by writing down your experiences; and, after reading your journal notes aloud to yourself, share your written words with others."

With the similarities between the Natural Systems Thinking Process and our take on Dream Tending in mind, after you sleep, record your dreams, and when you are ready to resume, head the next way-point: "NSTP."

28

NSTP

SHIFT OR GET OFF THE PATH

By using the Natural Systems Thinking Process along the specific route of the Heartwood Path one comes to the realization that for a "better earth" to be possible a "better you" is necessary. To make the person/planetary connection beneficial for all concerned (human and non-human alike) this "better you," cannot just be a person who is educated in ecology, she cannot just be a person who is passively concerned about environmental destruction, she cannot even just be a person who knows how to make ecologically sound purchases or knows the candidates endorsed by the League of Conservation Voters.

Although all of these attributes are important, they are merely some of the precursors to what is really needed because, being solely inner world shifts, they do not serve as a fulcrum for real, outer world movement towards bringing the civilization into balance with the environment. They will not help us realize that what Einstein knew: "all our lauded technological progress—our very Civilization—is like the axe in the hand of the pathological criminal" (Jensen, 2006) p. 663).

The above-mentioned inner world shifts will not, therefore, by themselves stem the tide of environmental destruction. In addition to all of these scattered inner world betterments, a concerned individual has to also have both an expanded psychological perspective (one that includes saint-like compassion—which means "feeling together with" (Zonar, 2000, p. 214)—for all sentient beings—and a workable, less random approach to activism that is personally doable, effective, inspires sustained involvement, and gets to the core of the problem: making the world's economy subordinate to the environment and helping people both psychologically and behaviorally regain their rightful, ecologically sound place in the scheme of things. Here's how to do it:

The Heartwood Path is a step-by-step program that involves learning universal principles, anchoring one's unique gifts to the world, integrating oneself into the whole, developing valued traits, going into action as an individual, persevering by connecting with the enchantment of daily life at home, reconciling self and other through sexual intimacy, going into action with a group, and learning to be a nature-centered life coach. Before going on further it may be useful for you to consider if the premise of the Heartwood Path—improving the environment by positively changing the happiness and giving character of the participant—is plausible to you. If so, stay with this book/course. If not, other courses of action may be more beneficial to you. I trust that your responses in the following activity will keep you heading down the Heartwood Path.

To Determine If You Need To Make A Change...

HumaNatureConnect Activity

Start-up Protocol

If this is not a day when you prefer to spend time in nature without an agenda, do the Heartwood Path Start-up Protocol found in the Appendix. Then return here to do the remaining portion of this activity:

Working On Your Character And/Or Circumstances

For this activity, ponder whether it is best for you to work only on changing the circumstances of your life that are external to your own character or if it would not be more prudent to also work on changing your perspective and character. If you say it is your situation and not your character, then you will likely be driven by your past rather than drawn by your future. This is because you will likely believe that most of your situation is the result of past occurrences that are separate from yourself. If you can blame your situation on circumstances from the past there will be no reason to become a responsible individual. If however, you state that your situation is the result of your own responsibility and free will, then your own character and choices will need to be addressed. So, which is it for you? Does your perspective and character need alteration? Is your life predicament the result merely of your situation and, therefore, there is no reason for personal growth? Could it be that there is reason to work on both your environmental situation and your personal growth? Write down your thoughts in your journal, using the following format and approach.

Follow-up Protocol

For best results, write down your impressions of this activity in your journal using the Heartwood Path Follow-up Protocol found in the Appendix. Afterwards, consider sharing your interpretations with others.

Heartwood Path Axioms

Key Assertions From Waypoint 1.28

1.28.1.

Consider helping to make the world's economy subordinate to the environment and helping people to both psychologically and behaviorally regain their ecologically-sound place in the

scheme of things by learning universal principles, anchoring one's unique gifts to the world, integrating oneself into the whole, developing valued traits, going into action as an individual, persevering by connecting with the enchantment of daily living at home, reconciling self and other through sexual intimacy, going into action with a group, and learning to be a nature-centered life coach.

1.28.2.

The premise of the Heartwood Path is that one can improve the environment by positively changing the happiness and giving character of the participant.

1.28.3.

If you can blame your situation on circumstances from the past there will be no reason to become a responsible individual.

Nocturnal Pilgrimage 1.28

For best results, write down your impressions of each night's dreams in your journal using the Heartwood Path Dreaming Time Protocols found in the Appendix. Afterwards, consider sharing your Dream Tending with others.

Remember to dream first, before continuing to the next waypoint. Here's an example to help you with dream amplification. If you dream of an Ocean for example, you may want to amplify it into the Source of All Life. Note how the image in the Dream—the Ocean can be psychologically amplified from its singularity (one ocean) to a universal archetype—Source of All Life. It could be amplified in numerous ways. Simply convert the image in the Dream to something that is global in scale, symbolic, pervasive, positive, and helpful. Do not worry about contradictions. Just make all of your amplifications into a network of archetypal connections, the best of which being universal patterns of thought represented by a superhero. As you do your amplifications, relate your emerging network of archetypes to your life by answering two questions:

1. What, continuing with our example, does the Source of All Life have for you today in terms of conversation, healing, and offered guidance?
2. What do you have for your archetype?

After recording your amplifications of dream impressions, continue on the Path by moving to the next waypoint: "Four Questions." As you do, remember that it is a prerequisite that you ask the right questions if you want to arrive at the right answers.

29

Four Questions

ANSWER THESE QUESTIONS AND TAKE AN IMPORTANT STEP TOWARD A STATE OF INTEGRITY

Having lived through the period of life from high school to parenthood and having also guided my daughters through much of this period, I am prepared to say that the main life question for adolescents and young adults is:

"What role will I play in life?"

Until later in life, when other questions loom larger in most people's consciousness, every other puzzle for the five to twenty years after high school seems to be subordinate to this main quandary. This question is typically answered as one, after careful planning or muddling through, finds a career or a long string of jobs. One's compensated work is the typical answer to the above question, one that leaves people and the world wanting. What I will attempt to do in this series of books is show readers a more comprehensive answer to that question, one that goes something like this: "I will learn how to become an ecologically minded person, mature spiritually in a way that gives me an uncommon depth of happiness and character, and then share my wisdom with others as a true and respected eartHeart or eco-centric life coach."

This answer helps people better answer the other two other questions that arise in most people in the so-called "middle years" of life. That is the time, often between the ages of thirty and sixty, when many people grapple with how to provide for themselves and their families while also caring for blossoming adolescents, diminishing parents, or both. Frequently feeling the tension of constant pressure to attend and to act, those in the middle years of life are neither too old nor too decrepit to be justified in dodging such responsibilities, and so, they come to question their role in life and even their life purpose with the hope that, at least, there is still time of fulfill their role. More often than not, at some point in most people's lives, this role proves to be less than perfectly satisfying, and so, people often ask:

"What can be done to improve my life?"

The answer to this question usually involves improving one's standard of living. But, while improving one's financial wealth and the amount of material objects one owns can be helpful, doing so is not totally fulfilling because one's quality of life and one's relationship with a greater reality are not adequately brought into the equation. This inadequacy frequently leads to a third key life question:

"What can I do to make the world better for everyone?"

Answering this question corrects the shortcomings that arise by only answering the first two questions. The third question arises usually after at least cursory solutions are put into effect regarding the previous two questions.

These three important questions typically arise separately and answers to these questions involve either greater effort to find a job or establish a career, earn a bigger salary, improve the mind through education and meditation, or serve others. Whether one chooses salary improvements, education, meditation, or service, the answers to all of these questions are, more often than not, less than satisfactory. One is typically left playing roles that do not meet one's goals. One is left personally wanting or overextended. Despite attempts to solve social or environmental issues, the world continues to face mounting problems.

Although there are plenty of roles to play, much money to be made, many schools to attend, numerous effective meditation techniques, and plenty of ways to serve others, satisfactory answers to the three big life questions are elusive because typically one does not bring them together in recognition of the interdependence of Self and other. Let me now propose just this sort of blended question that happens to be the central question of this series of books:

"How does one ethically and effectively both save the Earth and improve each person so that there can be happiness in one's newfound effectiveness?"

The answer to this question has to do with the fact that when any one of us reaches a full measure of spiritual maturity, a condition that we will define carefully subsequently, the whole world is a step closer to being saved, particularly from global problems caused by shallow and reckless people. I will in this writing attempt to demonstrate how, by using Dr. Cohen's methodologies along the Heartwood Path, one can, metaphorically speaking, earn the wings of an angel, ascend in one's spiritual maturity to an exalted level, and, thereby, significantly help the world's environment become more beautiful and more sustainable.

To Set A Beginning Point For Later Comparison Purposes...

HumaNatureConnect Activity

Start-up Protocol

If this is not a day when you prefer to spend time in nature without an agenda, do the Heartwood Path Start-up Protocol found in the Appendix. Then return here to do the remaining portion of this activity:

Marking Your Progress

For this activity, answer these four questions:

"What role will I play in life?"

"What can be done to improve my life?"

"What can I do to make the world better for everyone?"

"How does one ethically and effectively both save the Earth and improve each person so that there can be happiness in one's newfound effectiveness?"

Write down your answers in your journal. At the end of this series of books/courses, come back to these questions and answer them again. When you compare your answers now to the answers you give later you will be able to see the impact of these waypoints.

Follow-up Protocol

For best results, write down your impressions of this activity in your journal using the Heartwood Path Follow-up Protocol found in the Appendix. Afterwards, consider sharing your interpretations with others.

Heartwood Path Axioms

Key Assertions From Waypoint 1.29

1.29.1.

The main life question for adolescents and young adults is:

"What role will I play in life?"

1.29.2.

Those in the middle years of life often ask:

"What can be done to improve my life?" and "What can I do to make the world better for everyone?"

1.29.3.

A better question that happens to be the central question of this course of study is:

"How does one ethically and effectively both save the Earth and improve each person so that there can be happiness in one's newfound effectiveness?"

Nocturnal Pilgrimage 1.29

For best results, write down your impressions of each night's dreams in your journal using the Heartwood Path Dreaming Time Protocols found in the Appendix. Afterwards, consider sharing your Dream Tending with others.

Should answers to any of the key questions revealed in this waypoint show up in some way in your dreams, use the suggestions included in component of the After Dreaming Protocol titled "Book Of Dreams," namely: 1) talking in the present tense, 2) using verbs ending in "ing," 3) removing articles such as "an" or "the," and 4) using capital letters when naming the Dream Characters—which can be any notable people, places, or things that show up in your dream. Doing so will enliven your notes and allow them to influence you more positively.

As is our tradition, sleep, record your dreams, and then continue to the next waypoint. When you engage yourself in the "Predicaments" waypoint you will learn, among other things, how to assess your own ability to build expectations, to plan, and to make conscious choices.

30

Predicaments

LEARN ABOUT INVISIBILITIES AND VISIBILITIES, NEGATIVITIES AND POSITIVITIES

Over two decades of personal research and a lifetime of experience has demonstrated to me that working with roles, the paycheck, the mind, and the hand under the guidance of the heart would be an effective way to solve personal and global predicaments. Using the heart endows every activity with spiritual and symbolic meanings that help individuals connect with destiny-shaping universal forces and principles described subsequently.

These connections occur as one blends role, salary, mind, hand, and heart into a crucible of "miraculous" transformation—"miraculous" from the word "miracle," being defined here as a shift in perception. This blending occurs as one uncovers endless "visibilities"—outer world curiosities awaiting attention—and "invisibilities,"—the mysteries of the inner world where physical reality is translated into meanings that are afterwards acted upon.

One makes choices based on one's values. One is defined by the good that one chooses and the evil that one rejects. By spanning both realms —inner and outer—and by acting in ways that serve others one becomes *capable* of changing the world for the better by maturing spiritually to a higher, uncommon level. This *capability* arises when one sees outer world needs and reacts to such needs after careful introspection of not only one's "positivities" (the "cherubs" expressed as desires, goals, and objectives) but also one's "negativities" (the "fiends" expressed as fears, humiliations, rejections, and regrets).

To examine the visibilities and not the invisibilities, the positivities and not the negativities, and the mundane or obvious domain of Nature and not the obscure or transcendent grandeur of Nature is like trying to appreciate a musical composition by hearing all the notes individually and randomly. It is in the relationships between rather than in the individual elements where appreciation and meaning flourish. Improvements do not come solely by changing the relationships or the elements. One makes substantial discoveries and improvements not merely by modifying what is seen but also by altering the eyes that see. It is, therefore, best to not only turn one's attention outward.

Until one meets demons in the inner world one tries to massacre them in the outer world. Failing to encounter inner world fiends is how we humans make a mess of things.

Every thought leads to love, hate, or indifference. Thoughts of love are ones that cause the most constructive conversions of character. If one is going to transform the world by transforming oneself, one needs to reach deep within, even to the nasty corners.

The methodology you will learn in this series of books and courses will help you focus on altering mental patterns that are not working, will help you change unethical thoughts or behaviors, will help you improve one's rapport with the ecological and spiritual realms, and will help you enhance your imagination. Before learning this new methodology, take a moment to assess in the following activity your own ability to build expectations, plan, make conscious choices through three aspects of intelligence: speed, the management of anxiety, and the grit of self-control.

To Personal Beginning Assessments...

HumaNatureConnect Activity

Start-up Protocol

If this is not a day when you prefer to spend time in nature without an agenda, do the Heartwood Path Start-up Protocol found in the Appendix. Then return here to do the remaining portion of this activity:

Awakening

For this activity, write down your personal assessment of your unethical thoughts and behaviors, your rapport with the ecological or spiritual realms, your imagination, the speed of your mental functioning, your ability to build expectations, your ability to make plans, your track record with making conscious choices, your management of anxiety, and the grit of your self-control and self-discipline. Like in the previous activity, you can compare your written assessment now to your assessments after completing this book to determine its affect on your life.

Follow-up Protocol

For best results, write down your impressions of this activity in your journal using the Heartwood Path Follow-up Protocol found in the Appendix. Afterwards, consider sharing your interpretations with others.

Heartwood Path Axioms

Key Assertions From Waypoint 1.30

1.30.1.

One makes substantial discoveries and improvements not merely by modifying what is seen but also by altering both the eyes that see and the mind that discerns.

1.30.2.

Miraculous transformations occur as one uncovers endless "visibilities"—outer world curiosities awaiting attention—and "invisibilities,"—the mysteries of the inner world where physical reality is translated into meanings that are afterwards acted upon.

1.30.3.

Until one meets demons in the inner world one tries to massacre them in the outer world.

1.30.4.

Serving others and changing the world for the better is a capability that arises when one sees outer world needs and reacts to them after careful introspection of not only one's "positivities" (the "cherubs" expressed as desires, goals, and objectives) but also one's "negativities" (the "fiends" expressed as fears, humiliations, rejections, and regrets).

1.30.5.

If one is going to transform the world by transforming oneself, one needs to reach deep within, even to the nasty corners.

Nocturnal Pilgrimage 1.30

For best results, write down your impressions of each night's dreams in your journal using the Heartwood Path Dreaming Time Protocols found in the Appendix. Afterwards, consider sharing your Dream Tending with others.

Develop the intention to dream about your unethical thoughts and behaviors. Repeat over and over immediately before going to sleep that you will dream about your rapport with the ecological or spiritual realms. Think over the cherubs and fiends you would like to see visit in your dreams. After you dream, write down a title for it in your journal, as suggested in our After Dreaming Protocol.

After a night's dreamful sleep, record your dreams and move on to the next waypoint: "Better World." There, among other things, you will assess your satisfaction.

31

Better World

INVOKE THE WORLD YOU OPT TO SEE

The conception of a new world occurs in the womb of one's imagination. This statement is true only if one's imagination helps to remove the veils that give the illusion that makes one feel separate from the environment and the Absolute. Fortunately, one can learn to remove these veils—each described subsequently.

You and I and everyone else will invoke the world we opt to see. We have the power in us, but not of us, to miraculously save the world. We alone cannot create the miracle it takes for us to save the world by transforming ourselves. Nevertheless, by connecting to universal forces—the Absolute, the forces of Nature, and universal principles, for example—we can allow the miracle to occur.

Connecting with universal forces, working to save the Earth, and improving oneself requires a heroic journey guided by a fundamental truth. While engaging in a heroic journey of spiritual development or personal change it is handy to be able to identify the main maxim, the primary postulate, or the arch assumption that following the course will put into action.

Before getting to this main maxim, take the time for another personal assessment. This one will give you a current read on your overall level of satisfaction.

To Assess Your Self-contentment...

HumaNatureConnect Activity

Start-up Protocol

If this is not a day when you prefer to spend time in nature without an agenda, do the Heartwood Path Start-up Protocol found in the Appendix. Then return here to do the remaining portion of this activity:

Assessing Your Level Of Self-satisfaction

For this activity, undertake the following personal assessment: On a five point scale, with one being very dissatisfied, three being neutral, and five being very satisfied, how satisfied are you with your life as a whole, your work, your friends, the morale of your team, the morale of your friends, and the morale of your family. In a similar way, rate your application of novelty, creativity, ingenuity, and innovation in your life by answering the following questions with the use of a scale wherein 1 means never and 10 means always: how often do you use critical thinking, open-mindedness, and good judgement?; how often do you use bravery and courage? how often do you cheat, lie, or mislead?; how often do you use honesty?; how often are you persistent?; how often do you display enthusiasm, express love or attachment, and accept love?; how often do you use street smarts, social skills, and social awareness? How often do you show team work, use fairness, display leadership, use prudence or caution, and use self-control? Put your answers in your journal and share them with others as you wish via the Heartwood Path Exchange.

Follow-up Protocol

For best results, write down your impressions of this activity in your journal using the Heartwood Path Follow-up Protocol found in the Appendix. Afterwards, consider sharing your interpretations with others.

Heartwood Path Axioms

Key Assertions From Waypoint 1.31

1.31.1.

The conception of a new world occurs in the womb of one's imagination.

1.31.2.

You and I and everyone else will invoke the world we opt to see.

1.31.3.

We have the power in us, but not of us, to miraculously save the world.

1.31.4.

Connecting with universal forces, working to save the Earth, and improving oneself requires a heroic journey guided by a fundamental truth.

Nocturnal Pilgrimage 1.31

For best results, write down your impressions of each night's dreams in your journal using the Heartwood Path Dreaming Time Protocols found in the Appendix. Afterwards, consider sharing your Dream Tending with others.

With this activity, as you record notes in your Dream Journal, begin the habit that you will always date your journal entries. One reason this is a good idea is you might discover, upon looking over your entries, that you have the same or similar dreams on certain anniversaries. This alone may reveal a lot about yourself.

Record your impressions in your journal and take some time to reflect on what you have learned so far. Then move on to the primary postulate of the Heartwood Path, which you can find at the next waypoint: "Main Maxim."

32

Main Maxim

CONSIDER THE PIERCE PRINCIPLE

The Heartwood Path takes you on a heroic journey and it is based on one main axiom, one grand guiding tenet, the "PIERCE Principle, which is:

"Being happy and saving the earth requires an achievable high level of spiritual maturity."

Doubling as a credit line and an acronym, the PIERCE Principle contains all the main aspects of the Heartwood Path described in this series of books and courses:

P stands for the understanding of universal Principles and the Pondering of the origin and structure of integrity.

I stands for the contention that saving the planet and "perfecting" the person requires both the process of Individuation—which leads to becoming an individual—and the process of Integration—which leads to the formation of a Greater Self that includes the planet.

E stands for protecting the Environment.

R reminds one of the need to Ripen one's self into a state of spiritual maturity so that one can become a person with positive traits and, if one has a life partner, to Reconcile self and other, through a process described in a separate book, **Eros: Connecting Intimately For Transformation**.

C also has multiple meanings: it stands for developing enough Care to spur one into action as an individual or as a life Coach and, as described in a separate book, for Collaborating with others in ways that aid efforts (for oneself and others) to be Compassionate towards all sentient beings (those capable of perceiving) without Crashing.

E stands for the need to persevere in the above-stated efforts through the Enchantment one finds with Everyday life (enchantment defined as an opening of the mind to the wonder, sacredness, and magic of existence).

All statements made in this series of books and courses derive from the fundamental truth of the PIERCE Principle. This tenet is tantamount. Whether one considers it a universal truth, a code of conduct, or a mere literary thesis statement, the PIERCE Principle is, metaphorically speaking, the heading atop the main signpost at the outset of the Heartwood Path. It tells you, the pilgrim at the beginning of your pilgrimage down the Heartwood Path, where you are about to go and; if there is later confusion, reminds you of why you have embarked on this particular heroic journey. We humans tend to get lost on our journeys through life because of the elaborate means we have created to give ourselves misconceptions.

Often these misconceptions lead to the bad things. Take a moment to assess your own emotional fitness during negative events in the following activity.

To A Look At Your Temperament...

HumaNatureConnect Activity

Start-up Protocol

If this is not a day when you prefer to spend time in nature without an agenda, do the Heartwood Path Start-up Protocol found in the Appendix. Then return here to do the remaining portion of this activity:

Examining Your Emotional Fitness

For this activity, assess your emotional fitness using a scale where 1 is not like you at all, 3 is somewhat like you, and 5 is very much like you as you answer the following questions: Do you expect bad things to happen? Do you have control over things that happen? Do you respond to stress by making things worse? Do you expect good things to happen to you? Is work one of the most important aspects of your life? Do you find it difficult to adjust to changes? Do you keep your feelings to yourself? Look over your responses and write in your journal what they tell you about your emotional fitness.

Follow-up Protocol

For best results, write down your impressions of this activity in your journal using the Heartwood Path Follow-up Protocol found in the Appendix. Afterwards, consider sharing your interpretations with others.

Heartwood Path Axioms

Key Assertions From Waypoint 1.32

1.32.1.

PIERCE Principle:

"Being uncommonly happy and working effectively to help save the earth requires an achievable high level of spiritual maturity."

1.32.2.

Whether one considers it a universal truth, a code of conduct, or a mere literary thesis statement, the PIERCE Principle is, metaphorically speaking, the heading atop the main signpost at the outset of the Heartwood Path.

Nocturnal Pilgrimage 1.32

For best results, write down your impressions of each night's dreams in your journal using the Heartwood Path Dreaming Time Protocols found in the Appendix. Afterwards, consider sharing your Dream Tending with others.

You will not be able to use your dreams to help you determine your emotional fitness, to manage your expectations, to help you add a measure of control over your life, or to much of anything if you cannot recall and write down details about your dreams. The second step, after your initial recall of your night's dreams, is to be able to write down a short summary of your dreams before they are totally lost from your memory. This short description is usually enough to prod your memory of the Dream, enough so that you can do many of the suggestions in the Heartwood Path After Dreaming Protocol.

The next waypoint is called "Pierced Veils." Start it after a night's sleep. Be sure to record your dream associations and dream amplifications in your journal.

33

Pierced Veils

ASSESS HOW WELL YOU FIT IN

The sense that we humans are separate from nature is a mirage caused largely by what are metaphorically called the "veils of separation." These "veils," which are causes of the illusion of separation, occur because one's understanding is limited by the small amounts of perceptions made available through the use of human eyes, ears, mouths, noses, thoughts, and feelings.

The veils of separation—we will discuss seven—are made of the false data one gathers from one's deluded perceptions of the experience of life. These illusions are thus woven from the threads of one's assumptions, decisions, and determinations.

The process of removing the veils of illusion need not occur in a particular sequence. It matters only that, by the time the veils are removed, a sense of universal consciousness is remembered and one then naturally begins to think and behave on behalf of the whole (which includes the natural environment and the individual self).

The first veil makes one seek to conform to one's tribe at the expense of one's unique individuality. With this veil one forgets that life is created in divine perfection and that everything is part of a perfect plan. The Heartwood Path is designed to strip away this veil by the end of this book.

The second veil causes one to forget one's authentic identity, which is one's individuality and one's own unique emotional repertoire. Heartwood Path Book Three: **Egos: Connecting with the Individual Self** is designed to help readers remember and fortify their own spiritual essence—their own uniqueness. This illusion of separation is removed by anchoring one's uniqueness.

The third veil of separation makes one see the world primarily only as solid objects in a "real world." Against this apparent rigidity one feels powerless. This veil is removed by the discussions in the fourth Heartwood Path book—**Ecos: Connecting with the Ecological Self**—that informs the participant of the reality behind the surfaces of the real world, such as the spiritual aspects of nature, Nature's unseen powers, and appropriate power-producing rites used in Mother Earth Spirituality (such as the use of totems, sweat lodges, and medicine wheels).

The fourth veil of separation, created by feelings and emotions that have not been healed and released, masks one's ability to relate profoundly to another. Creating a common and valued pattern of behavior wherein such feelings and emotions can be healed and released is a key components of the fifth Heartwood Path book—**Ethos: Connecting with Valued Traits.** This book helps to lift the fourth veil by helping participants acquire traits that are valued highly in one's culture.

The fifth veil masks one's individual belief system, thoughts, theories, hypothesis, and mental computations. This masking occurs as one, over time, gives in to the dualistic beliefs, judgments, and unworkable learned patterns of behavior absorbed from one's family and peers. As one develops one's own will—including the will to differentiate oneself from one's family or peers—one is completing the set of assignments described in detail in later books, particularly **Volitos: Connecting with the Individual Will**. The result is a participant who has appropriately stripped away incorrect conclusions or false ideas so that the individual will can act forcefully and unencumbered. Once one has bolstered one's will one is able to speak out and act more clearly, creatively, and forcefully. This veil of illusion is lifted as one gets in better touch with one's own individual intentions.

The sixth veil of illusion blocks one's access to other worlds, other realities, other time periods, and other dimensions of awareness. Ways to remove this veil of illusion are included in the Nocturnal Pilgrimage sections, especially where dream interpretation helps readers access the vast reaches of human and universal consciousness. It is also addressed in Heartwood Path Book Eight: **Collectivos: Connecting with the More-Than-Individual Will.**

The seventh veil of illusion is created by one's sense of individuality, rigid ideas of one's identity, and an inability to experience oneness. Such illusions are taxing; and they are reasons why people procrastinate, become inactive, or fail to persevere. Those who follow the Heartwood Path's recommendation to find enchantment in everyday life—the main topic of Heartwood Path Book Seven: **Remeos: Connecting with the Enchantment of Home**—lower this veil and, therefore, are able to continue to serve others without crashing.

Such service depends, in part, on your social fitness. Take a moment to assess this aspect of your life in the following activity.

To Assess How Well You Fit In...

HumaNatureConnect Activity

Start-up Protocol

If this is not a day when you prefer to spend time in nature without an agenda, do the Heartwood Path Start-up Protocol found in the Appendix. Then return here to do the remaining portion of this activity:

Assessing Your Social Fitness

For this activity, assess your social fitness using a scale where 1 is not like you at all, 3 is somewhat like you, and 5 is very much like you as you answer the following questions: Does your work improve the world? Will your work companions look out for you? Are your closest friends from work? Do you trust your supervisor? Look over your responses and write in your journal what they indicate about your social fitness.

Follow-up Protocol

For best results, write down your impressions of this activity in your journal using the Heartwood Path Follow-up Protocol found in the Appendix. Afterwards, consider sharing your interpretations with others.

Heartwood Path Axioms

Key Assertions From Waypoint 1.33

1.33.1.

The sense that we humans are separate from nature is a mirage caused largely by what are metaphorically called the "veils of separation."

1.33.2.

There are seven veils of illusion: one that makes one seek to conform to one's tribe at the expense of one's unique individuality; one that causes one to forget one's individuality and one's own unique emotional repertoire; one that makes one see the world primarily only as solid objects in a "real world;" one that masks one's ability to relate profoundly to another; one that

masks one's individual belief system, thoughts, theories, hypothesis, and mental computations; one that blocks one's access to other worlds, other realities, other time periods, and other dimensions of awareness; and one that is created by one's sense of individuality, rigid concepts of one's identity, and an inability to experience oneness.

1.33.3.

Some important ways to remove the veils of separation include: remembering that life is created in divine perfection and that everything is part of a perfect plan; working to fortify one's own spiritual essence and uniqueness; becoming informed of the reality behind the surfaces of the real world, creating a common and valued pattern of behavior wherein unexpressed feelings and emotions can be healed and released; appropriately stripping away incorrect conclusions or false ideas so that the individual will can act forcefully and unencumbered; dream interpretation; and to find enchantment in everyday life so one is able to continue to serve others without crashing.

1.33.4.

By the time the veils of illusion (separation) are removed, a sense of universal consciousness is remembered and one then naturally begins to think and behave on behalf of the whole (which includes the natural environment and the individual self).

1.33.5.

Once one has bolstered one's will one is able to speak out and act more clearly, creatively, and forcefully.

Nocturnal Pilgrimage 1.33

For best results, write down your impressions of each night's dreams in your journal using the Heartwood Path Dreaming Time Protocols found in the Appendix. Afterwards, consider sharing your Dream Tending with others.

As always, be sure to tend to your nighttime reveries before heading to a new waypoint.

Now you are beginning to see that we will be going deep within during your sojourn down the Heartwood Path. This "going within" is further explained in the next waypoint: "Introspection."

34

Introspection

ASSESS YOUR SPIRITUAL FITNESS

Without the ability to listen or to be introspective, one misses vital signals the universe sends on one's behalf. When, metaphorically speaking, the dripping faucet of life's little warning signs fails to motivate us to do the preemptive work of a person-perfecting plumber, life sends a tidal wave just to stir us out of our slumber. Introspection, a crucial task of those who follow the Heartwood Path, is important because the fabric of life in the outer world is a precise weave of the thoughts and feelings in one's inner world.

Experiencing one's own inner world is a silent activity. Silence gives access to a clear mind; which, in turn, allows one to be more aware of the ebb and flow of energy and of the penetrating and projecting qualities of energy. Silence also allows for the revelation of negative energy often hidden by the clamor of life. Once revealed, negative energy can be processed and released. Thus, silence is not only golden; it is inspiring, as well.

Processing one's own psychological pain or emotional suffering brings a bonus. When those who have not engaged in such processing face danger or disaster they tend to panic and fail. Conversely, those who have already experienced and processed calamities garner the necessary inner strength to overcome adversity, succeed in their outer world goals, and grow towards spiritual maturity (perfection).

Such experiences and processing affect or indicate one's spiritual fitness. Assess yours in the following activity.

To Assess Your Present Spiritual Fitness...

HumaNatureConnect Activity

Start-up Protocol

If this is not a day when you prefer to spend time in nature without an agenda, do the Heartwood Path Start-up Protocol found in the Appendix. Then return here to do the remaining portion of this activity:

Assessing Spiritual Fitness

For this activity, use a scale where 1 is strongly disagree, 3 is neutral, and 5 is strongly agree with the following statements aimed at assessing your spiritual fitness: Your life has lasting meaning. Your life is connected to all of humanity and the whole world. Your job has lasting meaning. Look over your responses and write in your journal what they say about your spiritual fitness.

Follow-up Protocol

For best results, write down your impressions of this activity in your journal using the Heartwood Path Follow-up Protocol found in the Appendix. Afterwards, consider sharing your interpretations with others.

Heartwood Path Axioms

Key Assertions From Waypoint 1.34

1.34.1.

When the dripping faucet of life's little warning signs fails to motivate us to do the preemptive work of a person-perfecting plumber, life sends a tidal wave just to stir us out of our slumber.

1.34.2.

Silence gives access to a clear mind; which, in turn, allows one to be more aware of the ebb and flow of energy and of the penetrating and projecting qualities of energy.

1.34.3.

Silence also allows for the revelation of negative energy often hidden by the clamor of life.

1.34.4.

Once revealed, negative energy can be processed and released.

1.34.5.

The fabric of life in the outer world is a precise weave of the thoughts and feelings in one's inner world.

Nocturnal Pilgrimage 1.34

For best results, write down your impressions of each night's dreams in your journal using the Heartwood Path Dreaming Time Protocols found in the Appendix. Afterwards, consider sharing your Dream Tending with others.

For some time now you have been practicing dream association—correlating your dreams as signs of repressed anger or hidden wishes. You have also been amplifying your dreams, growing them into universal symbols, well known stories, and archetypes. Now it is time to start practicing the third way of dream tending. This stage, called "animating," will the most important way we will be tending to your dreams as you progress down the Heartwood Path. To animate a Dream Image, "you bring it to life in the here and now, rather than associating to the past or amplifying it into a myth of story" (Aizenstat, 2009, p. 23). Notice what the image is doing, how it is moving, how it is interacting with you, and how it affects you. Write your impressions in your journal.

You are now ready to continue. Move to the next waypoint, titled "The Journey," and prepare to grow up more fully. As an alternative, go someplace else and hope that you somehow learn how to act right in public. As we all know, it is not productive to fret over the good ole days. Nostalgia isn't what it used to be.

35

The Journey

GROW UP FULLY

The goal of traversing the Heartwood Path ought not to be achieving pre-given rules of perfection. There is no standard of perfection along the Heartwood Path. The goal ought to be to become impeccably aware of one's own feelings, thoughts, and actions so that one can find harmony, communicate with nature, be in a state of oneness with life, and use one's own individual gifts to serve others effectively and enduringly.

Like life, going down the Heartwood Path is not an experience that is selected and made. Rather, life and the Heartwood Path are experiences that involve ongoing selecting and making. The Heartwood Path is not about reaching a conclusion. It is, however, about helping humans in their efforts to work towards spiritual maturity. This path is necessary because, spiritually speaking, most people never develop into higher stages of maturity. Speaking plainly, the Heartwood Path does not make people perfect, not in any final sense; but it does help them grow-up more fully.

The Earth will never be finally saved, nor will you ever be made conclusively perfect. Still, working persistently towards both ends is the noblest of occupations. I cannot tell you where you are going, but this series of books and courses will help you determine what to pack.

Wherever you are going, your journey will affect your family fitness. Use the following personal assessment to strengthen of your family relationship.

To Assess Your Family Fitness...

HumaNatureConnect Activity

Start-up Protocol

If this is not a day when you prefer to spend time in nature without an agenda, do the Heartwood Path Start-up Protocol found in the Appendix. Then return here to do the remaining portion of this activity:

Evaluating Family Fitness

For this activity, use a scale where 5 is strongly agree, 3 is neutral, and 1 is strongly disagree with the following statements aimed at assessing your family fitness: I am close to my family. My job or insurance will take care of my family. My job puts too much burden on my family. My job enables my family to do well. Look over your assessments and write down what they tell you about your family fitness.

Follow-up Protocol

For best results, write down your impressions of this activity in your journal using the Heartwood Path Follow-up Protocol found in the Appendix. Afterwards, consider sharing your interpretations with others.

Heartwood Path Axioms

Key Assertions From Waypoint 1.35

1.35.1.

The Heartwood Path does not make people perfect, not in any final sense; but it does help them grow-up more fully.

1.35.2.

The Earth will never be finally saved, nor will you ever be made conclusively perfect.

Nocturnal Pilgrimage 1.35

For best results, write down your impressions of each night's dreams in your journal using the Heartwood Path Dreaming Time Protocols found in the Appendix. Afterwards, consider sharing your Dream Tending with others.

Congratulations for making it this far. There is much yet to come. Have a good night's sleep and record your dreams, and focus on animating them, as instructed before. Remember, the animating we are calling for is the act of converting your individual Dream Image into universally recognized patterns of positive thinking that have been brought to life as superheroes such as The Healer, The Innocent, The Genius, or the Adventurer. Once you have a group of Dream Archetypes, you can ask them what they have for you today in terms of conversation, information, healing, or guidance. One of my recurring Dream Images is the long-neglected parakeet, another is slow-moving turtle. In proper fashion, I animated the Dream Image of the parakeet to become the Wounded Healer and I animated the image of the turtle to become the Wise Sage).

After animating at least one Dream Image into a Dream Archetype continue to the next waypoint: "Three Paths."

36

Three Paths

FOLLOW PATHWAYS OF IMPROVEMENT AND HEED THE LITTLE THINGS THAT MAY BECOME THE BIG THINGS IN YOUR LIFE

We all spend too much of our time in fear, ignorance, indecision, lust, dependence, ineffectiveness, unrewarding labor, egoism, despair, insecurity, disease, debt, and domination. The Heartwood Path moves one away from these conditions by combining three pathways of improvement. One is the path people follow to improve the environment. Another is the trail people follow to improve their relationships. The third is the course to self-improvement.

At the confluence of these three trails begins the Heartwood Path, a multipart book/course that is already adding depth to your character and thus adding to your appeal—the attractiveness of character you can use during your journey along the Heartwood Path to find a mate or to motivate others to praise The Absolute and protect Its creation. When I recommend that participants praise The Absolute the action being encouraged is immersing oneself in nature rather than offering words of worship to Nature.

Praising the Absolute through heartfelt immersion in nature will add depth to your awareness and broaden your self-concept to the point that you will be driven easily to help others. You can use this series of books to help people love others or to at least keep yourself from hating those who don't. Use the Heartwood Path series of books also to enjoy the little things in life that you may one day realize are the big things in your life. Such reminiscing, like all reminiscing that is vivid, adds to happiness. The following activity will help you do both:

To Your Most Vivid Recollections...

HumaNatureConnect Activity

Start-up Protocol

If this is not a day when you prefer to spend time in nature without an agenda, do the Heartwood Path Start-up Protocol found in the Appendix. Then return here to do the remaining portion of this activity:

Reminiscing

For this activity, reminisce about loving others, the little things in life, or both. Write down the most vivid recollections possible.

Follow-up Protocol

For best results, write down your impressions of this activity in your journal using the Heartwood Path Follow-up Protocol found in the Appendix. Afterwards, consider sharing your interpretations with others.

Heartwood Path Axioms

Key Assertions From Waypoint 1.36

1.36.1.

We all spend too much of our time in fear, ignorance, indecision, lust, dependence, ineffectiveness, unrewarding labor, egoism, despair, insecurity, disease, debt, and domination.

1.36.2.

Praising the Absolute through heartfelt immersion in nature will add depth to your awareness and broaden your self-concept to the point that you will be driven easily to help others.

Nocturnal Pilgrimage 1.36

For best results, write down your impressions of each night's dreams in your journal using the Heartwood Path Dreaming Time Protocols found in the Appendix. Afterwards, consider sharing your Dream Tending with others.

Before going to sleep tonight meditate on how you feel about your loved ones. Focus your attention on the little things you like or dislike about your loved ones. Spread this meditation out to think about your feelings about other little things in your life. Write down your recollections. Read what you write over and over again as a way to prompt you to dream about the same topics. Record your feelings during and after dreaming and compare your before-dreaming feelings with your during and after-dreaming feelings. In doing so, you are following the suggestion of the component of our After Dreaming Protocol called "Mood."

Before moving on to the next waypoint, after a good night's sleep, animate your dreams, and record your impressions in your journal. When ready, head to the next waypoint, called the "Appropriate Path."

37

Appropriate Path

SEEK PERSONAL GROWTH FOR YOURSELF AND OTHERS AND MAKE A BETTER WORLD FOR EVERYONE

This series of books is for adults interested in making a difference in the world. It is for those who want to be guided down a pathway of reading and doing. It is for those who want to improve lives through the reciprocal nature of personal growth and environmental protection.

You need not be a nature-lover like me for the Heartwood Path to have significance. Although I will provide waypoints that are the result of the time I spend preserving, protecting, and restoring the environment, you need not be an environmentalist like me to glean value from the pages that follow. Most of what I will share here regarding my experiences as an environmentalist will be of value to you regardless of your own particular way to make a difference in the world.

The Heartwood Path is written for those who seek personal growth for themselves and a better world for everyone. It is also for those who, in their efforts to serve others, have in the past ended up "spending themselves for the cause."

The Heartwood Path is about a way to pursue personal and planetary improvement. Along this course you will discover what I call the "Law of Personal and Planetary Reciprocity," stated as follows: "While personal well-being depends on planetary health, the fate of the Earth depends on the health, happiness, and personal development of humans." To change something in your environment you need to become the change yourself.

Personal and planetary change and becoming the change you seek requires the suspension, usually as a temporary step leading to a desired result, of wanting. Human wants have created not only marvelous individual and cultural improvements but also widespread spiritual distraction and environmental destruction. I am speaking of both the wanting of positive things like security, acceptance, and survival and the negative wanting associated with conspicuous consumption, addictive consumption, overeating, and the like. My read of models in nature informs me that it is not enough to just get over my own negative wants. I need to also learn to release all wants, if only temporarily and if only the best I can, if I am to be able to find the junction of personal happiness and environmental sustainability. Some further elaboration is presented in the activity that follows:

To A First Attempt At Fleshing Out A Topic, Beginning With The Subject Of "Wanting"...

HumaNatureConnect Activity

Start-up Protocol

If this is not a day when you prefer to spend time in nature without an agenda, do the Heartwood Path Start-up Protocol found in the Appendix. Then return here to do the remaining portion of this activity:

Releasing Wants

For this activity, make physical contact with a tree, a rock, a lake, or any other natural being. Sense the essence of the natural being, not just with your typical senses of sight, sound, touch, smell, and taste, but also use Dr. Cohen's so-called natural senses such as his radiation senses (of color, of moods, and of temperature); his feeling senses (of the sensation of gravity, of air and wind pressure, and of motion); his chemical senses (of hormones, of pheromones, and of hunger for food, water or air); and his mental senses (of pain, of mental and spiritual distress of self, of power and of psychic capacity). Do not get bogged down in trying to understanding everything about these natural senses yet. Simply do what you can to feel the essence of the natural being and then do the best you can to corroborate or contradict the eleven statements below. If, however, you feel the need to review these natural senses right now, go back to Waypoint 1.27, entitled "Basis And Basics."

Getting to know the natural being through the typical and natural senses will naturally break down any resistance (and if it does not, simply go with the flow here) when I ask you to ask the natural being about the topic of "wanting." To make it easier for you to come up with an answer, in your imagination step into the essence of the natural being and, as best as you can as the natural being, give yourself an answer.

When I did this type of activity during Dr. Cohen's eco-psychology courses I got a multipart answer after I used my imagination in the afternoon and the experience entered my dreams that night and I interpreted my dreams the following morning. So we can provide elaboration on the topic of "wanting,"I would like you now, as the essence of your natural being, to ask your natural being cohort about "wanting." Glean answers from your imagination, from the intention to dream about the topic at night, and pick out any answers you may extract from your dream tending the next day. After doing these things, attempt to corroborate or contradict the responses you received. What do you think about what you garnered on the subject? Next, work on your wants:

1. Since wanting creates a sense of lack, let your wants go.
2. To let go, decide to drop it, welcome all attendant emotions, ask yourself or your natural being (you together are one awareness, if you have properly removed the veils of the illusion of separation) questions about letting go of a want.
3. Trust the facts of your experiences but consider that feelings tend to perpetuate the problems they appear to be preventing and often affect one's thinking.
4. As you give up your resistance to releasing your wants (both good and bad) you begin to feel a sense of ease and flow.
5. Aspects of wanting to be released include the desire to control or not be controlled, the desire to want approval and love, the desire for security, and the desire to want separation.
6. Releasing, if only temporary, adds to one's sense of freedom as one let's go of aversions and attachments.
7. It is easier to let go of wants when you consider that you are giving up the wanting and not the being or having—for example, the wanting to be thin rather than being thin.
8. Wants culminate in the emotional states of apathy, grief, fear, lust, anger, pride, courageousness, acceptance, and peace.
9. Since the elaborate "what ifs" we create because of fear interfere with our happiness and freedom and since what we fear tends to appear in our lives (because it becomes a sticking place in our minds in much the same way as visualization leads to actualization), ask yourself if you could and would give up your fear, and when.
10. Let go of your feelings about fear, guilt, shame, financial distress, relationship troubles, and keeping anything you do not like far away from what you do like.
11. Much of this seems counterintuitive until you remember that we are releasing the wanting—the wanting to be free of disease, for example, and not the having of health. Focus on having health rather than wanting to be free of disease. Giving up the wanting

frees one sufficiently to focus less on aversions and attachments and, thus, to be in an optimal state of functioning, to be happy, and to be productive.

Ask your chosen natural being about these topics and write down the responses in your journal. See if you can come up with similar or different responses regarding the value of releasing all wants—both good and bad.

Follow-up Protocol

For best results, write down your impressions of this activity in your journal using the Heartwood Path Follow-up Protocol found in the Appendix. Afterwards, consider sharing your interpretations with others.

Heartwood Path Axioms

Key Assertions From Waypoint 1.37

1.37.1.

The Heartwood Path is written for those who seek personal growth for themselves and a better world for everyone without spending themselves for the cause.

1.37.2.

The "Law of Personal and Planetary Reciprocity," states that while personal well being depends on planetary health, the fate of the Earth depends on the health, happiness, and personal development of humans."

1.37.3.

To change something in your environment you need to become the change yourself.

1.37.4.

Personal and planetary change and becoming the change you seek requires the suspension, usually as a temporary step leading to a desired result, of wanting—both the wanting of positive things like security, acceptance, and survival and the negative wanting associated with conspicuous consumption, addictive consumption, overeating, and the like.

Nocturnal Pilgrimage 1.37

For best results, write down your impressions of each night's dreams in your journal using the Heartwood Path Dreaming Time Protocols found in the Appendix. Afterwards, consider sharing your Dream Tending with others.

The otherworldly experience of dreaming demonstrates that circumstances that are not proven may still be true. Without having a known basis in reality dreams can still change one's life. If one feels the need to find a ground of reality in a dream one needs to look no further than one's own body, for that is the juncture between one's inner and one's outer dimensions.

In either of these directions, the pathways of experience—one "concrete" and the other "dreamy"—are one's various sensations. It is these sensations that allows one to have experiences, the most pertinent for this current discussion being the sensation of witnessing Images.

These Images can be either in one's dreams or in one's waking "reality." Thus, sensations are the two-way swinging doors that allow Images to make their impressions on a person. I say "two-way" because the Images can arise from within the mind or from outside of one's mind. In either direction, it is one's awareness, formed on a sort of bridge that spans between the mind and the source of the Image, that tempers one's impressions. This tempering is one's own Imagination.

The so-called "real world" and the so-called "dream world" affect each other at the point of one's bodily sensations, which are both a boundary and a link. In this way, one has access to and a measure of control over both worlds. As we will see, the two-way flow of information— one from the inside and the other from the outside— keeps the witness from sinking too deeply into one world or the other.

Be careful not to fall into the trap of thinking that only Images from the outside are worthy of your attention. Images from the Inside are neither worthless fantasy nor falsehoods. They are rather the bearers of great gifts.

To follow the Heartwood Path is to become an eartHeart. To become an eartHeart is to become a seer, a visionary, and a prophet. To become such a secular saint requires one to move along a path to the two-way door at the center of one's imaginal mind. Here sits Kavinah, the spiritual being that, by giving out through the two-way door and by taking in through the two-way door, is the source of one's Will.

Without Kavinah at the center of your imaginal mind you would have no intentions. And that would make you a very dull person, indeed.

Even if you want to keep moving ahead rapidly, I encourage you to sleep on what you have learned thus far before moving to the next waypoint: "Whole Character." Employing your Inner Kavinah tonight, develop a list of your five most important intentions. Write them in your journal right away, so you do not forget them. Do so tonight or first thing in the morning. Tomorrow will be soon enough to learn about adding depth to your character.

38

Whole Character

INCREASE YOUR LEVEL OF AWARENESS

The process of seeking added depth requires one to increase one's levels of awareness: the kind of increased consciousness that comes by adding depth to one's whole character. By "whole character" I mean both aspects of one's own inner realm (Interiority) and one's own behaviors and physical systems (the "real world" of Exteriority that appears to be "outside" of the mind and is both physiological and social). As we shall see, the hemisphere of "Interiority" is where one adds new levels of consciousness (either in intentions or in ethics) and the hemisphere of "Exteriority" is where one adds new levels of form (either in behaviors or in tangible physical systems).

Whether one is considering the internal realm of consciousness or the external realm of form, the process of moving up to the next level (stage of development) is the process of adding depth. Evolution adds depth by a three-part process of transcendence. This process involves fusing aspects of form and consciousness at one level, then differentiating and moving them up to the next level plus including all the aspects of the previous levels, and finally integrating the new level with the preceding levels.

The Heartwood Path mimics evolution's process of transcendence. With more layers of depth included in one's character, one becomes more vital. One matters more as the added layers of depth impart higher levels of intentions, ethics, behaviors, and physical systems that can be used to help one's self and others. This vitality is spurred as one's awareness expands to include a broader, more holistic view. This critically important process of adding depth to your own character—described throughout the pages that follow—enables you to be better prepared to help yourself and others without crashing.

You will become better prepared to help without crashing as a result of engaging in the activities at the waypoints along the Heartwood Path. In visiting these waypoints, novice trekkers tend to pack too much. The next series of activities will help you continue to unload your burdens and release your false perceptions. The letting go you will be working on will shift from unloading wants to clearing "space" so that you can walk the path unencumbered and, therefore, more easily reveal your own Authentic Self, a self that mirrors one's uncluttered source.

To The Well Spring...

HumaNatureConnect Activity

Start-up Protocol

If this is not a day when you prefer to spend time in nature without an agenda, do the Heartwood Path Start-up Protocol found in the Appendix. Then return here to do the remaining portion of this activity:

Finding Your Source

Imagine that you are not just visiting a natural place but also going to your spiritual source, which is a "place" without a locality. This "place" is more about a calling than it is about a location. This place, birthed by your source, helps you find sacredness and meaning. The "place" or primary role you are revealing to yourself will not be a temporary destination or a fleeting assignment. It will also not be a specific place like 3020 Linden Street, in East St. Louis. It will be universal in its application, infinite in its span, and eternal in its duration. It will be a place as in the statement: "It is my *place* to help others become happy and protect the environment." It may come to you in pieces, like memories that are tied to nature, and it will usually either be about air, water, fire, or earth.

Wait for impressions to form about hindrances that prevent you from identifying or acting on your soul purpose. Metaphorically speaking, by perceiving such hindrance-related impressions you are now cleansing your backpack amidst the cycles of nature as a way to bring you to your Source through the process of identifying and releasing your mental debris, your emotional trash, your burn-worthy hidden aspects of your Self, and anything that would weaken your physical and spiritual self (like an unneeded heavy object in your backpack).

You will not likely be able to find your source, your soul place, or your life purpose until you identify and rid yourself of your inner world burdens. Wait to perceive a message from your chosen natural being concerning your mental debris and your Source-produced place.

To facilitate your understanding of the nature of your soul place, start out simple by answering the following questions: What are your intentions for following this course? Are you ready to make changes in your life? Having answered these questions, continue to a more significant query: What inner world burdens do I need to dump? Then, as the essence of your chosen attractive natural being, ask yourself the most significant question: What is your source-provided place in life?

Follow-up Protocol

For best results, write down your impressions of this activity in your journal using the Heartwood Path Follow-up Protocol found in the Appendix. Afterwards, consider sharing your interpretations with others.

Heartwood Path Axioms

Key Assertions From Waypoint 1.38

1.38.1.

"Whole character" is both aspects of one's own inner realm of intentions and ethics (Interiority) and one's own behaviors and physical systems (Exteriority).

1.38.2.

The process of seeking added depth requires increasing levels of awareness: the kind of increased consciousness that comes by adding depth to one's whole character.

1.38.3.

The hemisphere of "Interiority" is where one adds new levels of consciousness (either in intentions or in ethics) and the hemisphere of "Exteriority" is where one adds new levels of form (either in behaviors or in tangible physical systems).

1.38.4.

Whether one is considering the internal realm of consciousness or the external realm of form, the process of moving up to the next level (stage of development) is the process of adding depth.

1.38.5.

Evolution adds depth by a three-part process of transcendence which involves fusing aspects of form and consciousness at one level, then differentiating and moving them up to the next

level plus including all the aspects of the previous levels, and finally integrating the new level with the preceding levels.

Nocturnal Pilgrimage 1.38

For best results, write down your impressions of each night's dreams in your journal using the Heartwood Path Dreaming Time Protocols found in the Appendix. Afterwards, consider sharing your Dream Tending with others.

Be sure to enter notes about your dream in your journal before you continue. These dreams are like a garden that will be tended later in this course of study. For now, just jot down what you can remember from your dreams, the more details the better. Pay attention to characters and what they are doing. You will receive more dream journaling advice as you continue.

Less burdened by life's "too-muchness," you are now better prepared for the next waypoint: "Unitive Perception."

39

Unitive Perception

RECORD YOUR OPERATIONS, BLESSINGS, AND AFFIRMATIONS

As you proceed through these pages, the boundaries of your Self will expand to include the Earth and your conception of the other will expand to include the animated Universe. By expanding your conception of "the Self" in this way you will have the opportunity to overcome the problematic duality of Self and other; learn to perceive "unitively" rather than dualistically, and learn how to accept awesome gifts from Nature—you can use to heal yourself, to grow spiritually, and to preserve the planet. It is through the self-discovery that comes with intimacy—intimacy with nature during the activities of this book/course—that you will be able to do these and other worthwhile things.

None of the worthwhile benefits of intimacy can occur very well when one follows old patterns of dualistic thinking such as the notion that Humans are separate from Nature. To keep from perpetuating this false aspect of reality I will often use the word "humaNature" when describing humans embedded in Nature. I use this term to help participants remember that, while there is a diversity of seemingly separate entities, "all is one."

The Heartwood Path fosters a strong spiritual sense of oneness—a sense that is, at once, expansive and ecological plus intimate and personal. Eventually as you continue down the Heartwood Path you will come to know that a strong spiritual sense arises spontaneously from the reciprocal nature of being nurtured by Nature and nurturing Nature.

To A Record Of Your Operations, Blessings, And Affirmations…

HumaNatureConnect Activity

Start-up Protocol

If this is not a day when you prefer to spend time in nature without an agenda, do the Heartwood Path Start-up Protocol found in the Appendix. Then return here to do the remaining portion of this activity:

Dividing Your Journaling Into Two Compartments To Lesson Your Perceived Load

As you proceed down the Heartwood Path, you will need to maintain a journal that is divided each day into two compartments: one for tending to your dreams (I put that on the right side of a two-page spread) and the other for recording awake-time revelations and occurrences (I put that on the left side of a two-page spread). Of the two, our suggested format for dream-time journaling is more elaborate, so we will discuss that over the course of several waypoints. For this activity, let us focus on the format for your awake-time journaling.

Begin the repetitive process of dividing a portion of each day's awake-time blank journal—be it one page or more than one page—into three sections as shown, one called "Blessings," another called "Operations," and another called "Affirmations." Make each section large enough for five entries each, and devote the largest space to the Operations section since these entries will likely require the most space. Each day in the

Blessings section of your journal write down five aspects of your life that deserve your gratitude. Each day in the Operations section write down any thoughts or actions you want to remember. Each day in the Affirmation section write down five present-tense statements about yourself, each beginning with the words "I am ... "

Some of the first entries in your Operations Journal will be about mental and emotional clearing (it is not wise to be carrying too much as you make your journey down the Heartwood Path). Your load will also appear lighter if you keep your own customized awake-time journalling separated into Blessings, Operations, and Affirmations.

Otherwise the jumble of entries will weigh you down. Each day you write in your journal enter your blessings, operations, and affirmations that are pertinent to the text of the Heartwood Path, the activities of the Heartwood Path, or anything else you are reading or doing in your life. Then, wait for a thought that seems to come from or be inspired by your chosen natural being, which has given you consent for this activity by remaining attractive to you for at least ten seconds.

Attend to this nature-inspired thought and, if not already in a "verbal" form, convert the signs, symbols, or nonverbal messages into words. These words are like wands that magically bring happiness and environmental sustainability to your life. Include in the Operations section your impressions about converting messages from (or thoughts inspired by) nature into words.

It is understandable that you may, at this early stage of the Heartwood Path, have some resistance to the notion of receiving guidance from nature. Simply write down whether your reception of such guidance is at this point considered by you to be accepted, questioned, or rejected.

Put what you accept in the Affirmations section. It can take some time and familiarity with the Natural Systems Thinking Process before one accepts the possibility of receiving guidance from nature. If you find that you are skeptical, and the stumbling block is your query about whether it is nature or your own mind offering the guidance, a way to move forward is to remember that nature and your mind are inseparable, with any distinctions being the result of an inaccurate veil of illusion (that causes you to perceive a separation that is not there). Your mind is an aspect of nature that gives you the guidance.

By engaging in these HumaNatureConnect Activities, your mind functions optimally and it becomes less fooled by the veils of illusion/separation put upon it by the stories and pervasive perceptions of one's indoor-dominated culture. You will soon learn how one's mind is not contained by one's brain but is instead an energy event that spans, chakra-by-chakra, throughout one's body and stretches, attractive natural being-by-attractive natural being, throughout nature and to various Earth Chakras around the world (Earth Chakras are explained in the Heartwood Path **Ecos** book, but it is best not to skip ahead now).

Follow-up Protocol

For best results, write down your impressions of this activity in your journal using the Heartwood Path Follow-up Protocol found in the Appendix. Afterwards, consider sharing your interpretations with others.

Heartwood Path Axioms

Key Assertions From Waypoint 1.39

1.39.1.

By expanding your conception of "the Self" to include the whole of nature you will have the opportunity to overcome the problematic duality of Self and other; you will learn to perceive "unitively" rather than dualistically, and you will earn how to accept awesome gifts from Nature—gifts you can use to heal yourself, to grow spiritually, and to preserve the planet.

1.39.2.

None of the worthwhile benefits of intimacy can occur very well when one follows old patterns of dualistic thinking such as the notion that Humans are separate from Nature.

1.39.3.

The Heartwood Path fosters a strong spiritual sense of one-ness—a sense that is, at once, expansive and ecological plus intimate and personal.

1.39.4.

A strong spiritual sense arises spontaneously from the recipro-cal nature of being nurtured by Nature and nurturing Nature.

Nocturnal Pilgrimage 1.39

For best results, write down your impressions of each night's dreams in your journal using the Heartwood Path Dreaming Time Protocols found in the Appendix. Afterwards, consider sharing your Dream Tending with others.

In the Blessings section of your journal write down the positive things that happened in your life. In the Operations sections of your journal write down what is going on in your life now that you would like to change. In the Affirmations section of your journal write down what you are doing now to improve your life. Read over these journal entries over and over again right before you fall asleep tonight (and possibly during the next few nights) as a way to prompt you to dream about your blessings, operations, and affirmations. As you dream, begin the habit of paying extra attention to the setting. After you dream, write down as much as you can remember about the place in which the Dream occurs—the surroundings or the location of the dream. In doing so, you are doing what is asked for in the component of our After Dreaming Protocol titled "Setting."

After recording another night time dream, continue making progress on the Heartwood Path by moving to the next waypoint: "Success." As we all know, if you are looking for success before work, the only place you can find it there is in the dictionary. There are many tempting parking places on the road to success. Real success is the person you become along the journey. No success makes up for failure in the home. There are two rules for success: 1) never tell everything you know.

40

Success

MAKE A SACRED CONTRACT

The Heartwood Path leads to success by helping you improve your health, character, relationships, and income, in part, by helping you examine your own inner world. Turning "inward" to your own psycho/ spiritual Self helps the "outward" tangible environment because when you turn your thoughts to the spiritual realm of The Absolute, the physical realm responds to Its higher call.

The Heartwood Path cannot, figuratively speaking, change a duck into an eagle; but it can make a duck into the best duck it can be. As you continue down the Heartwood Path you have an opportunity to benefit from the same process of "Spirit-in-Action" used by those who have made the greatest contributions to humanity—Confucius, Lao Tzu, Buddha, Jesus, Mohammed, Socrates, and others. All of these great individuals spent a considerable amount of time withdrawn from others while they soothed their own pains, cleared up private confusions, and advanced their own spiritual maturity. Once these great contributors withdrew from others for enough time to sufficiently fortify themselves, they were then ready to complete their own personal spiritual work by applying their own profound spiritual realizations to the service of others.

To The Vows Of Success...

HumaNatureConnect Activity

Start-up Protocol

If this is not a day when you prefer to spend time in nature without an agenda, do the Heartwood Path Start-up Protocol found in the Appendix. Then return here to do the remaining portion of this activity:

Withdrawing From Distractions And Making A Sacred Contract

For this activity, think of your time in nature as a withdrawal from distractions. Remain as long as you like. Note that your chosen natural being and the setting of your natural being is generally free of untrustworthiness and devoid of causes of reduced self-esteem. You are safe and esteemed when you engage in HumaNatureConnect activities. Appreciating the value of trustworthiness and self-esteem, make a contract with yourself that you will use what you glean from these activities in your everyday life. Write down your vows regarding being honest with yourself and others, uncovering the truth about the nature of your individual self and your self and its habitat—collectively referred to as your Greater Self. Vow to relax, eat well, drink plenty of water, exercise, take care of your emotional needs, or whatever else you will be committed to doing. In your written contract, mention that you accept that adhering to your pledges demonstrates your strength of character.

Follow-up Protocol

For best results, write down your impressions of this activity in your journal using the Heartwood Path Follow-up Protocol found in the Appendix. Afterwards, consider sharing your interpretations with others.

Heartwood Path Axioms

Key Assertions From Waypoint 1.40

1.40.1.

Turning "inward" to your own psycho/spiritual Self helps the "outward" tangible environment because when you turn your thoughts to the spiritual realm of The Absolute, the physical realm responds to Its higher call.

1.40.2.

The Heartwood Path cannot, figuratively speaking, change a duck into an eagle; but it can make a duck into the best duck it can be.

1.40.3.

Those who follow the Heartwood Path will use the time-tested model of personal withdrawal followed by a return to service used by those who have made the greatest contributions to humanity—Confucius, Lao Tzu, Buddha, Jesus, Mohammed, Socrates, and others.

Nocturnal Pilgrimage 1.40

For best results, write down your impressions of each night's dreams in your journal using the Heartwood Path Dreaming Time

Protocols found in the Appendix. Afterwards, consider sharing your Dream Tending with others.

Before moving to the next waypoint, sleep, dream, and record your dreams in your journal. Do not at this point attempt to find signs or meanings in your dreams, just focus on who is present and what is going on. Record as many details as possible. Write in your journal before you get out of bed. This quick-noting will prevent you from forgetting important details. The goal here is to get into the habit of recording your nightly dreams. After recording your dreams, go to the next waypoint, entitled "One Person At A Time," and continue your pilgrimage down the Heartwood Path.

41

One Person At A Time

DO WHAT IT TAKES TO AWAKEN REFRESHED AND BE STIRRED INTO ACTION

The Heartwood Path, supplemented as it is in this writing by Dr. Cohen's NatureConnect Methodologies, can move you in any of the following ways: from fear to love, from ignorance to knowledge, from indecision and stagnation to willfulness, from striving in lust to arrival in bliss, from dependence to interdependence, from ineffectiveness to effectiveness, from worry to peace, from egoism to selflessness, from despair to joy, from no place to some place, from detachment to belonging, from deception to truth, from toxicity to purity, from apathy to care, from alienation to bonding, from financial insecurity to financial freedom, from disease to health, from domination to partnership, from self-improvement to environmental improvement, and from environmental improvement to self-improvement. Each of these movements will be addressed later in this series of books. By its end you will be awakened refreshed and stirred into action.

Congratulations for making it this far. This path is designed to make you happier. It is also adding a new dimension to the environmental movement.

For the most part, the environmental movement focuses its attention on saving the Earth one place at a time (like Yosemite Valley in California or the Meramec River in Missouri, for example) or one resource at a time (like the air through the passage of amendments to the Clean Air Act or wildlife through the passage of conservation funding, for example). Those who follow the Heartwood Path, while recognizing the importance of saving places and resources, add a pivotal new dimension to the environmental movement: they undertake a spiritual odyssey focusing on saving the Earth one person at a time.

Like environmentalists, eartHearts—those who follow the Heartwood Path—concern themselves with air, but when eartHearts do it they are adding to the consideration of its mystical and metaphorical aspects, particularly those that relate to helping with personal well-being. The following activity will demonstrate what I mean:

To Breathe-in Self-acceptance And To Breathe-out Self-judgment...

HumaNatureConnect Activity

Start-up Protocol

If this is not a day when you prefer to spend time in nature without an agenda, do the Heartwood Path Start-up Protocol found in the Appendix. Then return here to do the remaining portion of this activity:

Breathing-in And Breathing-out The Air About You

For this activity, find an attractive aspect of the air such as a cloud, the sky, or oxygen, see if it retains its attractiveness for at least ten seconds, and, if so, imagine as you inhale that, along with the incoming air, you are also inhaling life force energy and self-acceptance. Then, along with your outgoing air, imagine you are breathing out self-judgement. Breathe deeply in this way for a long time. Feel the growth of self-acceptance as you inhale and the lessening of self-judgment as you exhale. Affirm that your self-acceptance and your self-judgments are not who you are.

Follow-up Protocol

For best results, write down your impressions of this activity in your journal using the Heartwood Path Follow-up Protocol found in the Appendix. Afterwards, consider sharing your interpretations with others.

Heartwood Path Axioms

Key Assertions From Waypoint 1.41

1.41.1.

The Heartwood Path can move you in any of the following ways:

from fear to love,

from ignorance to knowledge,

from indecision and stagnation to willfulness,

from striving in lust to arrival in bliss,

from dependence to interdependence,

from ineffectiveness to effectiveness,

from worry to peace,

from egoism to selflessness,

from despair to joy,

from no place to some place,

from detachment to belonging,

from deception to truth,

from toxicity to purity,

from apathy to care,

from alienation to bonding,

from financial insecurity to financial freedom,

from disease to health,

from domination to partnership,

from self-improvement to environmental improvement,

and from environmental improvement to self-improvement.

1.41.2.

By the end of the Heartwood Path you will be awakened
refreshed and stirred into action.

1.41.3.

Those who follow the Heartwood Path, while recognizing the
importance of saving places and resources, add a pivotal new
dimension to the environmental movement: they undertake a
spiritual odyssey focusing on saving the Earth one person at a
time.

Nocturnal Pilgrimage 1.41

For best results, write down your impressions of each night's dreams in your journal using the Heartwood Path Dreaming Time Protocols found in the Appendix. Afterwards, consider sharing your Dream Tending with others.

Immediately before falling to sleep repeat your expectation that you will dream of the ways the Heartwood Path will move you from separation to unity, ways the Heartwood Path will help you save the earth one person at a time, and ways the Heartwood Path will give you the integrity to sustain your efforts to make yourself and others happy in a sustainable environment. After dreaming, write down notes about what your dreams are telling you about the ways it is helping you move forward in positive ways. Also, affirm that you are a person who will give and record titles for your dreams about these and other matters, as suggested in our After Dreaming Protocol.

With the suggestions of this waypoint in mind, record your dreams before you move to the next waypoint: "Certitude & Development." Enjoy the journey.

42

Certitude & Development

BLEND MORAL CONVICTIONS
WITH "QUALIFIED" GROWTH

Altering behaviors and developing "improved" physical systems are matters of technology and science. These are important and worthwhile tools in the effort to protect humaNature. Two conditions are needed to accompany these tools, however: 1) a sense of what we want to do and 2) a sense of what we ought to do. The first condition falls in the realm of intentions. The second in the realm of ethics—where one finds the principles that guide behaviors in ways that cause the maximum amount of good for the maximum number of sentient beings. Both conditions fall in the realm of ideas—the thoughts that precede every revolution, every invention, and every transformation. Without changing the inner world of intentions and ethics the behaviors and physical systems we develop in the external world will likely end up being misguided, counterproductive, or inappropriate.

Information alone may not be enough to save the environment. "What is missing is the moral imperative, the conviction that assuring our own comfort at terrible cost to the future is not worthy of us as moral beings" (Moore and Nelson, 2010, p. xvi).

So it is, in part, our morality that calls us to environmental action. "No amount of factual information will tell us what we ought to do. For that, we need moral convictions . . ." (Moore and Nelson, 2010, p. xvii). Without certitude, there will be consequences, we will be failing in our duties as a species to avert harm to the earth, and we will fail to honor and celebrate our extraordinary world. There is not much factual data in this book because we as a species cannot rely on facts alone to guarantee environmental sustainability.

Nor can we rely solely on economic development to grow our way out of the global environmental predicament. Economic growth needs to be "qualified," by which I mean it ought to be authorized through democratic responses and made to fit within a world that sustains a quality of life for present and future generations. Rapid, ill-conceived economic growth is a strain on the environment; and, since corporate, governmental, or military elite usually end up with most of the spoils, grosser national products often spur social strife. The real problem is not a lack of physical resources. The real problem is a decline in human spirit.

To fix this problem and the environmental predicament we do not need greater quantities. Instead, we need the development of greater qualities. By this I mean humans involved in making a difference need to change their way of seeing, understanding, and acting. Use the following activity to assess but not judge (by saying something is good or bad) the qualities of your life right now.

To An Appraisal Of Your Character…

HumaNatureConnect Activity

Start-up Protocol

If this is not a day when you prefer to spend time in nature without an agenda, do the Heartwood Path Start-up Protocol found in the Appendix. Then return here to do the remaining portion of this activity:

Assessing Your Qualities

For this activity, use the good feelings you obtain from your outdoor setting or natural being to think clearly about the quality of your health, the quality of your relationships, the quality of your work, the qualities of life that your finances bring to you, the quality of your creativity, and the quality of your spiritual life. Simply make a mental assessment of your qualities by describing them without saying whether they are good or bad. Write about these in your journal and affirm that it is the qualities of your life that you will concern yourself with the most, leaving the counting to others. If you cannot think of the qualities to assess and write about, move on to the following waypoints for specifics and then come back.

Follow-up Protocol

For best results, write down your impressions of this activity in your journal using the Heartwood Path Follow-up Protocol found in the Appendix. Afterwards, consider sharing your interpretations with others.

Heartwood Path Axioms

Key Assertions From Waypoint 1.42

1.42.1.

Two conditions are needed to accompany science and technology: 1) a sense of what we want to do and 2) a sense of what we ought to do.

1.42.2.

Without changing the inner world of intentions and ethics the behaviors and physical systems we develop in the external world will likely end up being misguided, counter-productive, or inappropriate.

1.42.3.

Rapid, ill-conceived economic growth is a strain on the environment; and, since corporate, governmental, or military elite usually end up with most of the spoils, grosser national products often spur social strife. The real problem is not a lack of physical resources. The real problem is a decline in human spirit.

1.42.4.

To fix the decline in human spirit and the environmental predicament we need the development of greater qualities, not greater quantities.

1.42.5.

Humans involved in making a difference need to change their way of seeing, understanding, and acting.

Nocturnal Pilgrimage 1.42

For best results, write down your impressions of each night's dreams in your journal using the Heartwood Path Dreaming Time Protocols found in the Appendix. Afterwards, consider sharing your Dream Tending with others.

Before you fall asleep tonight assess your feelings about the growth you need to undergo in order to live up to your own moral convictions. Write down your before-dreaming mood regarding what you want to do with your life and about what you ought to do with your life. Develop the intention to dream about your self-development needs and the mood this realization put you in. Over and over again before you go to sleep state to yourself that you want to both dream about your own self-development and, while dreaming, lucidly monitor your mood. Upon completion of your self-development dream, as recommended in the After Dreaming Protocol titled "Mood," write down in your journal words about how you are feeling. Also note what you intend to do as a result of your mood. If you do not dream about your self-development on the first attempt, keep trying this activity until you are pleased with the results.

After you dream and write satisfactory notes about your dreams in your journal, move to the next waypoint: "Levels And Forms." Once there, you will learn about combining levels of personal development with higher forms of thinking, speaking, and acting. You will also learn how to assess the rift between where you are and where you would like to be regarding self-esteem.

43

Levels And Forms

COMBINE ALL LEVELS OF PERSONAL DEVELOPMENT— ARCHAIC, MYTHIC, AND RATIONAL —WITH HIGHER, TRANS-PERSONAL FORMS OF THINKING, SPEAKING, AND ACTING

The Heartwood Path is a route of study, worship, service, wealth (not just monetary), fulfillment of desires, right livelihood, and liberation of the Soul. Along this path, you will discover how to move from dependence to independence to interdependence. It is this last stage that makes this pathway unique.

Typically, self-help books encourage us to think of ourselves as individual agents needing improvement to succeed. This is true, but incomplete. We also need to work to improve the environment in which we live and we need to open ourselves up to the nurturing embrace of Nature. The Heartwood Path uses Nature's gifts and the concepts of self-help, relationship improvement, and environmental protection to create a new way to benefit humaNature.

The Heartwood Path is routed to allow a person to leave behind endeavoring in fear and dependency. The Heartwood Path helps people trade such striving for arriving at a "place" where love overcomes fear.

For those who find themselves at the mythic level of personal development and therefore have a certain set of religious-based responses, the frequent praising of The Absolute (which, by definition, can include the Judeo-Christian God) along the Heartwood Path will be welcome. While much of this book will be framed in rational and secular terms, it recognizes that to be fully developed one needs to integrate archaic, mythic and rational (scientific) modes of expression.

Embracing all levels—archaic (nature worshiping), mythic (deity worshiping), and rational (reliance on the scientific method) —within one's personal development leads, after the kinds of practices described in this series of books and courses, to a personal trans-rational transformation. Thus, the Heartwood Path does not encourage the denial of magic, myth, or reason, but a going beyond all shallower levels to deeper trans-personal forms (modes) of thinking, speaking and acting. These modes will be described later in this series of books and courses.

Those who do not undertake a spiritual quest such as the one undertaken along the Heartwood Path often end up feeling numb, traumatized, and valued for what they do rather than for who they are. Those who shun such pilgrimages may end up living their lives on distorted beliefs and with low self-esteem.

In doing the activities that follow, be sure to remember not to be self-critical. Inner peace comes from acceptance of your current qualities while also identifying, not in a harsh way, what aspects of your life you could stand to improve.

To A Look At Self-esteem…

HumaNatureConnect Activity

Start-up Protocol

If this is not a day when you prefer to spend time in nature without an agenda, do the Heartwood Path Start-up Protocol found in the Appendix. Then return here to do the remaining portion of this activity:

Assessing The Rift Between Where You Are And Where You Would Like To Be Regarding Self-esteem

For this activity, use the clarity and calmness imparted by your chosen natural being to help you assess your self-esteem. Write down where you are with self-esteem now. Then write down in your journal where you would like to be with self-esteem in the not-too-distant future. If you have difficulty or would like a second opinion, assume the essence of your chosen natural being and, as it, tell yourself what you need to know about your self-esteem. Identify the rifts between where you are now and where you want to be as either "Expansive," "Workable," or "Inconsequential." These are assessments of quality and not quantity. Affirm that your positive self-esteem makes you happier and, since you are not fighting low self-esteem with the false-comforts of excess consumption, your positive self esteem makes the environment more sustainable.

Follow-up Protocol

For best results, write down your impressions of this activity in your journal using the Heartwood Path Follow-up Protocol found in the Appendix. Afterwards, consider sharing your interpretations with others.

Heartwood Path Axioms

Key Assertions From Waypoint 1.43

1.43.1.

The Heartwood Path uses Nature's gifts and the concepts of self-help, relationship improvement, and environmental protection to create a new way to benefit humaNature.

1.43.2.

Embracing all levels—archaic (nature worshiping), mythic (deity worshiping, and rational (reliance on the scientific method) —within one's personal development leads, after the kinds of practices described in this series of books, to a personal trans-rational transformation.

1.43.3.

Those who do not undertake a spiritual quest such as the one undertaken along the Heartwood Path often end up feeling numb, traumatized, and valued for what they do rather than for who they are.

1.43.4.

Those who shun pilgrimages may end up living their lives on distorted beliefs and with low self-esteem.

Nocturnal Pilgrimage 1.43

For best results, write down your impressions of each night's dreams in your journal using the Heartwood Path Dreaming Time Protocols found in the Appendix. Afterwards, consider sharing your Dream Tending with others.

Tonight, when you dream, and tomorrow, when you record your dreams, approach the images with an open, accepting, dreamlike attitude. Notice how this approach to dreams brings them to life.

After making notes about your dreams in your journal, move to the next waypoint: "Stirring Irritations."

44

Stirring Irritations

PREPARE YOURSELF FOR SOME EMOTIONAL UNPLEASANTNESS

A journey down the Heartwood Path will inevitably cause self-reflection and some short-lived emotional pain. Give yourself permission to examine what is painful to you. Know that this examination is an integral part of the pathway that leads to ecstasy. Those who loiter in comfort often end up uncomfortable while those who loiter in discomfort often end up comfortable. The Heartwood Path will show you how to rapidly convert debilitating tribulations into strengthening solutions. You won't be stuck long in any bog of unpleasantness. Often such unpleasantness arises when parents, activists, and so-called "nice people" too often put the needs of others before the needs of themselves. When this happens consistently over a long period of time, one tends to become unpleasantly resentful and "burned-out."

To A Look At How You Put Other's Needs Ahead Of Your Own...

HumaNatureConnect Activity

Start-up Protocol

If this is not a day when you prefer to spend time in nature without an agenda, do the Heartwood Path Start-up Protocol found in the Appendix. Then return here to do the remaining portion of this activity:

Assessing The Rift Between Where You Are And Where You Would Like To Be Regarding Putting The Needs Of Others Ahead Of Your Own

For this activity, use the clarity and calmness imparted by your natural being to help you assess whether too often you place the needs of others ahead of your own. Write down where you are with deferring to the interests of others. Then write down in your journal where you would like to be in this regard in the not-too-distant future. If you have difficulty or would like a second opinion, assume the essence of your natural being and, as it, tell yourself what you need to know about putting the interests of others ahead of your own. Identify the rift between where you are and where you want to be as either "Expansive," "Workable," or "Inconsequential." These are assessments of quality and not quantity. Affirm that keeping your own interests in line with the interest of others makes you happier. Moreover, affirm that, since you are not over-buying to take away the emotional pain or ending your involvement in conservation due to burnout, staying happy and involved in conservation gives the environment a better chance to become more sustainable.

Follow-up Protocol

For best results, write down your impressions of this activity in your journal using the Heartwood Path Follow-up Protocol found in the Appendix. Afterwards, consider sharing your interpretations with others.

Heartwood Path Axioms

Key Assertions From Waypoint 1.44

1.44.1.

Giving yourself permission to examine what is painful to you is an integral part of the pathway that leads to ecstasy.

1.44.2.

Often unpleasantness in the form of resentment and "burnout" arises when parents, activists, and so-called "nice people" too often put the needs of others before the needs of themselves.

Nocturnal Pilgrimage 1.44

For best results, write down your impressions of each night's dreams in your journal using the Heartwood Path Dreaming Time Protocols found in the Appendix. Afterwards, consider sharing your Dream Tending with others.

Dream and record your dreams in your journal. Be sure not to try to explain away the dreams. Doing so will shrink them into logical signs when, in reality, they are much more.

After carefully making notes about your dreams in your journal, move to the next waypoint: "Connect With All."

45

Connect With All

FIND THE ENJOYMENT OF CONNECTING WITH THE GREATER SELF

By helping you add skill to your pleasure the Heartwood Path turns your pleasure into enjoyment. Every step is appropriate—whether pleasurable, enjoyable, thought-provoking, or charitable. Some steps lead to the possibility of ecstasy.

Along the Heartwood Path you are instructed to view your "self" not so much as a personal, isolated, and separate being but rather as a "Self" created from that spirit that in its infinite form is the Absolute Being, God, or the Universal Spirit. This Greater Self is also called the "Compound Self," the "Ecological Self," or the "Sacred Self." This Self is inviolable and indivisible from the cosmos. Great power and insight is available to those who connect with, or even seek to connect with, the universe.

Yet, those who use seeking as a means of achieving a "unitive" experience with the cosmos will likely fail to succeed. Unitive experiences are a gift from God and cannot be called up at will. Throughout the Heartwood Path, I will present numerous steps you can take to prepare yourself for such experiences. Instead of demonstrating how to use your own Will to achieve Oneness with the Universe on demand, this path will show you instead how to make yourself open to receiving the Universe and how to cope with the "unitive" experience when it does occur.

To A Look At Where You Stand With Torment And Exasperation...

HumaNatureConnect Activity

Start-up Protocol

If this is not a day when you prefer to spend time in nature without an agenda, do the Heartwood Path Start-up Protocol found in the Appendix. Then return here to do the remaining portion of this activity:

Assessing The Rift Between Where You Are And Where You Would Like To Be Regarding Worry And Frustration

For this activity, use the clarity and calmness imparted by your natural being to help you assess your level of worrying and your level of frustration. Write down where you are with worry. Then write down where you are with frustration. Then write down in your journal where you would like to be with both worry and frustration in the not-too-distant future. If you have difficulty or would like a second opinion, assume the essence of your natural being and, as it, tell yourself what you need to know about your own level of worrying and frustration. Identify the rifts between where you are and where you want to be as either "Expansive," "Workable," or "Inconsequential." These are assessments of quality and not quantity. Affirm that releasing your worries and frustrations make you happier. And affirm that, by not over-buying to take away the emotional pain of worry, or by not ending your involvement in conservation due to frustration, releasing your worries and frustrations gives the environment a better chance to become more sustainable. Ways to release your worries and frustrations will be presented later.

Follow-up Protocol

For best results, write down your impressions of this activity in your journal using the Heartwood Path Follow-up Protocol found in the Appendix. Afterwards, consider sharing your interpretations with others.

Heartwood Path Axioms

Key Assertions From Waypoint 1.45

1.45.1.

Along the Heartwood Path you are instructed to view your "self" not so much as a personal, isolated, and separate being but rather as a "Self" created from that same spirit that in its infinite form is the Absolute Being, God, or the Universal Spirit.

1.45.2.

Great power and insight is available to those who connect with, or even seek to connect with, the universe or their More-Than-Individual-Self.

1.45.3.

Unitive experiences are a gift from God and cannot be called up at will.

Nocturnal Pilgrimage 1.45

For best results, write down your impressions of each night's dreams in your journal using the Heartwood Path Dreaming Time Protocols found in the Appendix. Afterwards, consider sharing your Dream Tending with others.

Tonight, before you dream, and tomorrow, before tending to your dreams, remember the following key point from Aizenstat: dreams do not arise from the logical mind so using only the rational mind to explain dreams mutilates them. Rather than relying on rational analysis, connect (in ways presented subsequently) to the reality of the aliveness of dreams (Aizenstat, 2009, p. 25). An attitude of wonderment, curiosity, and presence is necessary.

To continue your pilgrimage down the Heartwood Path, go to the next waypoint: "Continue Fully." Enjoy your journey towards advanced spiritual maturity.

46

Continue Fully

READ THIS TEXT IN ORDER AND FOLLOW ITS NINE DIRECTIONS

Those who skip down the Heartwood Path without visiting its waypoints in order will most likely lose their way, fail to reach their destination, and perhaps even harm themselves in some way. Not reading the Heartwood Path sequentially is like wearing a hospital gown—you will only think you are covered. Therefore, it is best to study the following description of the trail so that while you are en route you will be prepared, safe, and pleased.

Like the center core of a tree, the Heartwood Path provides structure—the strength and direction needed to get to the "heart" of life's issues and meaning. Finding this strength is more possible if you do the practices, which are referred to here as "HumaNatureConnect Activities." These activities are a vital part of your spiritual pilgrimage down the Heartwood Path because of the truth in the popular experiential education adage: "Tell me and I will forget. Show me and I may remember. Involve me and I will understand." The reader will not fully comprehend the message of this book/course without engaging in its activities.

You are about to embark on a pathway that begins at the juncture of three other trails of betterment: the trail of self-help, the trail of environmental protection, and the trail of relationship improvement. Imagine yourself moving forward from where these three courses merge. At all points along the path you are continuing on is a view on the horizon that provides the Heartwood Path's one single unifying vision. This vision is: "People united in the praise of The Absolute through their heartfelt immersion in nature, in their effort to perfect themselves and others, in their love for each other, and in their efforts to protect The Absolute Spirit's creation."

Imagine before you a path that, along its length, has nine signposts that contain the main directions for continuing towards happiness and environmental sustainability. The directions are:

1. Prepare for the farther reaches of your pilgrimage down the Heartwood Path through the learning of universal principles and the origin and structure of integrity.
2. Anchor one's own individual character through self-examination.
3. Strengthen one's own universal aspect through nature kinship and environmental protection.
4. Develop positive traits.
5. Activate the individual will to seek justice through personal motivation.
6. Return home and persevere through daily enchantment.
7. Share love with another.
8. Put the collective will into effect to achieve joint goals. And
9. Increase one's own level of caring for one's self and others by being an eco-centric life coach.

Your visualization of the Heartwood Path is almost complete. The nine directions described above double as the Heartwood Path's Main Directions. Note that these directions double as the topics of the various courses of the Heartwood Path.

By following the whole Heartwood Path, one's satisfaction with life will go up as the improvements one finds along the way make one's resentments and bitterness go down. To verify this claim for yourself, you will need to make an assessment of these aspects of life at the outset and then again at the end of the book. For this reason, you may want to return to the previous three and the next three assessment activities after your pilgrimage down the Heartwood Path is complete, just to see in what ways your life truly is better due to your involvements along this trail.

To A Look At Where You Are With Petulance And Harshness...

HumaNatureConnect Activity

Start-up Protocol

If this is not a day when you prefer to spend time in nature without an agenda, do the Heartwood Path Start-up Protocol found in the Appendix. Then return here to do the remaining portion of this activity:

Assessing The Rift Between Where You Are And Where You Would Like To Be Regarding Resentment And Bitterness

For this activity, use the clarity and calmness imparted by your chosen natural being to help you assess your resentments and bitterness. Write down where you are now with resentments and bitterness. Then assess where you would like to be with your resentments and bitterness in the not-too-distant future. If you have difficulty or would like a second opinion, assume the essence of your natural being and, as it, tell yourself what you need to know about bitterness. Identify the rifts between where you are and where you want to be as either

"Expansive," "Workable" or "Inconsequential." These are assessments of quality and not quantity. Affirm that releasing your resentments and bitterness makes you happier. Moreover, affirm that, by not over-buying to take away the emotional pain of bitterness, or by not ending your involvement in conservation due to resentments, staying resent-ment-free, being and involved without bitterness in conservation gives the environment a better chance to become more sustainable.

Follow-up Protocol

For best results, write down your impressions of this activity in your journal using the Heartwood Path Follow-up Protocol found in the Appendix. Afterwards, consider sharing your interpretations with others.

Heartwood Path Axioms

Key Assertions From Waypoint 1.46

1.46.1.

Like the center core of a tree, the Heartwood Path provides.

1.46.2.

The main directions for continuing towards happiness and environmental sustainability are:

1. Learn universal principles and the origin and structure of integrity.

2. Anchor one's own individual character through self-examination.

3. Strengthen one's own universal aspect through nature kinship and environmental protection.

4. Develop positive traits.

5. Activate the individual will to seek justice through personal motivation.

6. Return home and persevering through daily enchantment.

7. Share love with another.

8. Put the collective will into effect to achieve joint goals. And

9. Increase one's own level of caring for one's self and others by being an eco-centric life coach.

Nocturnal Pilgrimage 1.46

For best results, write down your impressions of each night's dreams in your journal using the Heartwood Path Dreaming Time Protocols found in the Appendix. Afterwards, consider sharing your Dream Tending with others.

Tonight, when you dream, and tomorrow, when you record your dreams, greet the Dream Images "in an embodied way. . . Images have life force and walk about on legs of their own. Even the non-creature dreams. . . have a vitality that blossoms into visibility when met body-to-body" (Aizenstat, 2009, p. 26). To meet images in an embodied way pay particular attention to the feelings running through yourself. Take the time necessary to pay attention to your corporeal experience. Pay attention to the immediacy of your own animal body and your own instinctual sensitivities. (Aizenstat, 2009, p. 26).

When ready, click on "The Great Work" link to move to the next waypoint. You are making good progress.

47

The Great Work

ENGAGE YOURSELF IN ECOLOGICAL REFORMATION AND ASSESS INNER WORLD LIFE PARAMETERS

The Heartwood Path leads to knowledge, willfulness, arrival in bliss, interdependence, effectiveness, peace, selflessness, joy, belonging, truth, care, bonding, financial freedom, health, partnership, and people loving each other and praising and serving The Absolute and Its creation. This is a big job, perhaps the biggest. It is an occupation for both volunteers and paid staffers. The job is called by cultural historian Thomas Berry and others "The Great Work." Quoting eco-theologian Sallie McFague: "The Ecological Reformation is the great work before us" (Moore and Nelson, 2010, p. 249). This is why the eco-centric life coaches associated with the Heartwood Path are called "Great Work! associates." A considerable part of their job is to help clients become free of guilt and shame. To do so, prospective clients such as yourself will need to make an honest assessment of where they stand at this moment with guilt and various other life parameters included the following activity:

To A Look At The Aspects Of Your Interiority...

HumaNatureConnect Activity

Start-up Protocol

If this is not a day when you prefer to spend time in nature without an agenda, do the Heartwood Path Start-up Protocol found in the Appendix. Then return here to do the remaining portion of this activity:

Assessing Your Various Inner World Life Parameters

For this activity, use the clarity and calmness imparted by your chosen natural being to help you assess the nature of your guilt and shame, if any; your fear of failure, if any; your fear of intimacy, commitment, and risks, if any; your tolerance of busyness and whether you are overwhelmed; your capacity for self-motivation; your relationships with friends, lovers, family, and the Absolute; your capacity for forgiveness; your sexuality; your finances and job; your physical health; and your past. Write down in your journal where you are now with each of these life parameters. Then write down where you would like to be in this regard in the not-too-distant future. If you have difficulty or would like a second opinion, assume the essence of your chosen natural being and, as it, tell yourself the nature of the gulf between where you are now and where you need to be regarding each of these parameters. Identify the rifts between where you are and where you want to be as either "Expansive," "Workable," or "Inconsequential." As before, these are assessments of quality and not quantity. Make an affirmation about each of these parameters, stating it, as always, in the present tense—such as, I am benefitting by forgiving others (or name a specific person). Also, as we did in the previous activity, affirm that assessing each of your life parameters is making you happier and improving environmental sustainability.

Follow-up Protocol

For best results, write down your impressions of this activity in your journal using the Heartwood Path Follow-up Protocol found in the Appendix. Afterwards, consider sharing your interpretations with others.

Heartwood Path Axioms

Key Assertions From Waypoint 1.47

1.47.1.

The Heartwood Path leads to knowledge, willfulness, arrival in bliss, interdependence, effectiveness, peace, selflessness, joy, belonging, truth, care, bonding, financial freedom, health, partnership, and people loving each other and praising and serving The Absolute and Its creation.

1.47.2.

Linking the job of increasing human happiness with the Ecological Reformation is the great work before us.

Nocturnal Pilgrimage 1.47

For best results, write down your impressions of each night's dreams in your journal using the Heartwood Path Dreaming Time Protocols found in the Appendix. Afterwards, consider sharing your Dream Tending with others.

Continue recording your dreams. Do not attempt to analyze them. Just be with them as you would a good friend.

After a good dreamful night, move to the next waypoint: "The Experience."

48

The Experience

ALLOW NATURE TO WORK IT'S MAGIC ON YOU

The "Triple A" happiness that is found along the Heartwood Path arises from a very specific three-part circularity: a circle of outcomes where any one part leads to the other two parts. In this way along the Heartwood Path:

1. environmental sustainability leads to individual maturity and easy and enduring assistance to others;
2. personal maturity leads to both environmental sustainability and easy and enduring assistance to others; and
3. easy and enduring assistance to others leads to individual maturity and environmental sustainability.

These benefits sound a bit serious and heavy; but, as you will discover in this introduction, getting to them is actually very pleasurable and fun.

One way or another—by allowing nature to carry you where it may or by following the specific text and series of Heartwood Path Activities—those who follow the Heartwood Path will be moved beyond the ordinary and become uncommonly happy. And the world will become better off because you are making the necessary effort.

To The Benefits…

HumaNatureConnect Activity

Start-up Protocol

If this is not a day when you prefer to spend time in nature without an agenda, do the Heartwood Path Start-up Protocol found in the Appendix. Then return here to do the remaining portion of this activity:

Wandering In Nature Without An Agenda

For this activity, there is no instructions other than to take a walk in nature, to sit a while with an attractive natural being, to think about how, if at all, nature worked its spell on you without you having any sort of agenda, and to write down your impressions as suggested below.

Follow-up Protocol

For best results, write down your impressions of this activity in your journal using the Heartwood Path Follow-up Protocol found in the Appendix. Afterwards, consider sharing your interpretations with others.

Heartwood Path Axioms

Key Assertions From Waypoint 1.48

1.48.1.

Allow nature to work its magic on you.

1.48.2.

Finding a natural being that is attractive to you continuously for at least ten seconds can be thought of as that beings consent for you to receive its magic.

1.48.3.

Along the Heartwood Path, participants are free to take in nature's intelligence either by engaging in the waypoints or by wandering without an agenda in the wild.

Nocturnal Pilgrimage 1.48

For best results, write down your impressions of each night's dreams in your journal using the Heartwood Path Dreaming Time Protocols found in the Appendix. Afterwards, consider sharing your Dream Tending with others.

As part of your preparations for sleep say to yourself over and over again that you are a person who will tonight notice how events from your agenda-free nature walk or other events from your life are influencing your dreams. This activity is in line with our After Dreaming Protocol which calls for this same sort of attention: "Life Event Affecting Dream."

With the above before-dreaming suggestion, after you sleep, pay attention to your dreams. Record them in your journal. Do not attempt to analyze your dreams. Again, just be with them as you would a good friend. After doing these things, move to the next waypoint: "The Prerequisites."

49

The Prerequisites

UNDERSTAND THE EFFICACY AND PLAUSIBILITY OF THE HEARTWOOD PATH BY MASTERING ITS PREREQUISITES

The next book provides the theoretical background needed to explain both the efficacy and the plausibility of the material covered in all the waypoints that follow. By completing this waypoint and the first five in the next book you will have completed the prerequisites for beginning the "Great Work!"—a phrase I borrow and apply to the work to be done along the Heartwood Path; which is, working towards saving the Earth by encouraging enough people to secure significant and lasting personal and planetary change through working towards spiritual maturity.

Welcome To The End of the Prerequisites For The Training For The Great Work!

As always, here at the end of the prerequisites to the Great Work! as described in the Heartwood Path, I encourage you to transition to the next book, read the text, and participate in the numerous activities related to universal principles. Pay particular attention to Ken Wilber's Four Quadrants—intentions, behaviors, ethics and physical systems—and Hermes' Seven Universal Principles—everything is mental, as above, so below, all is in vibration, rhythm compensates, everything is dual, every cause has its effect and every effect has its cause, everything has masculine and feminine characteristic. To further one's examination of universal principles, use Cohen's Methods, summarized as follows: go to a natural place and gain consent to do the activity and, once consent is granted (as marked by one's continued attraction), ask what the natural attraction can share about universal principles. In doing so, you are encouraged to remain still, come into awareness of any of their fifty-three natural attraction senses (such as the sense of visibility or invisibility or the sense of proximity and space), psychologically assume the perspective of the natural area or a natural being in the scene, and glean from the scene information about universal principles. Noticing how the decaying of leaf matter becomes soil, for example, might lead the participant to the important principle "what goes around comes around." Noticing maple seeds landing in the middle of a pond might remind the participant of the principle "as you sew, so shall you reap." The principle "Whatever you do onto others, you also do onto your self" is demonstrated when a participant sees a man kill predators to stop them from eating his favorite trophy animal but then discovers that not having predators weakens the prey, making them unsuitable to the hunter.

Before moving on to the topic of universal life principles, take a moment to ask yourself whatever questions are pertinent to you at this moment. Additionally, spend some time now doing twenty squats while you answer the following "what's:"

1. What am I passionate about and what models of passion can I find in my environment right now?
2. What gives me joy inside of my home and outside of my home?
3. What in my inner world and what in my outer world gives me joy?

4. What is my relationship to the Absolute and how, if at all, does that differ from my relationship with nature?
5. What qualities do I have right now?
6. What qualities does my environment have right now
7. What qualities would I like to have right now?
8. What qualities would I like my environment to have right now?
9. What have I been putting off?
10. What seems about to happen in my environment?
11. What do I need to forgive about myself?, about people?, and about my environment?
12. What do I want to do with the rest of my life?
13. What do I want to do with my environment over the course of the remainder of my life?
14. What about myself is really important to me right now?
15. What about my environment is important to me right now?
16. What goals do I have for myself?
17. What goals do I have for my environment?
18. What are my personal blessings?
19. What are the blessings of my environment? And
20. What skills am I applying to enable me to use my environment appropriately?

If an answer to any of these questions does not emerge immediately do another squat or two. At least the exercise will do you some good. If you are not satisfied with your answers while multi-tasking as I suggest (tung-in-cheek), turn these questions into your own HumaNatureConnect Activity. Doing so will allow you to spend some time communing with nature and to see what develops. Note any improvement in your answering after this communing helps you to function optimally. As always, write down the answers to these questions in your journal and refer back to them periodically. Label this extra activity: "Twenty-Plus What's"

Make an affirmation about each of your answers to these questions, stating it, as always, in the present tense—such as: "I am using my environment in a nondestructive way." Affirm that answering each of these questions and the others of your own choosing is making you happier and improving environmental sustainability.

You have a choice: Engage in the Great Work! or be a part of the Great Ending—a miserable time in the not-to-distant future that would be marked by life system disruption, the catastrophic loss of species on earth, the resulting precipitous reduction in the numbers of human and non-human beings, and a big reduction in the levels of human happiness.

When you add your own "What" Questions, be sure to include some that encourage you to make inner world assessments. Suggestions include: 1) what makes me happy?, 2) what do I feel when I become aware of an environmental problem in my community?, what do I feel when I am always being busy?

While such inner world assessments are important, some of your happiness is affected by outer conditions, such as the way you organize your home or outer world physical environment. Now that you have made some important assessments of your inner world life, it is time to make similar assessments of your outer world life parameters by engaging in the following activity.

To A Look At The Aspects Of Your Exteriority...

HumaNatureConnect Activity

Start-up Protocol

If this is not a day when you prefer to spend time in nature without an agenda, do the Heartwood Path Start-up Protocol found in the Appendix. Then return here to do the remaining portion of this activity:

Assessing Various Outer World Life Parameters

For this activity, use the clarity and calmness imparted by your chosen natural being to help you assess the following outer world parameters: whether you feel nourished and safe in your bedroom; whether you sleep well in your bedroom; whether the objects in your bedroom contribute to your joy and balanced feeling; whether you get inspired when you cook a meal, whether you feel good about your body in the bathroom, whether you feel warm and inviting in your living room, whether you eat healthful food in your dining room, whether your garage is free of unwanted items, whether you feel great about being in your home, whether you listen to something inspirational in your car, whether you are growing and learning at work, and so forth. Write down in your journal where you are now with each of these life parameters. Then write down where you would like to be with these outer world parameters in the not-too-distant future. If you have difficulty or would like a second opinion, assume the essence of your chosen natural being and, as it, tell yourself the nature of the gulf between where you are now and where you need to be be regarding each of these parameters. As you did in some earlier activities, label the rifts as either "Expansive," "Workable," or "Inconsequential." As before, these are assessments of quality and not quantity. Make an affirmation about each of these parameters, stating it, as always, in the present tense—such as: "I am benefitting by forgiving others (or name a specific person)." Also, affirm that assessing each of your life parameters is making you happier and improving environmental sustainability.

Follow-up Protocol

For best results, write down your impressions of this activity in your journal using the Heartwood Path Follow-up Protocol found in the Appendix. Afterwards, consider sharing your interpretations with others.

Heartwood Path Axioms

Key Assertions From Waypoint 1.49

1.49.1.

Learn about universal principles, including Ken Wilber's Four Quadrants: intentions, behaviors, ethics, and physical systems.

1.49.2.

Learn about Hermes' Seven Universal Principles—everything is mental, as above, so below, all is in vibration, rhythm compensates, everything is dual, every cause has its effect and every effect has its cause, everything has masculine and feminine characteristics.

Nocturnal Pilgrimage 1.49

For best results, write down your impressions of each night's dreams in your journal using the Heartwood Path Dreaming Time Protocols found in the Appendix. Afterwards, consider sharing your Dream Tending with others.

It will be helpful to your assessment of your outer world parameters and to meet the challenges you face in life if you are able to witness, recall, and record the way Characters in your dreams respond to problems and situations. Look at the ways that Dream Characters respond to situations as clues for how you may or may not want to respond to your own outer world challenges. You will be reminded of this suggestion each time you see the component of our After Dream Protocol entitled "Culmination Or Response To The Problem."

Congratulations! After five more interesting and important required waypoints, presented as the conclusion of your prerequisites in the beginning of Book Two: **Logos: Connecting with Universal Principles of Integrity**, your preparations will be complete and your outbound sojourn to Gladandgreen Junction will begin in earnest.

This has been the Overture to the Heartwood Path. The topics in the next book will continue to be expansive. They all pertain to universal principles of integrity. Learn the teachings well: no sense trying to swim upstream all the time.

Be sure to get a good dream-filled night's rest before beginning the next book. Tend to your dreams, fight the urge to analyze them. Just pay attention to the details.

You are now done with **Kosmos**. **Logos** comes next. Enjoy!

References

Abram, David. (1987) The perceptual implications of Gaia, Revision, 9(2), 7-15).

Access to Insight Website: http://www.accesstoinsight.org/lib/authors/silananda/bl137.html

Aizenstat, Stephen, Ph.D. (2009). Dream tending. New Orleans, Louisiana: Spring Journal, Inc.

Barrett, Julie Langdon. Website: http://julielangdonbarrett.com/2011/08/11/how-to-tell-the-difference-between-intuition-and-your-imagination-or-ego/

Babauta, Leo. (2009) The power of less: the fine are of limiting yourself to the essentials . . . in business and in life. New York, New York: Hyperion.

Barasch, Marc, Ian. (2000). Healing dreams: exploring the dreams that can transform your life. New York, New York: Riverhead Books.

Beck, Larry and Cable, Ted (2002). Interpretation for the twenty-first century. Urbana, Illinois: Sagamore Publishing, Incorporated.

Beck, Martha (2012). Finding your way in a wild new world. New York, New York: Free Press

Bernard, Patrick. (2004). Music as yoga: discover the healing power of sound. San Rafael, CA: Mandala Publishing.

Borden, Richard, J. (2014). Ecology and experience: reflections from a human ecological perspective. Berkeley, California: North Atlantic Books.

Bosnak, Robert. (1986). A little course in dreams. Boston, Massachusetts: Shambala Publication, Inc.

Bosnak, Robert. (1996) Tracks in the wilderness of dreaming. New York, New York: Delacorte Press

Boston, John Website: (https://www.american.edu/spa/cep/upload/jonathan-boston-lecture-american-university.pdf).

Bowden, Jonny, Ph.d, C.N.S. (2009). The 150 most effective ways to boost your energy. Beverly, Massachusetts: Fair Winds Press.

Buddy, Cathal Br. ofm. Website: www.praying-nature.com.

Buechner, Frederick. (1993). Wishful thinking. A theological abc. San Francisco, California: Harper.

Buhner, Stephen Harrod. (2004). The secret teaching of plants. Rochester, Vermont: Bear and Company, Inner Traditions International.

Bunzl, John M. (2004). Evolutionary Biology and Simultaneous Policy: Vision-Logic for the Next Stage in our Evolutionary Future, Website: http://www.integralworld.net/bunzl.html

Byzant Kabblah Website (www.byzant.com/mystical/kaballah/Path.aspx?number=31)

Care2.com

Cairns, John Jr. (2001) Equity fairness, and the development of a sustainability ethos. Blacksburg Virginia : Ethics in Science and Environmental Politics, February 1., Blacksburg Virginia. www.mnforsustain.org/cairns_j_equity_and_a_sustainability_ethos.htm

Cameron, Julie. (2006). Finding water: the art of perseverance. New York, New York: Jeremy P. Tarcher.

Cannon, Walter B. (1963). The wisdom of the body. New York, New York: W.W. Norton & Company, Inc.

Cengagesites Website: http://www.cengagesites.com/academic/assets/sites/4713/Chapter%2015.pdf

Capra, Fritjof. (1996). The web of life. New York, New York: Anchor Books, Random House.

Castro, Dr. Anthony J. (2009). Creating space for happiness: the secret of giving room. Amherst, New York: Prometheus Books.

CGJungPage Website: http://www.cgjungpage.org/learn/articles/technology-and-environment/683-robert-romanyshyn-on-technology-as-symptom-a-dream

Chakra Tones and Notes Website: http://www.wingmakers.co.nz/Chakra_Tones_and_Notes.html

Chalquist, Craig, editor (2010). Rebearths: conversations with a world ensouled. Walnut Creek, Caliifornia: World Soul Books.

Chapman, Alan. (2003) website: http://www.businessballs.com/maslowtest.pdf

Childre, Doc and Martin, Howard. (1999). The heartmath solution. San Francisco, California: Harper Collins Publishers, Inc.

Chopra, Deepak. (2000). How to know god: the soul's journey into the mystery of mysteries. New York, New York: Harmony Books.

Chopra, Deepak. (2004). The book of secrets: unlocking the hidden dimensions of your life. New York, New York: Three Rivers Press.

Millaka Chopra Website: http://www.huffingtonpost.com/mallika-chopra/finding-serenity_b_868151.html

Cialdini, Robert B. (2009) Influence: science and practice. Boston, Massachusetts: Pearson Education, Inc.

Clark, Rawn. (2002) Journal of Wester Mystery Tradition, No. 3, Vol 1 (Website www.jwmt.org/v1n3/32 paths.)

Cohen, Michael J. Ecopsych Website: http://www.ecopsych.com/iupsmswaiver.html.

Cohen, Michael J. Ecopsych/Ecopsychology Journal Website: http://www.ecopsych.com/ecopsychologyjournal.html.

Cohen, Green Wave, ecopsych.com

Cohen, Michael J. Ecopsych/Lifeweb Website: www.ecopsych.com/lifeweb.html.

Cohen, Michael J. Ecopsych Thesis Quote Website: www.ecopsych.com/thesisquote.html.

Cohen, Michael J. (1993) Integrated ecology: The process of counseling with nature. Humanistic Psychologist, 21(3), 277-295.

Cohen, Michael J, Ed.D. Personal email dated December 23, 2010.

Cohen, Michael J, Ed.D. Project NatureConnect Website: http://www.ecopsych.com/insight53senses.html.

Cohen, Michael J, Ed.D. Project NatureConnect Website: http://www.ecopsych.com/earthstories101.html).

Cohen, PNC Website: www.ecopshych.com/universealive.html

Cohen, Michael J, Ed.D. Green Wave Information: (Project NatureConnect Website: http://www.ecopsych.com/journalaliveness.html and personal email June 8, 2016)Comaford-Lynch, Christine. (2007). Rules for renegades. New York, New York: McGraw-Hill.

Cohen, Michael J. (2018). Principles of Organic Psychology. The Eco-Arts and Science of Unconditional Love Friday Harbor, Washington: Project Nature Connect

Cook, Charles. (2001). Awakening to nature: renewing your life by connecting with the natural world. New York, New York: Contemporary Books, MacGraw-Hill

Cope, Stephen. (1999) Yoga and the quest for the true self. New York, New York: Bantam Books.

Copenhagen Qabalah Website: www.qabalah.dk/paths.html.

Csikszentmihalyi, Mihaly. (1993) The evolving self: a psychology for the third millennium. New York, New York: HarperCollins Publishers, Inc.

Csikszentmihalyi. http://psychology.about.com/od/PositivePsychology/a/flow.htm)

Dangerfield, Dr. J. Mark Website. https://www.smashwords.com/.../how-to-love-nature-when-you-live-in-the-city.

Delaney, Gayle, Dr. (1994) Sexual dreams: why we have them, what they mean. New York, New York: Fawcett Columbine.

De Stefano, Matias, Three Earth Chakra Videos on You Tube. https://m.youtube.com/watch?v=IcfOwlVQGec.

Discovery Fit and Health Website. http://health.howstuffworks.com/wellness/stress-management/finding-serenity-in-your-life2.htm

DreamTending Website: http://dreamtending.com/naturedreaming.pdf

Dyer, Wayne, Ph.D. (2005) The power of intentions: learning to co-create your world your way. Carlsbad, California: Hay House.

Dwoskin, Hale. (2009). The Sedona Method. Sedona, Arizona: Sedona Press.

Eat, Taste, Heal: an Ayurvedic Guidebook website: http://www.eattasteheal.com/ETH_6tastes.htm

Edge Magazine Website: http://www.edgemagazine.net/1995/11/robert-sardello/

E-How. http://www.ehow.com/how_2338305_develop-character.html.

EnglishClub.com Website: http://www.englishclub.com/vocabulary/fl-making-request.htm

Evernden, Neil. (1985). The natural alien. Toronto, Canada: University of Toronto Press.

Ewolt, Dave and Weeks-Ewolt, Alison. (2001) Rational spirituality: evidence of the web of life, Attraction Retreat Website: http://www.attractionretreat.org/Writings/RationalSpirituality.html

Farley, Kent M. (2002) Developing character traits through sport/athletic participation. The Sport Digest- ISSN: 1558-6448. The United States Sports Academy Website: http://thesportdigest.com/archive/article/developing-character-through-sportathletic-participation

Ferlic, K. (2007). Tapping and sustaining the source. Website: http://ryuc.info/common/creation_process/tap_sustain_source.htm

Ferlic, K (2009) A bottom line about sex and our creativity. Website: http://ryuc.info/creativesexuality/bottom_line_about_sex.htm

Fitness Health Zone Website: http://www.fitnesshealthzone.com/meditation/walking-meditation-and-its-benefits/

Fiorenza, Nick Anthony (2010). Planetary harmonics & Neurobiological resonances, Website: http://www.lunarplanner.com/Harmonics/planetary-harmonics.

Flickstein, Matthew. Online Website: Swallowing the River Ganges: http://innerself.com/Meditation/mindfulness.htm?phpMyAdmin=1IAC4WZXEVp9XvKg-Nokyjpr3el1.

Franden, Nathaniel. (1996). Taking responsibility, New York, New York: Simon and Schuster.

Franklin Institute Website: http://www.fi.edu/learn/brain/exercise.html.

Gallup, Inc: (http://www.gallup.com/poll/190916/americans-identification-environmentalists-down.aspx)

Gardner, Howard. (1999) "Intelligence reframed: multiple intelligences for the 21st century." New York: Basic Books.

Garon, Henry A. (2006). The cosmic mystique. Maryknoll, New York: Orbis Books.

GDRC Website: https://www.gdrc/uem/ee/Tbilissi.html.

George, James. (1995) Asking the Earth. Saftsbury, Dorset; Element Books Limited.

Goldman, Jonathan. (2002) Healing sounds: the power of harmonics. Rochester, Vermont: Healing Arts Press.

Goodreads Website: www.goodreads.com. Alan_Wilson_Watts

Grand, David, (2001) Emotional healing at warp speed. New York, New York: Harmony Books.

Gunther, Folke, and Folke, Carl, "Characteristics of Nested Living Systems," Journal of Biological Systems, 1:3, Stockholm: Sweden. Website: http://library.uniteddiversity.coop/Systems_and_Networks/Nested%20Living%20Systems%20(Holons)%20.pdf

Hargrove, Eugene C. (1988) Foundations of environmental ethics, Englewood Cliffs, New Jersey: Prentice Hall.

Hawkes, Joyce Whiteley, Ph.D. (2012) Resonance, nine practices for harmonious health and vitality, Carlsbad, California: Hay House, Inc.

Henning, Sequoia. Website: http://www.feelingsoulgood.com/index.php?id=2

Howerton, Mari and Sorensen, "Maya." Website: http://www.singandhum.com/educational-development/humming-for-health.html

Inner.org. The Gal Einai Website: http://www.inner.org/Institute of HeartMath. Online Website. Global Coherence Initiative. http://www.glcoherence.org/about-us/about.html

Hauser, Marc D. (2006) Moral minds: the nature of right and wrong. New York, New York: Harper Collins.

Helm, Russell Buddy. (2001). The way of the drum. St. Paul, Minnesota: LLewellyn Publications.

Hindu Temples and Gods Website: http://hindutemplesandgods.blogspot.com/2013/03/sri-yantra.html

Hubbard, Barbara Marx. (2001). Emergence: the shift from ego to essence. Charlottesville, Virginia: Hampton Roads Publishing Company

Huning, Barb. (2-28-11) Personal email: "Re: Editorial Help with Instructions and Marketing."

InnerVision Yoga Website: http://www.innervisionyoga.com/what-is-my-sacred-work/

Institute of Human Conceptual and Mental Development. Online Website. Experiences and Feelings: http://www.ihcmdonline.com/mentalproblems/experiences.htm.

Institute for Social Ecology Website: www.social-ecology.org/199.

Jackson, Brooks and Jamieson, Kathleen Hall. (2007). Unspun: Finding Facts In A World Of Disinformation. New York, New York: Random House Trade Paperbacks

Jensen, Derrick. (2000) A language older than words. White River Junction, Vermont: Chelsea Green Publishing Company

Jensen, Derrick. (2006) Endgame volume I: the problem of civilization. New York, New York: Seven Stories Press.

Jensen, Derrick. (2006). Endgame volume II: resistance. New York, New York: Seven Stories Press.

Jung Atlanta: http://www.jungatlanta.com/articles/winter02-decoding-hillman.pdf

Jurado, Anthony. (2010) Cracked.com Website: http://www.cracked.com/article_18405_7-insane-ways-music-affects-body-according-to-science_p2.html

Kahn , Pete3r H Jr. and Hasbach Patricia H. (2012) Ecopsychology: science, totems, and the technological species, Cambridge, MA: MIT Press.

Kawasaki, Guy (2004). The art of the start. New York, New York: the Penguin Group.

Kawasaki, Guy. (2012). Enchantment. New York, New York: Penguin Group.

Kaza, Stephanie. (1993) The attentive heart: conversations with trees. New York, New York: Fawcett Columbine.

Kittleswon, Mary Lynn. (1996). Sounding the soul: the art of listening. Einsiedeln, Switzerland: Daimon.

Kohn, Alfie (1990). The brighter side of human nature. New York, New York: Basic Books, Inc.

Kroeber, Theodora. (1961) Ishi: in two worlds. Berkeley, California: University of California Press.

Krutch, joseph Wood. (2009) The voice of the desert. New York, New York, General Books.

Kundalini Yoga Info Website: http://www.kundalini-yoga-info.com/humming.html.

Lachance, Albert (1997). "The Architecture of the Soul: Sacred Process Ecopsychology," from the book The Greening of religion: god, the environment, and the good life, edited by Carrol, John E., Broclelman, Paul, and Westfal, Mary. Hanover, New Hampshire: University Press of New England

Lama Dalai. (2011) How to be compassionate. New York, Neew York: Atria Books..

Lame Deer and Erdoes, John. (2009). Lame deer: seeker of visions. New York: New York: Simon and Schuster.

Leopold, Aldo. (1949) . A sand county almanac. London, England: Oxford University Press.

Leopold, Aldo and Flader, Susan L. (editor). (1991) The river of the mother of god and other essays by aldo leopold. Madison, Wisconsin: University of Wisconsin Press.

Lesser, Elizabeth. (2009). The seeker's guide. Website: www.oprah.com/spirit/10-Signs-of-Progress-on-Your-Spiritual-Path/10 - God is Optimistic - Oprah.com.

Lessmann, Kevin. (2004) Emotions of the Musical Keys Website: http://www.grad-free.com/kevin/some_theory_on_musical_keys.htm

Lewis, Dennis. Website: http://www.authentic-breathing.com/breathing_tips.htm

Levey, Joel and Michelle. (2003). The fine arts of relaxation, concentration & meditation: ancient skills for modern minds. Somerville, Massachutsetts: Wisdom Publications.

Levi, Renee. (2003). Group magic; an inquiry into experiences of collective resonance, doctoral dissertation executive summary: http://resonanceproject.org/execsum.cfm

Lovelock, James. (2010) The vanishing face of gaia. New York, New york: Basic Books.

Luks, Allen and Payne, Peggy. (1991). The healing power of doing good.   New York, New York: Fawcett Columbine.

Luskin, Fred and Pelletier, Kenneth R. (2005) Stress free for good. San Francisco, California: Harper Collins Publishers.

Maathai, Wangari. (2010). Replenishing the earth. New York, New York: Random House.

MacGregor, Catriona. (2010). Partnering with nature: the wild path to reconnecting to the earth. New York, New York: Atria Paperback.

Macy, Joanna and Johnstone, Chris. (2012) Active home: how to face the mess we're in without going crazy. Novato, California: New World Library.

Mander, Jerry (1979) as quoted in the website: http://www.eco-action.org/dt/elimtv.html

Marc and Angel Website Practical Tips for Productive Living: http://www.marcandangel.com/2013/04/21/8-effective-ways-to-let-go-and-move-on/

Mayo Clinic/Ranges of Self-Esteem. www.mayoclinic.org

McCraty, Rollin Ph.D., Atkinson, Mike, Tomasino, Dana and Bradley, Trevor Raymond, Ph.D. (2006). The coherent heart: heart-brain interaction, psychophysiological coherence, and system-wide order. Boulder Creek, California: Institute of Heartmath.

McCraty, Rollin Ph.D. and Tomasino, Dana. (2006). Emotional Stress, Positive Emotions and Psychophysiological Coherence, Institute of HeartMath Website: alternativeworldwidehealth.com, Heartmath_Stress_chapter.pdf

McKay, Kim and Bonnin, Jenny. (2007) True green. Washington D.C: National Geographic Society.

McKay, Pip. (2009). Website: http://www.evolvenow.com.au.

McIntosh, Steve (2007) Excerpt from Integral consciousness and the future of evolution. Website: http://www.stevemcintosh.com/books/integral-consciousness/chapter-five-integral-politics/

McTaggart, Lynne. (2002). The field: the quest for the secret force of the universe. New York, New York: HarperCollins Publishers, Inc.

Mellick, Jill. (1996). The art of dreaming. Berkeley, California: Conari Press.

Michigan Online Website. http://web1.msue.msu.edu/4h/charcoun.html

Mindbodygreen Website: mindbodygreen.com

Montgomery, Pam. (2008) Plant spirit healing. Rochester, Vermont: Bear and Company.

Morris, Jill. (1985). The dream workbook: discover; the knowledge and power hidden in your dreams. Boston, Massachusetts: Little, Brown, and Company.

Murray, William H. From the website: http://innerself.com/content/social-a-political/environment/3934-for-those-who-would-save-the-earth.html

Myersbriggs.org

Myth-Dream-Symbols Website: http://www.mythsdreamssymbols.com/432.html

Nahko Bear (Medicine for the People). Song lyrics to "Aloha Ke Akua," (Onecommunityglobal.org).

Naiman, Rubin R. Ph.D. (2006). Healing night: the science and spirit of sleeping, dreaming, and awakening. Minneapolis, Minnesota: Syren Book Company.

National Catholic Reporter Website: http://ncronline.org/blogs/eco-catholic/fr-thedreamoftheearth.

Neubauer, Joan, R. (1985). Dear diary: the art and craft of writing a creative journal. Nashville, Tennessee: Turner Publishing Company.

New Oxford American Dictionary. Online Edition.

Noll, Doug. Website: http://lawyertopeacemaker.com/heartmath.html

Norbu, Namkhai. (2002). Dream yoga and the practice of natural light. Ithaca, New York: Snow Lion Publishing.

Nordhaus, Ted and Shellenberger, Michael. (2010). Break through: why we can't leave saving the planet to environmentalists. New York, New York: First Mariner Books.

Oelschlaeger, Max. (1991). The idea of wilderness. New Haven, Connecticut: Yale University Press.

Oestreich Associates. www.teamtrustsurvey.com

Oktar, Adnan. website: http://www.secretbeyondmatter.com/ourbrains/the-worldinourbrains3.html

Orloff, Judith (2003) Website: Trust your hunches: 5 steps to develop your intuition - Intuitive Advice: http://findarticles.com/p/articles/mi_m0NAH/is_8_33/ai_108786014/

Ortiz, John M., Ph.D. (1997) The tao of music: sound psychology. York Beach, ME: Samuel Weiser, Inc.

Ortner, Nick. (2013). The tapping solution: a revolutionary system for stress-free living. Carlsbad, California: Hay House, Inc.

Ouderkirk, Wayne and Hill, Jim editors. Land, value, community: Callicott and environmental philosophy. State University of New York Press. Internet: Callicott_My_Reply_to_Land_Value_Community.pdf

Parker, Jonathan (2011). The soul solution: enlightening meditations for resolving life's problems. Tiburon, California: H J Kramer.

Partridge, Ernest, Ecological morality and nonmoral sentiments. Internet: 60477.pdf.

Partridge, Ernest and Holmes, Ralston III. (1984 ad 1996) The Online Gadfly: http://gadfly.igc.org/papers/values.htm

Peaceful Mind. (2011) Website: http://www.peacefulmind.com/music_therapy.htm

Peaceful Rivers Online Website. Eckhart Tolle Quotes: http://peacefulrivers.home-stead.com/EckhartTolle.html

Pearson, Carol S. (1991) Awakening the heroes within: twelve archetypes to help us find ourselves and transform our world. New York, NY: HarperCollins Publishers.

Peat, F. David. Nature and Ethics. http://www.paricenter.com/library/papers/peat23.php

Plotikin, Bill (2008). Soul craft: crossing into the mysteries of nature and the psyche. Novato, California: New World Books.

Plotkin, Bill. (2010). Nature and the human soul: cultivating wholeness and community in a fragmented world. Novato, California: New World Books.

Plotkin, Bill (2013). Wildmind: a field guid to the human psyche. Novato, California: New World Books.

Pratt, Vernon (Unknown) website: http://www.vernonpratt.com/211/

Reverso Online English Dictionary and Thesaurus: http://dictionary.reverso.net/english-cobuild/linear

Ricard, Matthieu. (2006) Happiness: A guide to developing life's most important skill. New York, NY: Little, Brown and Company.

Robbins, Stephen P. Organizational behavior, Chapter Six: website: http://www.gobookee.net/organizational-behavior-stephen-p-robbins-14th-edition/

Root-Bernstein, Robert and Michele. (1999). Sparks of genius. Boston, Massachusetts: Houghton-Mifflin Company.

Rudd, Vols, Aaker Website: http://faculty-gsb.stanford.edu/aaker/pages/documents/TimeandAwe2012_workingpaper.pdf

Scull, J (n.d.) Eco-psychology: Where does it fit in psychology? Website: http://www.island.net/~jscull/ecopsych.htm

Scully, Matthew. (2002), Dominion. New York, New York: St. Martin's Press.

Second Journey Website, "Itineraries:" http://www.secondjourney.org/newsltr/NDX/Sullivan_frameset.htm

Selhub, Eva M. and Logan, Alan C. (2012). Your brain on nature: the science of nature's influence on your health, happiness, and vitality. Ontario, Canada: John Wiley and Sons Canada Ltd.

Seligman, Martin E.P. (2011). Flourish: a visionary new understanding of happiness and wellbeing. New York, New York: Free Press, Simon and Schuster.

Sewell, L. (1995). The Skill of ecological perception, In T. Roszak, M.E. Gomes, & A.D. Kanner (Eds.). Eco-psychology: Restoring the earth, healing the mind (pp. 201-215). San Francisco, California: Sierra Club.

Sewall, Laura Ph.D. (1999). Sight and sensibility: the ecology of perception. New York, New York: Jeremy P. Tarcher/Putnam.

Shannahoff-Khalsa, David S. (2006) Kundalini yoga mediation. New York, New York: W.W. Norton & Company

Sharp, Jonathan. (2002). Diving your dreams. New York: Simon & Shuster.

Silva Therapy Website: http://www.silvamindbodyhealing.com/articles/mind-body-healing/healing-colors/

SingingToThePlants Website: http://www.singingtotheplants.com/2014/01/dreaming-with-open-eyes/

Songwriting-guide.com Website: http://www.songwriting-guide.com/basic-music-theory.html

Sound Essence Website: http://www.soundessence.net/chakras.php

Sound-PHYSICS.com: http://www.sound-physics.com/Sound/Resonance-NaturalFrequency/

Spoto, Donald (2003). Reluctant saint: the life of francis of assissi. New York, New York: Penguin Books

Spurgeon, C.H. (1871) http://www.spurgeon.org/sermons/1005.htm

State of California, Department of Education, Regional Occupation Centers, and Department of Developmental Disability. (2014). Student Resource Guide: Direct Support Professional Training. http://www.dds.ca.gov/DSPT/Student/Student-Year1_FullVersion.pdf

Steep Path Online Website: http://www.steeppath.com/article.php?ID=6

Sun Bear. (1980). Medicine wheel: earth astrology. Austin, Texas: Touchstone.

Sunstein, Cass, R. and Nussbaum, Martha C. (2004) Animal rights. Oxford, England: Oxford University Press.

Székely, Edmond Bordeaux. The Essene Gospel of Peace. International Biogenic Society, 1981.

Tebra's Writer's Blog Website: http://www.thepensters.com/tebra/secular-saints-philosophy.html.

Templin, Steven, D.O.M Website. http://www.innerbalanceconsulting.com/wp-content/uploads/2011/11/HeartMath-Guide.pdf

Tharp, Twyla. (2003). The creative habit. New York, New York: Simon and Schuster.

Thomashow, Mitchell. (1996). Ecological identity: becoming a reflective environmentalist. Cambridge, Massachusetts: MIT Press.

Thompkins, Peter and Bird, Christopher. (1973) The secret life of plants. New York, New York: Harper and Row, Publishers.

Thoms, Justine. (2008) Small pleasures: finding grace in a chaotic world. Charlottesville, Virginia: Hampton Roads Publishing Company.

Thornton, James. (1999). A field guide to the soul: down-to-earth handbook of spiritual practice. New York, New York: Bell Tower

Thoreau, Henry David. (1965) Walden and on civil disobedience. New York, New York: Harper and Rowe.

Thoreau, Henry David. Excerpt from Journal, quoted from online website: http://www.mothwingarts.com/waldenvisionquest/excerpts.html

Thorncraft, Sylvan. 2006. Website: http://www.emeraldspritestudio.com/articles_toning_and_sacred_sound.htm.

TotalWellnessWorldwide Website: www.totalwellnessworldwide.com/ions.html

Twenge, Jean M. and Campbell, Keith, W. (2009). The narcissism epidemic. New York, New York: Free Press, Simon and Schuster. United States Conference of Catholic Bishops, Themes from Catholic Social Teaching" Washington, D.C., 2005. Website: http://www.cchdbaltimore.org/soc-teach-color-inst.pdf

Uphanishads. Uphanishads quotes and sayings. Website: http://spiritquotes.com/quotes/upanishadsquotes/upanishads_quotes1.htm.

Van Dyke, Deborah.Mantras Sacred Sounds Website: http://www.kirtancommunity.com/html/mantras_sacred_sound.html

Vedicyagyacenter Website: http://www.vedicyagyacenter.com/mantras-chant/Devi-Khadgamala-Stotram-lyrics-with-meaning.pdf

Veracious. Wikihow.com Website: http://www.wikihow.com/Choose-the-Right-Life-Coach

W, Karen. How to overcome fear. Website: http://www.wikihow.com/Overcome-Fear.

Wallace, Alan B. (2012). Dream yourself awake. Boston, Massachusetts: Shambala Publications, Inc.

Webster's Online Dictionary. http://www.websters-online-dictionary.com/definitions/Ethos

Weissman, Darren, R. (2005). The power of infinite love and gratitude. Carlsbad, California: Hay House, Inc.

Whitfield, Charles, L., Whitfield, Barbara H., Park, Russell, and Prevatt, Jeneane. (2006). The power of humility. Deerfield Beach, Florida: Health Communications, Inc.

Whitworth, Laura, Kimsey-Shouse, Karen, Kimsey-House, Henry, and Sandeahl, Phillip. (2007). Co-active coaching: new skills for coaching people toward success. Mountain View, California: Davies-Black Publishing.

Wholistic Healthworks Website: www.wholistichealthworks.com/healing%20with%20colors.htm

Wilber, Ken. (1995). Sex, Ecology, and Spirit: the spirit of evolution. Boston, Massachusetts: Shambala Publications, Inc.

Wilber, Ken, (1998). The essential ken wilber: an introductory reader. Boston, Massachusetts: Shambhala Publications, Inc.

Wilber, Ken (2007) Chapter 14. Integral Politics, or Our of the Prison of Partiality . . . KenWilber.com Website: http://www.kenwilber.com/Writings/PDF/14-integral%20politics.pdf

Wilber, Ken; Patton, Terry; Leonard, Adam; and Morelli, Marco. (2008) Integral life practice: a 21st –century blueprint for physical health, emotional balance, mental clarity and spiritual awakening. Boston, Massachusetts: Integral Books.

Williams, Ernest H. Jr. (2005). The nature handbook: a guide to observing the great outdoors. New York, New York: Oxford University Press.

Wikia Website: http://synchromystic.wikia.com/wiki/432

Wiki-How. http://www.wikihow.com/Strengthen-Character

Wikipedia. David Hume. website: http://en.wikipedia.org/wiki/David_Hume

Wikipedia. Theory Z: webssite: http://en.wikipedia.org/wiki/Theory_Z

Wilderness Survival Sills for Save Wilderness Travel Website: http://www.wilderness-survival-skills.com/how-to-predict-weather.html

Wilson, Carol. (1997) Online Website. Mindfulness: Gateway Into Experience: http://www.dharma.org/ij/archives/1998b/carol_wilson.htm

Wilson, Edward O. (2002). The future of life. New York, New York: Vintage Books.

Winter, Deborah Du Nann and Koger, Susan M. (2004) The psychology of environmental problems. New York: Psychology Press

Wohlforth, Charles. (2010). The fate of nature: rediscovering our ability to rescue the earth. New York, New York: Thomas Dunne Books: St. Martin's Press.

You Tube: Caposiena, Nicholas. (2011) You Tube Podcast: https://www.youtube.com/watch?v=o-r_sMYzW_w

Zeleski, Inessa. North Star Wellness Center Website: http://www.calmness.com/chakras.htm

Zohar, Dana and Marshal, Dr. Ian. (2000). Spiritual intelligence: the ultimate intelligence. New York, New York: Bloomsbury Publishing.

Appendix

Online Resources

Your senses and the Heartwood Path will all come alive as you use the following online resources:

Read the **Glossary** and watch your sense of reason come alive. (www.heartwoodpath.com/glossary)

Use your sense of language when you connect online with other EartHearts at a variety of locations:

- **EartHeart Networking Forum** (www.heartwoodpath.com/connect)
- each **online waypoint** (learning station)
- our **Instagram** account (@heartwoodpath)
- our **Facebook** Page (Heartwood Path)

Your sense of light and sight will be activated when you watch our informative and visually appealing podcasts on **YouTube** (www.youtube.com/user/heartwoodpath).

Inside or outside, online or offline, the Heartwood Path helps you overcome any breaches in your well-being that hinder increasing your happiness and the sustainability of the natural environment.

HumaNatureConnect Activity Protocols

The full meaning of each protocol is revealed as you progress, waypoint by waypoint.

Start-up Protocol

- Read The Text — Use your literary sense, your mind sense, and your reason sense to move towards happiness and sustainability by reading the Heartwood Path text but also go outdoors to the backyard or to the backwoods, where the higher levels of negative ions in the air will improve your mood and well-being.
- Attention Restoration — With a pen and journal in hand, go to a natural area that is attractive, has a variety of plants and animals, and is tranquil enough to leave room for reflection.
- Source — Spend time wandering without an agenda in nature or, if you don't have time to receive nature's magic in this way, follow the instructions in the text at each learning station.
- Attractive Natural Being — Once you are in a natural area (the wilder, the better), look to find a natural being that is attractive to you and remain near that being until the end of the activity.
- Appreciation And Gratitude — While communing with your chosen natural being, appreciate it as you inhale and show it gratitude as you exhale.
- Consent — Once you find an aspect of nature that is attractive to you continuously for at least ten seconds, think of your continued attraction as your consent to have a connection experience that will help you function optimally; receive information, guidance, and healing; and establish in your mind a more helpful egalitarian relationship with the natural being.
- The Natural Senses — Beyond seeing, hearing, and the three other commonly recognized senses, use as many of the fifty-four

Natural Senses as you see fit and prepare to document the ones that you use in your journal.

- Great Trustable Truth — Experience what is happening at the present moment in nature, paying particular attention to the role of both beauty and balance; remember that the impressions you form about attractive natural beings and natural areas, coming from your experiencing of them in the Now, are trustable; and recognize that the natural processes and features witnessed are a source of special, substantial, and irreplaceable truthfulness about both nature and yourself.
- Recall — Place the great trustable truth and any other insights that you discover in a mental lock-box so you can later record them in your journal.

Follow-up Protocol

- Date — Write down the date of your outdoor nature-communing experience.
- Activity — Write down the waypoint title and number each time each you do an activity.
- Location — Write down the location of your outdoor nature-communing experience.
- Natural Being Indicator — Draw a picture or write down in your journal a nameless way to remember your chosen attractive Natural Being; for example, call it your "____ ____ Connection Experience."
- The Natural Senses Used — Write down all of the Natural Senses you used for this activity.
- General Description — Write a general description of how you did the activity and what happened.
- Freeform — Write, in freeform, what you found attractive about your natural being.
- Three Qualities — Write down three qualities you found attractive about your natural being.

- Three Learnings — Write down three things you learned from this activity.
- Self-esteem & Trust — Write down how, if at all, this activity changed your self-esteem or trustfulness of NNIAAL (Namelessness, Now, Intelligence, Alive, Attraction, and Love).
- Changes To Self — Write down what aspects of your Self, if any, were changed by this activity.
- Honor Yourself — Praise yourself and your commitment to making another stop along the Heartwood Path good for yourself and the world.
- I'm A Person Who. . . — Write down three different so-called "G/G Statements" using the following format: "This connection experience tells me that I am a person who_____."
- Feelings If Activity Taken — Write down a sentence about how you would feel if you lost your ability to experience this connection.
- Nature Compared To Self — Create a sentence that reads: "I love this (insert words that identify the attractive natural being) because it is (insert words that refer to the qualities you like about the natural being); then, create a parallel sentence that reads: "I love (insert the word "myself") because I am (insert the same qualities as before)."
- Name Your Discomforts — Make a list of aspects of your negative emotional residue, if any, that lifted simply by being in nature.
- Two-word Summary — Write down two words that summarize your response to this activity.

Heartwood Path Exchange

- Comment — Post your impressions and photos in the Comments section of this waypoint—the place for on-going discussion regarding this waypoint.
- Join — Engage with others in a Heartwood Path course or salon.
- Create — Start your own Heartwood Path salon that meets regularly online, by phone, or in person.
- Talk — Share your impressions with trusted family members and friends.
- Network — Post your impressions and photos on our EartHeart Networking Forum.
- Post — To see what conversations you can ignite, upload on social media your photos and impressions about anything pertaining to your journey down the Heartwood Path.
- Connect — Follow our account on Instagram, Like our Page on Facebook, Subscribe to our Channel on YouTube, and use hashtags such as "#heartwoodpath", "#eartHeart", and "#waypoint(insert book)(insert waypoint number) i.e."#waypointkosmos5").

Dreaming Time Protocols

The full meaning of each protocol is revealed as you progress, waypoint by waypoint.

Before Dreaming Protocol

- Dream Prep — Prepare yourself for productive dreaming by de-cluttering your mind before sleeping.
- Journal Ready — Prepare to record your dream impressions by placing your journal so that you can make initial recordings in it without changing your dreamtime sleeping position.

Dreaming Protocol

- Remember This — Look to your dreams to tell you what you need to remember.
- Open To Dream — Be receptive, fluid, interactive, and grounded as you dream.
- Shape-shifters — Watch characters that change in your dream to see into the possibilities of your own transformation.

After Dreaming Protocol

- First Off — Recall your dream by staying in your sleeping position as you make your first attempt to remember your dream.
- Book Of Dreams — Create an entry in your dream journal using the following linguistic tools: 1) talking in the present tense, 2) using verbs ending in "ing," 3) removing articles such as "an" or "the," and 4) using capital letters when naming the Dream Characters—which can be any notable people, places, or things that show up in your dream.

- Title — Give your dream a memorable title.
- Date — Write down the date of your dream.
- Description — Write down a short, general summary of your dream.
- Mood — Write down how the dream affected your mood upon waking.
- Life Event Affecting Dream — Write down any events in your life that may have influenced your dream.
- Dream Characters — List all remembered notable "actors" in your dream, whether they are people, places, or things.
- Setting — Describe the location of your dream.
- Statement Of Problem — Write down the complication, challenge, predicament, situation, obstacle, plight, quandary, or misadventure presented in your dream.
- Culmination Or Response To The Problem — Describe what you or another Dream Character did in your dream to respond to the problem presented in the dream.
- Conclusion — Describe how your dream ended.
- Beings Revealed — Write down how your dream seemed to be, if at all, linked in some way to your chosen attractive natural beings.
- Freud's Approach — Associate the actions of your Dream Characters with latent, infantile, repressed, or sexual drives.
- Jung's Approach — Amplify your Dream Characters into Archetypes that are global in scale, symbolic, pervasive, positive, and helpful.
- Hillman's Approach — Recognize your Dream Characters as animated, living beings by honoring their presence, place, and body.
- The Richest Treasures — Do not force narrow interpretations upon the natural being impressions that reappear in your dream by condensing them into limited signs when it is more fruitful to simply engage with them as living beings that reside in your dream, possibly with infinite symbolic value.

- Privacy — Store your dream journal in a safe place and, where appropriate, share your dream with others.

Natural Senses

The Radiation Senses

- Sense of light and sight, including polarized light.
- Sense of seeing without eyes such as heliotropism or the sun sense of plants.
- Sense of color.
- Sense of moods and identities attached to colors.
- Sense of awareness of one's own visibility or invisibility and consequent camouflaging.
- Sensitivity to radiation other than visible light including radio waves, X rays, etc.
- Sense of temperature and temperature change.
- Sense of season including ability to insulate, hibernate, and winter sleep.
- Electromagnetic sense and polarity which includes the ability to generate current (as in the nervous system and brain waves) or other energies.

The Feeling Senses

- Hearing including resonance, vibrations, sonar, and ultrasonic frequencies.
- Awareness of pressure, particularly underground, underwater, and to wind and air.
- Sensitivity to gravity.
- The sense of excretion for waste elimination and protection from enemies.
- Feel, particularly touch on the skin.
- Sense of weight, gravity, and balance.

- Space or proximity sense.
- Coriolis sense or awareness of effects of the rotation of the Earth.
- Sense of motion, body movement sensations, and sense of mobility.

The Chemical Senses

- Smell with and beyond the nose.
- Taste with and beyond the tongue.
- Appetite or hunger for food, water, and air.
- Hunting, killing, or food obtaining urges.
- Humidity sense including thirst, evaporation control and the acumen to find water or evade a flood.
- Hormonal sense, as to pheromones and other chemical stimuli.

The Mental Senses

- Pain, external and internal.
- Mental or spiritual distress.
- Sense of fear, dread of injury, death or attack.
- Procreative urges including sex awareness, courting, love, mating, paternity and raising young.
- Sense of play, sport, humor, pleasure, and laughter.
- Sense of physical place, navigation senses including detailed awareness of land and seascapes, of the positions of the sun, moon, and stars.
- Sense of time.
- Sense of electromagnetic fields.
- Sense of weather changes.
- Sense of emotional place, of community, belonging, support, trust, and thankfulness.
- Sense of self including friendship, companionship, and power.
- Domineering and territorial sense.

- Colonizing sense including compassion and receptive awareness of one's fellow creatures, sometimes to the degree of being absorbed into a superorganism.
- Horticultural sense and the ability to cultivate crops, as is done by ants that grow fungus, by fungus who farm algae, or birds that leave food to attract their prey.
- Language and articulation sense, used to express feelings and convey information in every medium from the bees' dance to human literature.
- Sense of humility, appreciation, and ethics.
- Senses of form and design.
- Sense of reason, including memory and the capacity for logic and science.
- Sense of mind and consciousness.
- Intuition or subconscious deduction.
- Aesthetic sense, including creativity and appreciation of beauty, music, literature, form, design, and drama.
- Psychic capacity such as foreknowledge, clairvoyance, clairaudience, psychokinesis, astral projection, possibly certain animal instincts, and plant sensitivities.
- Sense of biological and astral time, awareness of past, present, and future events.
- The capacity to hypnotize other creatures.
- Relaxation and sleep including dreaming, meditation, and brain wave awareness.
- Sense of pupation including cocoon building and metamorphosis.
- Sense of excessive stress and capitulation.
- Sense of survival by joining a more established organism.
- Spiritual sense, including conscience, capacity for sublime love, ecstasy, a sense of sin, profound sorrow, and sacrifice.
- Sense of homeostatic unity, of natural attraction aliveness as the singular essence-diversity attraction dance of all our other senses (NNIAAL). (Cohen, website: http://www.ecopsych.com/insight53senses.html).

Acknowledgments

I would like to thank everyone who helped me blaze the trail that has become the Heartwood Path. Initially, David Brower got me going, after asking me to "write a piece" to combat "burnout" in environmentalists. Roger Fritz helped me with my conversion from corporate executive to author. Paula Badger was a good listener on our frequent walks. Michael J. Cohen helped me to add nature's intelligence to the methodology. "Forest Maiden" Sylvia Shelton served as my "muse"—always with humor, tenderness, intelligence, and love. I started out thinking I was writing traditional books. My daughter Courtney Logue converted my text into an interactive website. Without her efforts—in editing, in creating the format, and in providing important encouragement—there would not be a Heartwood Path. To these people, and many more, I am forever grateful.

About The Author

Pierce has spent nearly his whole life working to protect the environment. After decades of work as a professional environmentalist, Pierce concluded that a new approach—one focused on the environmentalist and not just the environment—was needed.

When famed conservationist David Brower asked him to write "a piece" to show environmentalists how to persevere, the result was a series of books and courses that are good for both environmentalists and anyone seeking happiness and the preservation of nature. This series—the Heartwood Path—helps people to develop spiritually, helps people discover the benefits of communing with nature, and helps people find the abundant, abiding, and authentic happiness that comes from helping others, including natural beings.

Pierce formed his first environmental group—a tree planting club—when he was nine. After that, he was president of both his high school and college environmental organizations. After a few years as a professional river conservationist, he was hired by Brower to be the Midwest Representative of Friends of the Earth. Pierce has led numerous conservation groups, including the Illinois Chapter of the Sierra Club. He was a governor-appointed member of the Illinois Nature Preserves Commission.

He has a Bachelor's Degree in environmental science, a Master's Degree in political science, and Master's Degree in social work. When he was not working to protect the environment or guiding people down the Heartwood Path, Pierce—a qualified life coach and mental health practitioner—served those who needed his care—including those who are young, aged, mentally ill, or mentally disabled.

Currently working on his PH.D in eco-psychology, Pierce divides his time between Santa Barbara, California and St. Louis, Missouri. He is a professional drummer, an avid canoeist, and a photographer. He loves to walk in nature. He has two grown daughters (one, the mother of his two granddaughters, in Missouri and another one somewhere on a sailboat that is often close to Santa Barbara).

Heartwood Path One-On-One Guidance

(30 minute or 60 minute sessions)

Don Pierce will move you to an extraordinary awakening of personal happiness and ecological sustainability.

"Make a difference, happily."

To do so, go down the Heartwood Path under the skilled guidance of its creator, Don Pierce. Don's education and experience will help you turn your advocacy into a source of abiding, abundant, and authentic happiness. His years as an active environmentalist will enable him to teach you how to become both happy and effective in your own causes. His years as a social worker will help you fit better into your own environment. His experience as a life coach will help you set your own agenda towards meeting your goals. His years as a mental health practitioner will enable him to help you achieve the integrity that comes when your inner world enables you to be "glad" as you endeavor to make the outer world "green." By signing up for guidance, you will have Don at your side to answer questions, provide encouragement, and avoid wrong turns.

In productive and easy-to-afford steps, Guidance moves you to an extraordinary awakening of personal happiness and ecological sustainability. Guidance moves you beyond a common state of separation to an extraordinary awakening of oneness that is experienced as personal happiness, ecological sustainability, and spiritual maturity.

Sessions, which are purchased in thirty minute and one hour segments, occur online, on the phone, or in person with Heartwood Path creator Don Pierce. Elements of Heartwood Path guidance include:

- making checklists of topics or actionable items
- establishing guidelines
- setting and reviewing deadlines
- explaining and reviewing practices
- responding and questioning journal entries
- instructing
- providing individualized templates of models
- supporting individuals and teams in the field
- defining terminology and elaborating on Heartwood Path text
- mentoring on related subjects and
- assistance in interpreting signs and symbols.

Complementary Guidance sessions are available when you sign up for any Heartwood Path course.

Further Action

REVIEWS APPRECIATED AND OTHER HEARTWOOD PATH BOOKS

If you enjoyed reading **Kosmos**, please leave a review on Amazon. I would appreciate any comments you may wish to share. Positive reviews go a long way in spreading our important message.

For further reading, the next book in the Heartwood Path series is **Logos**, on universal principles of integrity. Then comes **Egos**, on connecting with the Individual Self. Another book in the series is **Ecos**, on connecting with the Ecological self.

All Heartwood Path books are available on Amazon. Together, Heartwood Path books provide important personal preparations necessary for the creation of happiness and a regenerated environment.

In recognition for all that you do along the Heartwood Path, I say "thank you" and "Great Work!"